Outside
the
Limelight

OUTSIDE
THE
LIMELIGHT

Basketball in the Ivy League

KATHY ORTON

Foreword by
John Feinstein

Rutgers University Press
New Brunswick, New Jersey, and London

Library of Congress Cataloging-in-Publication Data

Orton, Kathy, 1968–
Outside the limelight: basketball in the Ivy League / Kathy Orton.
p. cm.
Includes bibliographical references and index.
ISBN 978-0-8135-4616-2 (hardcover : alk. paper)
1. Ivy League (Basketball conference) 2. Basketball—Atlantic States.
3. College sports—Atlantic States. 4. Private universities and colleges—
Atlantic States.
I. Title.
GV885.415.I88O78 2009
796.323'630973—dc22
2008051478

A British Cataloging-in-Publication record for this book is available from
the British Library.

Visit our Web site: http://rutgerspress.rutgers.edu

Manufactured in the United States of America

For my parents,
Audrey and Duane Orton

Contents

Part III Tournament Hoopiness

Foreword

John Feinstein

When I was a kid growing up in New York City, my favorite college basketball team was the Columbia Lions. Frequently, I would ride the subway up to 116th Street and hope to find an unobstructed seat in University Gym to watch Jack Rohan's teams play. I still remember 1968 when Columbia finally beat Penn and Princeton and won the Ivy League title with a team that was led by Jim McMillian, Heyward Dotson, and Dave Newmark. (The other two starters, for those of you scoring at home, were Roger Walaszek and Billy Ames).

To me, Columbia was just a very good basketball team. After winning the Ivy League championship, the Lions went on to beat La Salle in the first round of the NCAA tournament before losing to Davidson in overtime in the round of sixteen. I can still remember Davidson coach Lefty Driesell calling a time-out with the score tied at 55 with one second left in regulation when Columbia's Bruce Metz had a one-and-one that could have won the game. Metz missed, Davidson won in overtime and, forty years later, I'm still a little bit upset about it.

What I didn't understand—couldn't understand—at that point was how special that Columbia team was. I was a little too young to follow Princeton and Bill Bradley in 1965, but I was aware of the fact that Princeton made the Final Four that year and that Bradley scored fifty-eight points in the third-place game (still a Final Four record) and then went on to something called a Rhodes Scholarship before coming home to play for the New York Knicks.

Now, I understand.

Bill Bradley was a once-in-a-lifetime person, not just a great basketball player. What Columbia achieved in 1968 was extraordinary. The Penn team that went to the Final Four in 1979 was the best college basketball story this side of George Mason in 2006, and Princeton's upset of defending NCAA champion UCLA in 1996 was the perfect climax to one of the great coaching careers ever—that of Pete Carril.

Those stories, of course, are the ones that a lot of basketball fans already know. Everyone knows who Bill Bradley is, and most remember Penn's run under Bob Weinhauer in 1979 with a concert pianist playing center. And, if you follow basketball, you know that most of the Ivy League's glory, especially during the last forty years, has focused on two teams: Penn and Princeton.

In the 2005–2006 season, Kathy Orton set out to tell the Ivy League stories that people don't know. One of the great myths about athletics is the notion that only the most gifted athletes are driven. People talk about the work ethic of Michael Jordan and Tiger Woods, athletes with once-in-a-lifetime talent, who were driven to be the absolute best at their sports. Jordan and Woods combined their natural ability with their work ethic and their smarts to become multi-multi-multi-millionaires.

But there are other athletes, far less gifted, who care every bit as much and who work every bit as hard as Jordan and Woods. They work in obscurity, knowing that if they give their absolute best, they may help Brown finish second in the Ivy League or keep Harvard in the top half of the league for another season. They're all very smart, so they understand that 999 out of 1,000 of them aren't a Bradley or McMillian or, for that matter, a Matt Maloney or Jerome Allen, the Penn guards of the early 1990s who both went on to play in the NBA.

Most Ivy League basketball players understand that when they play their last college game, that's the end for them as serious athletes. A few might play overseas for a couple of years; others will continue to play pickup ball or rec ball for a long time. But the time when a large chunk of their lives are focused on being part of a team, on preparing for the next game or the next season, will be behind them. It is just as hard for an Ivy League basketball player to walk away from the game as it is for a guy who plays ten years in the NBA. Harder, perhaps, because it comes so much sooner, when one's passion for the game is still at its peak.

Kathy Orton first fell in love with the Ivy League at a Penn-Princeton game in the Palestra. That makes absolute sense because there is no college gym like the Palestra and Penn-Princeton is as special and as intense a rivalry as there is in college basketball. But she knew there was a lot more to the Ivy League than Penn and Princeton. She wanted to find out what it was like at the other six schools—Brown, Columbia, Cornell, Dartmouth, Harvard, and Yale—grinding away year after year in pursuit of the league's two icons. She knew there were plenty of stories to be told about the kids at those other schools, each of whom begins each season believing this will be the year when someone other than Penn or Princeton wins the league title.

She also learned how grim it could be in February for the players when their dreams have been washed away and they still have to get on the bus for the ride from Dartmouth to Columbia; Harvard to Cornell; Brown to Penn. The Ivy League is unique—mostly for good; on rare occasions for bad. The best example of the league not being perfect is the lack of a conference tournament.

A conference tournament gives everyone hope. Every year, a team comes from at or near the bottom of some league and makes a run in early March that lands it in the NCAA tournament. All the disappointments of the regular season are forgotten; injured players may get another chance; everybody has hope. In the Ivy League, however, hope often dies in a cold, half-empty gym in late January because there is no conference tournament—which is really too bad for those involved. Someday, maybe the Ivy League presidents will realize that the best thing for their student-athletes is to keep hope alive throughout the long winters and those long bus rides.

As we all know, the kids who play basketball in the Ivy League are, in fact, student-athletes, unlike so many of the players on the so-called big-time teams that are ranked in the top twenty-five, week in and week out. The graduation rate for Division I basketball players in the NCAA is about 44 percent. In the Ivy League, as we would expect, it is closer to 100 percent.

Most of those who play in the league will go on to major success away from the basketball court. They will become CEOs, doctors, lawyers, judges, and distinguished professors. Many will end up flying their own planes and owning fabulous homes around the world. But all of them will sit back and tell stories about their days playing in the Ivy League, about riding the buses, about the tiny locker rooms, about walking into the Palestra and Jadwin Gym and feeling the history of those places. They'll talk about tough losses and great wins—wins that perhaps only they and their teammates could truly understand—and they *will* call those The Good Old Days.

That's the way it is for every athlete, whether he is Jordan or Woods or the walk-on at Columbia or Brown who got into one game and missed a wide-open three-pointer at the buzzer that would have sliced the final margin to 83–65. Ivy League basketball players work every bit as hard, care every bit as much, and revel in victory and are saddened by defeat at the same level as—perhaps even a little higher than, because the end for them is nearer—the guys Dick Vitale is always screaming about.

I guess the biggest difference is that when it is time to tell their stories, they can sit down and do so without ever saying: "We gave 110 percent," "We needed to step up," or "We just didn't execute." They are smart, they are funny, and they are also pretty good basketball players.

Their stories are well worth hearing. Or, in this case, reading. Enjoy.

Preface

I wasn't always obsessed with Ivy League basketball. I didn't grow up watching any of the teams, nor did I know any of the players. Frankly, until I went to college, I'm not sure I could have named the eight schools in the league.

This fascination I developed grew out of my love for basketball. I am one of those hoops junkies who can watch the sport anywhere, anytime. I'll sit entranced for hours in a sweaty gym while a group of fifth-graders play a game most of their parents would prefer to avoid. Of all the sports I've covered through the years, none fascinates me as much as basketball does. And college basketball completely captivates me.

Still, I was only a casual follower of Ivy League basketball in February 1999, when my editor at the *Washington Post* assigned me to cover the Penn-Princeton game at the Palestra. The focus of the story wasn't to be about the game; instead, I was to capture how unusual the rivalry between the teams was.

After the first half ended, was I glad I wasn't writing about the game. Even a basketball fanatic like me had a hard time staying interested, with Princeton unable to make a basket and Penn ahead, 33–9, at halftime. With the outcome all but decided, I figured it would be an easy night for me—no overtime, no dragging out the game with late fouls, and no frantic push to make a 10 P.M. deadline.

Well, it didn't quite work out that way. Princeton staged a record comeback, winning 50–49. I've covered Super Bowls, Final Fours, and U.S. Opens featuring Tiger Woods. This game topped them all. To this day, it remains the most thrilling athletic contest I have ever watched live.

From that point on, I couldn't get enough of the league. It wasn't just the Penn-Princeton rivalry. It was the other six teams, which reminded me of that figure from Greek mythology, Sisyphus, pushing a boulder up a hill throughout eternity. Time after time, one of these teams would come close to seizing the title from Penn or Princeton, only to fall short. It was the lack of a conference tournament, which created a fourteen-game, winner-take-all endurance test to determine the league champion. Such a format in a league that receives only one berth in the NCAA tournament means that even minor injuries can ruin a team's season. As Harvard coach Frank Sullivan once put it, most Ivy League teams are "an ankle sprain from average."

It was also the Friday-Saturday schedule for league games. A nod to the importance of academics, the arrangement creates logistical difficulties for teams. No other league plays its regular-season games on back-to-back nights. It was the absence of athletic scholarships, which means if a student-athlete wants to play for an Ivy League team, he or his family must pay upward of $45,000 per year for the privilege. It was the travel-partner arrangement, which pairs the two traditionally toughest teams in the league, forcing the other teams to play them on consecutive nights. It was the bus travel between the schools. While many Division I teams are flying around in charter jets, the teams that play for the wealthiest schools in the nation ride buses to and from their league games.

But most of all, it was the players: young men who will become doctors, lawyers, and leaders of government and industry. Overachievers who have been successful in every aspect of their lives—except one. Basketball humbles them. It treats them with disdain. The prosperity that comes easily to them in other areas proves far more elusive on the court. They pursue their sport even though few expect their playing days to extend beyond college. And they sacrifice for this most fickle mistress even though she rarely rewards them. They spend sleepless nights poring over textbooks and writing papers to make up for the time spent lifting weights, watching game film, and traveling to and from away games. Most will have more setbacks than successes on the basketball court, and as a result, few will still be playing their senior years. The demands are too great. Even those determined to stick it out all four years—such as Cornell's Khaliq Gant, whose devastating injury cut short his career—discover how difficult it is to keep going.

Those who remain are the ones whose love of basketball supersedes nearly everything else. They enjoy the challenge of driving the length of the court as much as deriving the Fibonacci sequence, of breaking down a defender as much as breaking down Kant's *Critique of Pure Reason*, of penetrating a zone defense as much as penetrating the Riemann hypothesis. Along the way, basketball imparts lessons they probably won't learn in a classroom: how to work with others, how to fail, and how to move past that failure.

Because Ivy League players labor in obscurity most of their college careers, they often are lightly regarded by those outside the conference. They may not run as fast or jump as high as many of their big-school brethren, but that doesn't mean there aren't plenty of talented players in the league. What they lack in athleticism they make up for with solid fundamentals and court savvy.

Some industrious parents, who view Ivy League basketball as a mere step above an intramural sport, see basketball as a way to sneak their children into a prestigious school, not realizing how good the league's players are. The offices of Ivy coaches are littered with boxes of videotapes and DVDs of jump-shot-challenged kids who can barely make a layup yet think their skills are good enough to earn them a spot on the team.

Another widely held misperception is that Ivy League rosters are filled with privileged white kids from upper-class backgrounds. In reality, the league's players are a collection of ethnic, religious, and socioeconomic backgrounds from across the country and around the world. Few Division I basketball rosters boast as much diversity as those in the Ivy League.

Gone are the days of Bill Bradley, Corky Calhoun, Chet Forte, Jim McMillian, and John Edgar Wideman. They were student-athletes in every sense, excelling at their sport and in the classroom. Forte was the national player of the year. Bradley took Princeton to the Final Four before becoming a Rhodes Scholar. Wideman led Penn to its first Big 5 title before he, too, became a Rhodes Scholar. The Ivy League hasn't attracted basketball players of this caliber in recent years. Smart kids with strong basketball skills tend to play for Stanford, Duke, or Vanderbilt, schools that will pay for their education. Ivy League loyalists lament the decline of talent in the league, fearing the conference's better days are behind it.

Yet, the league has lost neither its relevancy nor its distinctiveness. Although highlights from its games do not appear nightly on *Sports-Center* and its teams often bow out in the first round of the NCAA tournament, Ivy League basketball is at turns wildly entertaining, utterly exasperating, fiercely competitive, gut-wrenchingly emotional, artistic, and unsightly—sometimes within the course of a single game. In an era when Division I basketball is corrupted by recruiting scandals, star players' jumping to the NBA, and huge television contracts, the Ivy League has managed to steer clear of these pitfalls by steadfastly adhering to its principles. It has become one of the last refuges for players and coaches who truly respect the game.

Before taking readers on my journey through the 2005–2006 season of Ivy League basketball, I would like to include a note about why I selected that particular season and why I focused on the teams that I did. When deciding to write a book about Ivy League basketball, I realized that the 2005–2006 season was the fiftieth season of the league. (The league celebrated its fiftieth anniversary the following season, but if you do the math, the league played its fiftieth season in 2005–2006.) Second, Harvard looked like it might win the league that season. The possibility of the Crimson winning its first Ivy title presented an opportunity that was too historic to pass up.

With those story lines in mind, I quickly realized it would be foolhardy to try to chronicle the entire seasons of all eight teams. The book would be too unwieldy. Instead, I picked four teams—Cornell, Harvard, Penn, and Princeton—that I felt had the most compelling themes. I then tried to include the other four—Brown, Columbia, Dartmouth, and Yale—as much as I could. My sincerest apologies to those teams if they feel overlooked.

All interviews were conducted by me unless otherwise noted in the text. When not present at the games, I relied on press releases from the Ivy League schools and recaps from the following for background on what happened at the game. These sources included *Brown Daily Herald, Columbia Spectator, Cornell Daily Sun, Harvard Crimson, Daily Pennsylvanian, Daily Princetonian, Yale Daily News, Ithaca Journal, Philadelphia Inquirer, Philadelphia Daily News, Providence Journal,* Ivy .basketball-u.com, Princeton Basketball News, ESPN.com, and Associated Press.

In the following pages, I describe a typical Ivy League basketball season, showing how teams come together and how they ultimately succeed or fail. Starting with the October practices, moving into the pre-conference competition, then the league games, and finally the NCAA tournament, this book offers a chance to get to know the players and coaches that make this league special.

Outside
the
Limelight

Chapter 1

Origins

of a

League

"The Ivy League is frequently accused of several kinds of snobbery, but never in athletics. Ivy League people, in fact, have a considerable sense of inferiority about the quality of their teams in contrast to those schools in other parts of the country."
— John McPhee, *A Sense of Where You Are*

The most popular explanation of how the Ivy League got its name dates back to October 14, 1937. As the story goes, George Daley, the sports editor of the *New York Herald-Tribune,* and his assistant editor, Irving Marsh, were assigning writers to upcoming college football games. The weekend's big game was Pittsburgh against Fordham at the Polo Grounds. They assigned their veteran football writer, Stanley Woodward, to that one. Caswell Adams, the paper's boxing writer, drew the Columbia-Penn game at Baker Field. Adams, none too thrilled about the assignment, groused, "Do I have to watch the ivy grow every Saturday afternoon? How about letting me see some football away from the ivy-covered halls of learning for a change?"

Woodward was said to have overheard Adams's complaint and inserted the phrase "Ivy League" into a later column, thus introducing the term into the lexicon. It's the sort of tale one might expect to be associated with this venerable league. Unfortunately, it's a fable. This bit of fiction was so well crafted that even the Ivy League bought into it, publicizing the anecdote until facts disproved it.

Another theory about the Ivy League's etymology stems from the belief that it was once a four-team league. Some say Harvard, Princeton, Yale, and Columbia; others insist Penn, not Columbia, was part of the group. These teams apparently formed the "Four League" or, using Roman numerals, the "IV League." Yet, there is no evidence that a four-team league existed.

Alan Gould, an Associated Press sports editor, reportedly was the first person to apply "Ivy League" in a story that appeared on February 8, 1935—well in advance of the league's official formation. Although others, including Woodward, made reference to ivy in earlier articles about the schools, no one apparently put "ivy" and "league" together until Gould did. What's more, Ivy League isn't the official name of the conference. The proper title is the Council of Ivy Group Presidents, which makes abundantly clear who runs this league. But by the time the presidents got around to forming the conference in 1954, with competition slated to begin in 1956, the Ivy League label was so strongly attached to these schools that it became the de facto designation.

From its inception, the Ivy League—or Ancient Eight, as it is sometimes affectionately known—has distinguished itself from the rest of Division I by eschewing athletic scholarships. For a time, the Patriot League followed the Ivy League's example and shunned athletic-based aid, but eventually it, too, succumbed to pressure to remain competitive in Division I in 1998. Now the military academies, where all students are on scholarship, are the only schools outside the Ivy League not to grant athletic aid.

"The Ivy League, partly because of the scholarship issue, sees itself as different and therefore needs to make a number of its own rules in addition to those the NCAA imposes," said Hunter R. Rawlings III, the president of Cornell from 1995 to 2003 and its interim president from 2005 to 2006. "As a result, the Ivy League often works by a different standard. It's usually a tougher standard."

Despite their emphasis on academics, Ivies have a long history of sports competition and boast more varsity teams than most college campuses. Harvard and Yale met in the first athletic event contested between two U.S. universities—a boat race on New Hampshire's Lake Winnipesaukee in 1852. Harvard fields the largest Division I athletic program with forty-one varsity sports and more than 1,500 student-athletes. Dartmouth, which has the smallest undergraduate enrollment of the Ivy schools (approximately 4,100 students), has thirty-four varsity, twenty-four intramural, and seventeen club sports. Nearly three-quarters of Dartmouth's undergraduates participate in some form of athletics.

The eight schools share several traits. They are all elite educational institutions located in the northeastern United States with highly selective entrance requirements. They are privately owned and controlled, and they rank among the wealthiest private universities in the world with endowments ranging in the billions of dollars. They also are some of the oldest colleges in the country. Seven were founded before the American Revolution.

And they have their differences.

- Brown is known for an unconventional curriculum that allows students to individually tailor their studies rather than requiring them to take specific core courses. The school, located in Providence, Rhode Island, also shuns the traditional grading system by allowing students to take any class pass/fail.

- Columbia has the smallest campus—a mere thirty-six acres, or about six city blocks, tucked into the Morningside Heights neighborhood of New York City. It was the last Ivy school to become co-ed (1983).

- Cornell, the youngest Ivy (founded in 1865) and the only one that was co-ed from the beginning, boasts the largest campus. Its 745-acre grounds in Ithaca, New York, resemble a midwestern state school more than a stereotypical New England college.

- Dartmouth, situated in Hanover, New Hampshire, is the northernmost Ivy. Its motto, "a voice crying out in the wilderness," gives one an idea of its remoteness.

- Harvard is the oldest and richest college in the United States. Founded in 1636, the Cambridge, Massachusetts, school has an endowment of $25.9 billion (as of 2005).

- Penn, a large, urban school located in the heart of Philadelphia, has the largest undergraduate population among the Ivies (close to 10,000 students).

- Princeton, a small, suburban school situated in the middle of New Jersey, has the third-smallest Ivy undergraduate body (4,700 students).

- Yale is the second-wealthiest university and the third oldest in the United States. Founded in 1701, the New Haven, Connecticut, school has a $15.2 billion endowment (as of 2005).

Just as the schools' personalities differ, so do their basketball histories. Some are rich and enduring; others are sparse or faded. And even though Ivy League teams aren't regularly mentioned among the sport's top powers, that doesn't mean their pedigrees aren't as regal as some of the country's most storied programs. When Street & Smith's released its publication *100 Greatest College Basketball Programs of All Time* in the spring of 2005, nearly half of the Ivy League was included: Penn (No. 16), Princeton (No. 19), and Dartmouth (No. 66). Columbia just missed the list at No. 104.

Ask the average basketball fan to name some of the top college programs in the country, and he would probably list UCLA, Kentucky, Kansas, Duke, and North Carolina, among others. It is doubtful that Penn would be included. But the Quakers should be part of any conversation involving college basketball nobility. Entering the 2005–2006 season, Penn ranked in the top ten in all-time victories among Division I basketball teams and had made twenty-one NCAA tournament appearances. Its most memorable NCAA run came in 1979 when Tony Price and James Salters propelled the Quakers through the East region and into the Magic Johnson–Larry Bird Final Four. Penn also left its mark on basketball's highest honor, the Naismith Memorial Basketball Hall of Fame. Chuck Daly, who coached the Quakers for seven seasons before leading the Detroit Pistons to two NBA titles and Team USA to an Olympic gold medal, was inducted in 1994.

Princeton produced two Hall of Fame members: Pete Carril and Bill Bradley. Although the program is known as much for its near upsets as its wins—just ask Alonzo Mourning and Georgetown about that opening-round game in the 1989 NCAA tournament—the Tigers have had some notable victories. Gabe Lewullis's backdoor layup knocked defending champion UCLA out of the first round of the 1996 NCAA tournament, and Carril led Princeton to the 1975 NIT championship. The Tigers' twenty-three NCAA tournament appearances included a trip to the 1965 Final Four, that team led by Bradley.

Dartmouth's inclusion in the top 100 programs by Street & Smith's may have surprised those unaware of its basketball lineage. The Big Green played in the national title game twice, losing to Stanford in 1942 and falling in overtime to Utah in 1944. Dartmouth, which won two of the first three Ivy League championships, has made seven NCAA tournament appearances but none since Rudy LaRusso, a future NBA all-star, led the Big Green in 1959.

Columbia's basketball glory has dimmed in recent years, but the Lions once featured some of the top players in the nation. Chet Forte, who later as sports director at ABC helped launch *Monday Night Football*, narrowly beat Wilt Chamberlain for national player of the year honors in 1957. Jim McMillian led Columbia to its only Ivy title in 1968—one of three NCAA tournament appearances by the Lions—then was the Los Angeles Lakers' first-round draft pick in 1970.

Yale has fielded a basketball team longer than any other Ivy school. The Bulldogs began competing in the sport just five years after James Naismith first hung peach baskets on the wall of a YMCA in 1891. Yale, which won the first of its four Ivy titles in 1957, also produced the Ivy League player with the longest NBA career. Chris Dudley may not have made many free throws during his time in the NBA, but he lasted sixteen years, playing for five teams.

Brown celebrated its one hundredth year of basketball in the 2005–2006 season, but has had few highlights during that century. The Bears won their only Ivy League championship and made their lone NCAA appearance in 1986. Their most famous player is best known for his coaching accomplishments on a different field of play. Joe Paterno played basketball for two years at Brown before becoming Penn State's longtime football coach.

Cornell and Harvard also lack strong basketball traditions. The Big Red won its only Ivy championship in 1988, making it the last school not named Penn or Princeton to hold the Ivy title outright. Bryan Colangelo missed out on that championship by a year, but found success in the NBA, becoming the team president and general manager of the NBA's Toronto Raptors and the Phoenix Suns. Harvard is the only school not to have won an Ivy League championship. James Brown did his best to win a title for the Crimson, leading it to three consecutive winning seasons. But the host of CBS's *The NFL Today* came up short of the ultimate prize.

Part I

GREAT
EXPECTATIONS

Chapter 2

A Mom-
and-Pop
Store

D roplets of water trickling down from the ceiling collected into
puddles on the court. These slick spots—a result of a cold,
steady rain pelting Lavietes Pavilion and seeping through the
glass-paned roof—proved no more than a nuisance to the Harvard basketball team as it went through its first practice of the 2005–2006 season. Harvard's home court, Ray Lavietes '36 Pavilion at Briggs Athletic
Center, opened in 1926 and is tied with the University of Oregon's
McArthur Court as the second-oldest basketball arena among Division I
schools. (Harvard's basketball team didn't move into Lavietes until 1981.
Before that time, the Crimson played at the Indoor Athletic Building.)
Only Fordham's Rose Hill Gymnasium is older, by two years. While
Lavietes's roof is an architectural marvel, it doesn't provide much of a
barrier to the cold and damp on raw October mornings like this one.

As players slipped and slid through practice, the task of mopping
up the constant moisture on the court was handled by one of the assistant

coaches or a player temporarily sidelined with an injury. At most schools, this duty would fall to a team manager, but Harvard has no managers. As Division I basketball programs go, Harvard has one of the more bare-bones operations. With just a head coach, two assistants, and a trainer, the Crimson is the mom-and-pop store in the corporate world of college basketball.

Harvard, the nation's first college and one of its most prestigious universities, has earned a well-deserved reputation of excellence. Included among the school's long and impressive list of accomplishments is producing thirteen U.S. presidents, six Supreme Court justices, and an astronaut. It boasts the nation's largest varsity sports program, which has won a total of 123 Ivy League titles in eighteen sports. The women's basketball program holds the distinction of being the only No. 16 seed to upset a No. 1 seed in the NCAA tournament.

Compared with the lofty standards set by the rest of the school, the men's basketball program doesn't measure up. Harvard is believed to be the only Division I program never to have won a conference championship. In its ninety-five seasons of college basketball, the Crimson has been to exactly one NCAA tournament, in 1946. Some people thought that might change in the 2005–2006 season, particularly Harvard's three seniors, whose sole objective was to win the school's first Ivy League title. Michael Beal, Zach Martin, and Matt Stehle had gone through a lot during their three years, including a 4–23 season as sophomores. They weren't about to let this chance slip away. Fearing that the six freshmen didn't share their resoluteness, they called a players-only meeting on the eve of the first practice. "We were telling the younger guys, 'You can always say there's always next year. We ourselves said that,'" Stehle said. "But we finally realized—it's too bad it took us this long to realize—the fact that there isn't a next year for us. This is our last shot. We're trying to impart that on the freshmen. 'You guys are going to have three or four more years, but this is it for me. I don't care whether you like it or not, but this is what we're going to do, and this is how we're going to do it.'"

Coaches often talk about wanting upperclassmen to take ownership of a team. In Harvard's case, the seniors embraced that philosophy whole-heartedly. "Sometimes things can get awkward around here," coach Frank Sullivan said. "We say, 'Everybody wants to be management. Nobody wants to be labor.' Sometimes that can happen at an Ivy League school. A lot of people who are going to be management in the future want to be management now, and you have to tell them, 'You are rank and file.' But those three guys I'll allow to be management. They've heard me say, 'You three guys have been waiting to take this team over.' Their eyes are all like, 'Yeah, we have been.' It's good to see. What's even better with this group here, they are three guys I truly trust. I truly trust them in all respects. If they tell me it's black, then it's black. I believe them. They're unique in that sense."

Sullivan, who began his fifteenth season at Harvard in the fall of 2005, is one of the old-guard Ivy coaches and the Crimson's most successful coach. Only Penn's Fran Dunphy had been around the league longer. An affable fellow, Sullivan is well liked and well respected by his coaching peers. After thirty-plus years in the business, working for well-known coaches such as Rollie Massimino, Brian Hill, and P. J. Carlesimo, Sullivan could have used his connections to obtain a more high-profile position. But he was happy at Harvard. The Ivy League suited him and allowed him to do what he enjoyed most: coach. Unlike at a bigger program, where his time would be eaten up by media requests, administrative demands, fundraising, and community relations, Sullivan could devote himself to teaching his players. With limited resources, Sullivan quietly had built Harvard into a strong program. The Crimson had finished .500 or better in the league in seven of the last ten seasons and in the top half in four of the last five. In the past ten seasons, only Penn and Princeton had better Ivy records.

Under Sullivan, Harvard was known for its guard play. In the 2005–2006 season, however, the Crimson's frontcourt of forward Stehle and center Brian Cusworth had led many prognosticators to call this Harvard's year. Stehle and Cusworth, who would have been a senior had he not suffered a stress fracture in his foot his sophomore year and elected to drop out of school to preserve his eligibility, were the top returning scorers and rebounders in the Ivy League.

Stehle, pronounced STAY-lee, was the poster boy for Harvard basketball. Every preseason publication lauded him. Harvard magazine wrote a glowing profile, calling him an "All-Court Wonder." The nickname stuck, and his teammates teased him relentlessly about it. In many ways, Stehle was the classic stereotypical Harvard man—clean-cut, smart, and serious, traits perhaps passed down from his two uncles who graduated from Harvard. Although Stehle was confident, he was not overtly arrogant. He wasn't one who craved attention. He would rather be one of the guys. Stehle ended up at Harvard in part because Sullivan happened to live on the same street as Stehle's high school coach. At Newton South High School, he started out as a five-foot-ten point guard before a growth spurt caused him to shoot up nearly a foot. But it wasn't until he was a junior, when mostly Ivy and Patriot league schools began showing interest in him, that Stehle thought about playing Division I basketball.

At Harvard, Stehle was the team's best player and starting power forward. There wasn't much power to his game, however. At six-feet-eight, 215 pounds, he was more wiry than muscular. In comparison with other power forwards in Division I basketball, Stehle was an inch shorter and about thirty pounds lighter than Duke's Shelden Williams and twenty pounds lighter than Texas's Brad Buckman. But what Stehle lacked in speed and jumping ability, he made up for in court awareness. His strength lay in his versatility. Stehle could play any position on the court, including point guard.

You didn't have to be around Stehle long to realize how intense and driven he is. No one demands more or is as critical of Stehle than Stehle himself. When his teammates selected him captain—the first Massachusetts native to be voted Harvard's basketball captain in more than fifty years—Stehle took the job seriously. Unlike other schools, where the coach may select the captain or two or more players may be co-captains, Harvard chooses its leader by a secret ballot of the players in the spring. The coaches have no input. If there is a tie, the players vote until it is broken. There are no co-captains. "One of the things that's really important at Harvard is the role of captain," Sullivan said. "It's a very tradition-soaked role. Captains are highly respected by our administration. The role of captain is always a big deal here, but for me personally, it's always been a significant thing."

Stehle had no illusions of playing basketball professionally. He knew his days of competitive basketball would end after this season. A government major mostly because Harvard made him decide early, Stehle had intended to follow his mother to law school. Lately, though, he was leaning toward jobs in finance. The summer before his senior year, he interned for an asset management company in Spokane, Washington. A political career was another possibility. "This year I'm trying to put [basketball] in the driver's seat," Stehle said. "Now that I'm a senior, I'm trying not to worry too much about the classroom, but my mom will kill me if I don't come home with good grades. It's a real pain because there's a lot of good students here so it's very competitive."

Harvard's optimism about the 2005–2006 season was bolstered by the release of the league's preseason poll in early November. The prognosticators picked the Crimson to finish second behind Penn, the defending champion. In four of the last seven years, the team picked second had won the league.

Suddenly, there was a buzz around campus. People were taking notice of the basketball team—a rarity at a school where hockey is the most popular winter sport. The recognition was nice, and most of the players enjoyed it—except for Stehle. "Right now, people are coming up to me saying, 'Wow, Harvard is picked No. 2. That's great,'" Stehle said.

"It's not great. It doesn't mean anything. Preseason rankings, preseason accolades don't mean anything."

Not all of his teammates were as dismissive of the preseason poll. Beal, a fellow senior, was pleased Harvard was receiving recognition, but like Stehle, he wasn't letting it go to his head. "We believe that's where we should be," Beal said. "It's good to have that pressure. It's good to have people realize the things that we have, but it's more on us. Obviously, we have the top two returning scorers in the league [Stehle and Cusworth], but that doesn't do anything unless we're in practice every day working. I think that's something that our maturity has kind of shown us. That one sophomore season taught us a lot."

None of the seniors, least of all Beal, had forgotten their sophomore season. Beal wears the number 23 on his jersey, a popular number for basketball players since Michael Jordan made it famous. But in Beal's case, his crimson numeral also could have represented the basketball version of Hester Prynne's scarlet letter—a constant reminder of the number of losses Harvard endured during the 2003–2004 season. The team's 4–23 mark was Harvard's worst under Sullivan and the Crimson's worst in fifty-five years.

Beal was the more reserved and introspective of the three seniors. Aside from an occasional fist pump, he wasn't prone to displays of emotion. It was hard to tell at times what he was feeling because he kept such a tight rein on his demeanor. Growing up in Brooklyn, the son of a Wall Street investment banker, Beal had developed an interest in the fast-paced world of finance. He was an economics major and had interned with Morgan Stanley, where he hoped to work after graduation. "It's always been the Brooklyn edge that I've liked about him," Sullivan said. "Even though he went to Collegiate School, he still had a city edge, he still had a Brooklyn edge to him. For us, it's good to have a kid from New York City on the team. There are not that many New York City players in the Ivy League right now."

Sullivan had recruited Beal as a small forward but was forced to play him at point guard out of necessity. Beal started twenty-three games at point guard his sophomore season until he tore the medial collateral ligament in his knee that February. His knee never fully healed, quelling any thoughts of playing professionally. Besides his ability to run an offense, Beal also was one of Harvard's better defenders. He usually was assigned the task of guarding the opponent's top scorer.

As much as he enjoyed playing basketball, Beal made an effort to downplay his athletic status to the rest of the student body. Rarely would he wear his basketball apparel to class. He didn't want to be defined that way, especially since he had many interests outside of basketball. He was co-president of the Aspiring Minority Business Leaders and Entrepreneurs (AMBLE), a Harvard student group, and was the executive producer for "Eleganza," a fashion show production of BlackCAST, the Black Community and Student Theater, a nonprofit student group that promotes diversity in the arts. "I get angry when people tell other people that I'm a basketball player," he said.

Athletes at Ivy League schools are not glorified. Sometimes, they are treated with disdain. Other students and even some professors wonder whether the athletes would have been admitted had it not been for sports. Some probably wouldn't have been. Studies have shown that recruited athletes at Ivy League schools have SAT scores and grade-point averages lower than the rest of the student body, yet they are accepted at a rate twice that of the other students. The concern is that underqualified athletes are taking spots away from more deserving academic minds. William G. Bowen, a former president of Princeton, wrote two books— *The Game of Life* in 2001 with James L. Shulman and *Reclaiming the Game* in 2003 with Sarah A. Levin—that skewered the Ivies, among other elite institutions of higher education, for allowing athletics to overshadow the mission of these schools. Bowen asserted that because athletes perform worse academically than the student body as a whole they undermine the school's commitment to academic excellence.

Jere R. Daniell, a professor emeritus of history at Dartmouth, admires Bowen, saying his books "warrant against excess." Yet, Daniell noted that Bowen happened to pick a year that best served his argument and that the data for 1999 enabled him to "make his most exaggerated point about the, from his point of view, the negative components of the relationship between athletics and academics. From a combination of formal and personal evidence, the low point was the year at which Bowen gathered data, and since then . . . there's no basically softening of criteria for athletes.

"There is some suggestion in that second book, which is specifically about [the New England Small College Athletic Conference] and Ivy League, that even given adjustments for admissions criteria, recruited athletes do worse than you could project their academic expectations. Well, to begin with, that's not surprising. The number of hours they are expected to put in[to their sport]. And what no one has done is project this five, ten, twenty years out." In the second book, Bowen briefly mentioned that though athletes underperformed against their peers during college, they tended to outperform them after leaving school.

Bowen's books caused much hand-wringing and brought about meaningful changes in the Ivy League, most notably to the Academic

Index (AI). The AI is a combination of a recruit's grade-point average, SAT score, and class rank, and it must fall within an acceptable range for the athlete to be admitted. Most Ivy League basketball players have SATs in the 1300s and GPAs between 3.5 and 4.0. In the rest of Division I, an athlete only needs an SAT score between 620 and 800 and a GPA between 2.5 and 3.0. The uproar over Bowen's books led to much higher AI averages, resulting in a smaller pool of eligible recruits, and some would argue, a much less diverse group of athletes. Critics of Bowen cite his books as the reason the Ivy League no longer competes as strongly as it once did against the rest of Division I basketball. They claim the new standards make it more difficult to admit talented athletes. "I would say that first [book] had a good impact in the sense that it brought to the presidents' attention some long-term trends that the presidents perhaps had not been fully aware of and therefore raised some real questions that seemed legitimate and valid to study in more detail," said Hunter R. Rawlings III, the president of Cornell from 1995 to 2003 and its interim president from 2005 to 2006. "That book did lead to some real reflection about the overall impact of Ivy League athletics."

Like Beal, Zach Martin fought the athlete stereotype. Of the three seniors, Martin was the most outgoing. He was good-natured, easy to be around, and seemed to be friends with everybody, including Princeton's senior point guard Scott Greenman. The two had known each other since seventh grade and had thought about attending the same school. Princeton recruited both of them for a time but then lost interest in Martin, who eventually chose Harvard over Cornell and Lafayette. "I know that some people feel that 'Oh, you only got into Harvard because of basketball,'" Martin said. "It's kind of annoying. Harvard doesn't take just the smartest people. They take people with merit, diversity, whatever. As athletes, we bring that. It's not just academics. We bring something to the college that the others can't."

Martin was in the midst of applying to law schools in the fall of 2005. He had worked at a law firm the previous summer and wanted to study sports law with the goal of becoming an agent. As part of his application, he was required to submit a personal statement. The topic he chose to write about was how being an athlete at Harvard helped him with time management. "The point I made is, yeah, I have five less hours a day than other students" because of practices and workouts, Martin said. "That's why I have to work so hard to keep up. That's why I'm so proud of my GPA, how well I've done in school."

Martin, a 3.47 student, wasn't the only talented basketball player in his family. His older sister Aimee played at Georgia Tech and then professionally overseas. Coming out of Shawnee High School in Medford,

New Jersey—the same school that produced NBA player Malik Allen and Princeton standout Brian Earl—Martin was Harvard's most highly touted recruit going into the 2002–2003 season. One scouting service ranked him among the top 100 seniors in the country. A four-year starter and three-year captain at Shawnee, he led the school to a state title his junior year and finished as the second-leading scorer in school history.

"The thing that sticks out in my mind about Zach is he's a real basketball player," Sullivan said. "He grew up around basketball. It means so much to who he is. It clearly is how he defines himself. Here he is at Harvard, and he's a really bright guy. In Zach's case, I've always felt he was a real basketball guy who happened to go to Harvard. We don't get those guys too often. That kid loves basketball." Martin never found the same success at Harvard that he found in high school. He failed to break into the starting lineup, instead becoming a solid player off the bench for the Crimson. His contributions, however, showed up in ways that couldn't be measured on a stat sheet. Martin was a good guy to have in the locker room. He kept everyone loose.

As the 2005–2006 season opener against Vermont approached, the three seniors—Beal, Martin, and Stehle—knew this was their last chance to make their mark on Harvard basketball. They were tired of losing. They wanted to go out as winners. "We haven't had four great basketball years," Martin said. "We've had three let-down years, especially our sophomore year. We haven't had the best collegiate careers. It would be disappointing not to play up to our potential this year."

Chapter 3

Great

Scott

After a rocky first season, some observers expected Princeton coach Joe Scott to take a low-key approach this year. But anyone who thought that didn't know Scott. It didn't take him long to cause a stir. Five days into practice, Scott dismissed two players from the team, cut and then reinstated another, and asked two more to remain even though they wouldn't play much. As personnel moves go, these were minor. The players who were cut rarely came off the bench the previous season. The two who wouldn't play much were on the junior varsity squad anyway.

For all the brouhaha created by the dismissals, one would have thought Scott sent packing some of the most important players on the team. The players were shocked even though Scott had told them cuts would be made. Ivy League coaches and players outside of Princeton wondered what was going on. It was simple. Scott did not believe in having a player on the roster just for the sake of having him there. He wanted players committed to his way of doing things. If a player wasn't committed, he was gone.

Princeton was less than a week into its season, and already Scott had given his critics another opportunity to question his coaching methods. Many Princeton basketball observers grumbled that Scott was too strict, too rigid, too hard on his players. They felt today's players needed to be coddled. Scott believed otherwise. He was convinced that the more he demanded, the more he would get and the more success Princeton would have. It wasn't that he was indifferent toward his players. Rather, it was a form of tough love.

"There's no way that they're [not] going to know—and this is the ultimate goal—that I don't care about them," Scott said. "I don't think they're something special inside. That we together have to bring that out. It's not my job to bring that out. It's your corresponding commitment, the same commitment that I have. Together that's our job over four years."

Many hailed Scott's return to Princeton in 2004 as the second coming of longtime Princeton coach Pete Carril. Scott had spent twelve years at Princeton with Carril, first as a player, then as an assistant coach, before leaving to take over a dormant Air Force program. In his fourth season at the Colorado school, Scott led the Falcons to a 22–7 record, their first Mountain West Conference regular season championship, and their first NCAA tournament appearance in forty-two years.

Viewed as the strictest adherent of Carril's Princeton offense, Scott was going to be the coach to return the school to its glory days. Princeton wouldn't just contend for Ivy League titles; it would challenge the best teams in the country. The Tigers wouldn't just participate in the NCAA tournament; they would make a deep run. Scott didn't try to disabuse fans of this notion. Instead, he fed their grandiose visions and high expectations with his own talk of Princeton superiority.

Such boasting didn't seem misplaced, considering that Scott inherited a Princeton squad that had four starters—including two first-team all-Ivy selections—returning from a 20–8 team that won the Ivy League title and reached the NCAA tournament. Nearly everyone expected Scott's first season at Princeton to be special. It turned out to be special, just for all the wrong reasons. The Tigers stumbled to a 15–13 overall record and 6–8 in the league, their most Ivy losses in twenty years and their first below-.500 finish in league history.

Princeton is accustomed to being the lead horse in the Ivy League, not its also-ran. The Tigers have won or shared more than half of the Ivy basketball titles. This inexplicable decline rocked everyone associated with the proud program, especially Scott. Now in his second season, he was taking a different tack. "We're starting from scratch only because I made mistakes last year," Scott said. "I thought we could skip steps. You can't skip steps when you're trying to build something special, something that's going to last forever and going to stand for something."

Scott exudes an intensity and passion so great that it's best to hold on to a fixed object when you're around him so that you don't get blown away. The zeal that served him well at Air Force, however, was abrasive to the Princeton players. Coaching changes are usually disruptive, and Princeton's situation was one of the more difficult. Taking over a successful program is almost a bigger challenge than taking over a losing one. When a coach comes to a team that has no history of success, the players will do whatever he says because they want so badly to win. If Scott had told the Air Force players they had to dye their hair pink in order to win, they probably would have done it because they were tired of losing. But at Princeton, the players had won or shared three Ivy League titles and gone to two NCAA tournaments under John Thompson III, Scott's predecessor. When Scott walked in and started telling them they had to play his way in order to be successful, they balked. They had won without doing things his way, so they saw no reason why they should conform to his methods now. That clash of agendas proved to be Princeton's undoing.

"There's definitely players who had difficulty adjusting [to the coaching change] and it was definitely a distinct contrast in [coaching styles], two completely different coaches," senior point guard Scott Greenman said. "The dynamic on this year's team is so much different. We have just a completely different team, different expectations."

Greenman was Joe Scott's staunchest defender. And in many ways, the two seemed cut from the same cloth. They were a couple of Jersey guys, who grew up about an hour apart from each other along the Garden State Parkway—Scott in Toms River, Greenman in Linwood. They both were point guards. They both stood less than six feet tall. And both had a wry sense of humor. But while Scott always appeared to know where he was going and how he was going to get there, Greenman seemed more willing to let life take him along for the ride.

Growing up, Greenman was the kind of kid who always had a ball in his hands. Although he played several sports, he was drawn to basketball. His father, Allan, played basketball at Bucknell for Jim Valvano in the early 1970s and imbued his son with a love of the game. When it came time for him to choose a college, Greenman was recruited by several Ivy League schools, but selected Princeton because of the program's history of success. After he committed to the Tigers, he was offered a scholarship by Stanford. He turned it down, preferring to remain close to home. "It was definitely enticing, obviously, Stanford, Pac-10, but this is pretty big time," Greenman said. "We play on ESPN two or three times a year against some of the best teams in the country. We're usually in the top one hundred, top fifty every year. I wanted to go to a school that challenged me both academically and athletically. I would not have forfeited the athletics for academics so it was extremely important that it was a great basketball school as well. It wasn't a thing where I was saying, 'Oh my god, I have to play in the Ivy League.' That wasn't the case at all. Basketball is the main thing in my life, so I was really trying to go with the best situation, and obviously that it was the Ivy League didn't hurt."

Greenman was majoring in sociology, which seemed the perfect course of study for someone with his range of interests. As a junior, he wrote a paper on the evolution of and trends in crimes committed by females over the last fifty years. For his senior thesis, Greenman was writing about interfaith marriages, specifically between Jews and Christians. But with his college career winding down, Greenman was uncertain what he would do with his degree. He hoped to do something with basketball after college, perhaps play overseas or maybe coach. He also had thought about following the same path as his coach and going to law school. After Scott graduated from Princeton, he received his JD from Notre Dame and then worked at a law firm before turning to coaching. For the moment, though, Greenman's primary goal was making sure Princeton didn't suffer through a season similar to his junior year. "It was one of the worst seasons I've had in my playing career," Greenman said. "A lot of guys felt the same way. I'm sure a lot of coaches felt the same way. But it's over, and it's something that everyone deals with in their life. I'm sure everyone has one bad season, but yeah, it was extremely frustrating, and we'll try not to have that happen again."

Scott didn't recruit Greenman to Princeton, but he won him over with his perfectionism. No one is allowed to slack off at one of Scott's practices. Mistakes are not tolerated. If a player messes up a drill or a play, he can expect Scott's rapier sarcasm—no matter if he is the star or the last man on the bench. Greenman, who described playing for Scott as challenging and fun, craved this kind of accountability. He needed to have himself and his teammates held to a high standard.

"He's a very funny guy," Greenman said of Scott. "He's completely different off the basketball floor than he is on the court. He's relaxed. But even on the court, I mean, it's his job. He has to get a bunch of eighteen- to twenty-two-year-old guys to get on the same page. He has to try to make us the best we can be. I don't know why everybody sees somebody who's demanding, people automatically see it as a negative where I don't think it is. If someone is trying to make you the best you can be at what you really like to do, how is that a bad thing?

"We go through tough times. We might get mad at Coach. But at the end of the day, he's our coach. We're all on the same page. He's trying to get the most out of us. If we really care about basketball and this is what we love to do, then we shouldn't have any problems with that. He's trying to make us better. That's not to say that's the only way that works. Other styles of coaching work, but he's proven at Air Force that this way does work. That's the way he does it, and it works."

In the 2005–2006 season, Scott believed he had more players who were willing to play his way and comfortable with his coaching methods. He also had a lot of inexperienced players. Greenman was the only senior on the roster. Two starters from the previous season, junior Luke Owings and sophomore Noah Savage, had been solid complementary players, but neither had shouldered much of the offensive burden. Owings, an economics major from Hyattsville, Maryland, who attended the same high school as his former Princeton coach John Thompson III, led the Ivy League in three-point percentage in his sophomore season but averaged only 6.3 points per game. Savage, who came out of the Hun School, located just a mile from the Princeton campus, was the team's top returning free-throw shooter. He averaged 6.4 points per game as a freshman. Sophomore Harrison Schaen, an athletic player out of basketball powerhouse Mater Dei in Santa Ana, California, had shown flashes of promise during his freshman season but then took a year off from school. The rest of the roster was a mix of freshmen and role players.

"We're going to be young, which is good," Scott said. "This is the right time to be young. When you're a new coach trying to build your program, it's good to be young so you can grow old together. . . . In my opinion, we might have more leadership this year because there's more knowledge as to what that word means. Last year, we might have had seniors. I don't know if that equaled leadership. That equaled being old."

Chapter 4

Multicultural Quakers

College basketball rosters tend to be regional. Except for a few elite programs, most teams recruit mainly in their backyards, and as a result, the players often come from the same geographic area. That's not the case in the Ivy League. Ivy coaches cast a wide net, searching across the country and around the world for players. In the 2005–2006 season, Ivy rosters comprised players from thirty-one states, the District of Columbia, and eight foreign countries. California was the most represented among the states, sending eighteen players to the Ivies. There were more Canadians (four) than any other nationality. Although more than a third of the players came from the eastern part of the United States, there were as many Ohioans as New Yorkers and as many North Carolinians as Massachusetts residents.

Penn had one of the more eclectic rosters. Eric Osmundson, an anthropology major, is an easygoing Californian with a passion for surfing. Friedrich Ebede, who is concentrating on finance at the Wharton School, speaks eight languages and is the son of a Cameroon political prisoner. Steve Danley, a philosophy, politics, and economics major, is a devout Roman Catholic from Maryland who was home-schooled until high school. Ibrahim Jaaber, a sociology major, is a Muslim from New Jersey who enjoys spoken-word poetry.

As might be expected from a group with such distinctive upbringings and intellectual curiosity, lively discussions often ensued. While the discourse could deteriorate into the ribald banter typical among young men their age, it did sometimes veer to topics usually not talked about in Division I locker rooms. "We're guys, and we screw around a lot like any other guys but some of the conversations I have with Ibby are unbelievable," said Danley who shared an apartment with Osmundson and Jaaber. "He's just a very intelligent kid, and he'll be pointing out patterns [of behavior]. We love to discuss patterns. We had a big discussion about [Malcolm Gladwell's] *The Tipping Point* book."

On a team of colorful characters, Danley is a true individualist. He purposely defies labels and refuses limitations. Blessed with an outgoing and friendly personality, he wants to experience all that life has to offer. He is active in his church and has his priest's phone number programmed into his cellphone, yet he enjoys attending Hillel services occasionally. He participates in spoken-word poetry with Jaaber and has written a novel. He was awarded a fellowship to the Center for the Study of the Presidency and has put himself on track to earn a Rhodes Scholarship. "My life is split into very different compartments, more than I feel like most people's lives are," Danley said. "I see myself being involved in a bunch of very different crowds. I really enjoy that. I like the fact that I can go from basketball to spoken word to church. . . . I wouldn't want to get myself in one circle with one set of circumstances. Someone said a liberal arts education at an Ivy League school is more about who you meet than what you learn."

Danley chose Penn because it allowed him to explore his many interests. It also was the place he felt most comfortable. Before Penn, Danley attended DeMatha, a private all-boys Catholic high school in suburban Washington, D.C., where he was coached by Morgan Wootten, one of the most successful high school basketball coaches ever. Even though he liked DeMatha, Danley felt out of place at times. "By the end, it was like everywhere I went, people would talk about my academics and not about my basketball," he said. "It was really important for me to go to a school where I wouldn't be the one academic kid. Here, I feel like I'm very much more one of the crowd. . . . When I'd pull out my books on the bus at DeMatha, it was 'Oh, Steve—dork.' But when I pull out my books here, it's just more expected. That was good. That was one of the reasons I loved the Ivy League as a whole."

Now that he's at Penn, the situation often gets reversed. Instead of being thought of as the smart kid, he is sometimes regarded as the dumb jock. Rather than letting it upset him, he has fun with it. "I almost set it up to take advantage of it because I think that's an incredibly good time," Danley said. "I enjoy very much playing off those [athletic] stereotypes. I think that's a lot of fun. There's probably a negative stigma that comes with it sometimes, but I'm six-eight. People know I play basketball. I wouldn't want to try to hide it."

Because his parents paid for him to go to a private high school, Danley chose to pay for Penn himself. So, in additional to his classes, basketball, and other extracurricular activities, Danley has a work-study job. Fortunately, it is one that accommodates his schedule. Danley does the laundry at the Palestra. He will throw in a load of wash before going to a shoot-around and then move it to the dryer after practice. "I worked in the office that does the Rhodes Scholarships my freshman year," Danley said. "That was great. I made contacts, but I just couldn't get enough hours in. Laundry lets me do an hour or two after practice and an hour before practice. It's really a lot more lenient."

Penn coach Fran Dunphy admires Danley and even says he has learned a lot from him. Yet, their relationship is not particularly close. Dunphy doesn't see it as his job to be Danley's buddy; and Danley, who is accustomed to praise, struggles at times with Dunphy's criticism. "I have to watch myself here," Danley said. "Dunph likes to say it's his job while we're here to be an asshole, and then he can be a friend to you after you graduate. That's very much his style to be hard on you now. That's his way of pushing you. I'm not going to say I always agree with it or it's the best way. It's kind of the opposite of what Coach Wootten did. Coach Wootten was more of a pat-you-on-the-butt [coach].

"Ultimately, I think in a lot of ways we need a lot less coaching as a team than a team of guys who don't have as high a basketball IQ. When I got here, Charlie Copp called as many sets as Dunph did. He was on the floor. He was the point guard. Dunph trusts that. He puts the guys in situations, and they're going to be able to make the right plays."

Danley was one of four starters who returned from Penn's 2005 Ivy League championship team. The Quakers' title—their third in four years—came as somewhat of a surprise. Not because few expected them to contend for the championship. They do so almost every year. But it wasn't supposed to be their year. They were too young, too inexperienced. Princeton, with its veteran lineup, was the prohibitive favorite to win it all. (Princeton fans would contend that Penn was the fortunate beneficiary of the Tigers' implosion.)

The upside of Penn's championship was that its starting lineup remained nearly intact going into the next season. The Quakers had a steady point guard, Osmundson, and a solid front line in Danley and Mark Zoller. They also had one of the league's more talented and athletically gifted players in Jaaber. Their biggest loss—and it was a significant one— was leading scorer and Ivy League player of the year Tim Begley, who had graduated. But given their experience plus Penn's longtime superiority in the league, it was hard not to make the Quakers the favorite to win the league again. "We respect that they honored us [with] the No. 1 position, but [in] the past few seasons, the favorite hasn't won, so we've got to remain focused," Osmundson said.

Being selected the front-runner was not an unfamiliar position for Penn. Since winning their first Ivy championship in 1966, the Quakers had accumulated twenty-three titles. Only four times in the past forty years had they finished in the bottom half of the league standings. Though their 1,592 victories put them behind Kentucky and North Carolina on the all-time victories list, they were ahead of Indiana and UCLA.

Penn's most celebrated basketball achievement came in 1979. The Quakers knocked off North Carolina and Syracuse in the NCAA tournament, then beat St. John's in the Eastern Regional final to reach the Final Four. Eventual champion Michigan State, led by future NBA great Magic Johnson, ended Penn's extraordinary campaign in the semifinals. Since then, the Quakers have won only one NCAA tournament game— a first-round victory over Nebraska in 1994—but they have remained mostly competitive against the scholarship schools.

The Quakers' success, inside and outside the league, has left them in an enviable place. Winning has its perks. People love a winner, and Penn has the strongest following in the league. The Quakers draw the biggest, most enthusiastic (and often the most amusingly clever) crowds among the Ivy teams. Every team wants to be them, but at the same time, every team wants to beat them. Some say Penn has it easy. Because of their success, the Quakers tend to attract top players. The best players, however, don't always make the best team. And winning when you're supposed to win isn't easy.

Because of the challenges that come with success, there is something to be said for being the underdog. There is less pressure as well as fewer expectations. The feeling of having to win can be as suffocating as the dread of losing. When Osmundson was asked if he enjoyed being on the team that the rest of the league was chasing, he gave a mixed response: "Yes and no. Yes, because the fans always come to support the team; and no, because you're never going to be under the radar. When you're under the radar, you can kind of slip in sometimes."

If the 2004–2005 season had been one of those rare occasions when Penn was overlooked, that would not be the case this year. Nobody was taking the Quakers lightly, but already Penn's title defense had gotten off to an uneven start. At its intrasquad scrimmage in early November, Penn had only eight healthy players and had to play four-on-four. Several players were out with ankle injuries, most notably starters Zoller, Osmundson, and David Whitehurst. Two more players had painful blisters on their feet. Another had a strained Achilles tendon. Greg Kuchinski had a stress fracture in his left foot. Whitehurst's injury was the most serious. Whitehurst, also a first-team all-Ivy hurdler on the track team, was still recovering from September 1 ankle surgery to repair a torn ligament. "For a while, it seemed like practice was almost a death march," said Danley, one of the few starters not felled by injury. "It seemed like people were going down every day."

With so many players injured—Jaaber was another who missed practice time because of an ankle injury—it had been difficult to develop any cohesion. Fortunately for Penn, the Quakers were the last Ivy League team to open the 2005–2006 season. Their first game wouldn't come until November 21 against Siena, plenty of time for everyone to heal. But this endless stretch of preseason practices with no games in sight was trying on the players. They were eager to defend their Ivy championship and return to the NCAA tournament, both of which seemed a long way off. "You do get antsy," Osmundson said. "You want to get out there and see where you stand. The preseason for us is long—six weeks. You can't wait to get on the court. It's what you work for, to get out and play in front of fans, play for your team. It's the best feeling."

Chapter 5

Getting

Under Way

E very college basketball team breaks its season into four parts: preseason practice, nonconference games, league games, and post-season. Preseason practice lasts from mid-October until early November. The nonconference schedule typically runs from early November until early to mid-January. The league season can begin as early as mid-December and runs through early March. The postseason starts in March and, as every team hopes, can last until early April.

In years past, when teams waited until after Thanksgiving to start playing games, preseason practice was a time to work on the fundamentals of passing, shooting, and dribbling. Teams would learn new offenses, defenses, and out-of-bounds plays. These days, with games beginning in early November, they are lucky if they have time to learn their base offenses and defenses. The first part of the season flies by so quickly that when the nonconference season starts, few teams look ready.

When it comes to scheduling nonconference games, some coaches are better at it than others. All teams play opponents outside of their league before their conference season begins, and coaches view this time as a chance to prepare for conference play, though they differ on how best to get their teams ready for what lies ahead. Some feel it is important, especially if they have inexperienced teams, to schedule easy opponents during the nonconference season so that when the league season rolls around, their players aren't discouraged by too many losses. Others, particularly those with experienced teams, want to challenge their players and therefore will schedule difficult games. Most coaches, including Ivy League ones, try to schedule a mix of games—some they're confident they'll win, some they hope they'll win, and some they have almost no chance of winning.

Cornell had opened practice less than a month earlier, and already the Big Red was headed to its first game of the 2005–2006 season. Cornell was set to play Saint Francis of Pennsylvania on this temperate Tuesday night in early November in the first game of a doubleheader, part of the College Hoops Classic—a tournament benefiting the Coaches vs. Cancer charity. Syracuse was hosting the regional, one of four tournament sites, and Cornell hoped to meet its intrastate rival in the second round.

On the hour-long bus ride to the game, Cornell coach Steve Donahue received a call on his cellphone from Columbia coach Joe Jones wishing him luck. Donahue and Jones knew each other from their days in Philadelphia when Donahue was an assistant at Penn and Jones was an assistant at Villanova. Although the two men weren't particularly close and were now Ivy League rivals, Jones nonetheless wanted Cornell to do well. He knew that a win by the Big Red would be good for the league.

In the Ivy League, there are the haves and the have-nots, and Donahue has been on both sides. For ten years, he was Fran Dunphy's assistant at Penn. During his time in Philadelphia, the Quakers won six league titles. They also went through the conference undefeated four times, including three consecutive years when they didn't lose an Ivy game. Then in September 2000, Donahue left Penn to become Cornell's head coach. The contrast between the two programs couldn't have been greater.

By the time Donahue arrived in Ithaca, it had been twelve years since Cornell's one and only Ivy League championship, and the intervening years hadn't been kind to the Big Red. The season before Donahue took over, Cornell won just three Ivy games. It is understandable why a coach from outside the Ivy League might go after this job, naively thinking that with hard work and good recruiting he can turn the program around and win a title. For someone within the league to willingly become Cornell's head coach, well, it took guts and plenty of optimism.

Reviving Cornell basketball hadn't been easy. In Donahue's first two seasons, the Big Red won a combined five league games. Cornell steadily improved, however, and in the 2004–2005 season finished alone in second place—its most Ivy wins since it won the title. That impressive showing had Donahue believing that the Big Red could win it all this year. "When I first got here, I coached every dribble," he said. "Last year, I coached every pass. Now, I can coach to win."

Donahue's strategy for restoring Cornell's program was no different than that of any other coach at any other school. He needed to recruit talented players. It sounds simple enough. But when dealing with Ivy League admission standards, it never is. There are only a finite number of players whose jump shots are as strong as their SAT scores, and every coach in the Ivy League knows who they are. It is not unusual to see Cornell battling Penn and Yale for a player, or Dartmouth going after the same player as Columbia and Brown. Sometimes, the decision isn't made by the coach or the player but by the admissions department. Every coach has a story about a player who didn't pass muster with the admissions department at his school but wound up at another Ivy League institution.

Donahue has tried as much as possible to avoid competing for the same players as the rest of the league coaches by carving a niche for himself. Early on, he realized that two types of players were attracted to Cornell—farmers and Canadians—and he targeted his recruiting efforts in their direction. Nearly a third of the Big Red roster either grew up on or near a farm or hails from Canada. Donahue found that these kids feel the most comfortable at Cornell because of its size and location. They aren't the only players he goes after—California native Lenny Collins fits neither category—but over the years Donahue has had the most success persuading players from these backgrounds to come to Cornell.

Donahue had every reason to be optimistic about the upcoming season. Two of Cornell's top three scorers from last season had graduated and another player had transferred, but the Big Red brought back a good mix of veterans, role players, and newcomers. Collins, a senior forward out of San Juan Capistrano, California, tended to be a player who didn't stand out during a game—until the stat sheet revealed he somehow finished with twenty points. His quiet versatility—a knack for making a three-point basket when his team needed it or coming up with a steal at a crucial time—earned him the Ivy League freshman of the year award in 2003, then first-team all-Ivy honors his junior season. Collins, an industrial labor relations major, planned to go to law school. "I feel like basketball has just become a part of me," Collins said. "The reason I do it is just because I've gotten so much from basketball, and I've learned so much, and I'm continually learning about myself and building character from basketball. The reason I still do it is pretty much that I've made a commitment. I'm not going to quit on it just because there's no real future in it for me."

Ryan Rourke, meantime, had finally found a home at Cornell after a vagabond career that began at the Air Force Academy and took him to Mesa (Arizona) Community College before he wound up in Ithaca. Rourke had the athleticism that could lead to an overseas professional career if his tendency to overthink the game didn't stand in his way. David Lisle was one of the Canadians. A guard from Wingham, Ontario, Lisle was a deft shot maker, but his future plans included medical school, not professional basketball. Donahue's biggest concern going into the season was at point guard. Because Graham Dow had not fully recovered from a pelvic injury, Donahue was forced to start freshman Adam Gore. "I understand what this group is going to give me, day in and day out, more than any team we've had," Donahue said.

Cornell arrived in Syracuse about two hours before tip-off. Donahue wanted to give his younger players plenty of time to adjust to the cavernous Carrier Dome. At roughly seven times the size of the Big Red's home court, Newman Arena, the Carrier Dome typically is a tough place for shooters. The sightlines in a dome are different than in a traditional basketball arena, and the vast emptiness behind the basket can be disconcerting. Although many teams have struggled in this spacious environment, Cornell had shot the ball well here in the past. A year earlier, the Big Red set the Carrier Dome single-game record by sinking fifteen three-point baskets.

The Cornell players, wearing their gray long-sleeved warm-up shirts with the big red C on their chests, didn't seem to have any trouble putting the ball through the net before the game, especially Gore. The point guard with the wisp of blond hair on his chin seemed unperturbed by his surroundings, calmly making shot after shot as if this were just another high school game back in Indiana. Gore is from Monrovia, whose entire population of 625 would fit into one section of bleachers at the Carrier Dome. In minutes, he would start his first Division I college basketball game. If he had any sense of the magnitude of what lay ahead, he betrayed no hint of it.

This was the earliest Cornell had opened its season. Not only was the Big Red the first Ivy team, it also was the first Division I team to play a game in the 2005–2006 season. After a rough start, Cornell beat Saint Francis, 75–54. For a couple hours, the Big Red had the best record in Division I. Rourke finished with twenty-five points, and Jason Hartford, a junior college transfer out of the coastal town of Tillamook, Oregon, added sixteen points and eleven rebounds in his first game for Cornell.

Gore also had an impressive debut—eleven points, two assists, and no turnovers—which thrilled his parents, Doug and Kathy, who watched from the stands. "It was exciting, especially in a place like this. It's a little different than your average high school gym, obviously," Gore said, displaying none of the excitement he purported to have felt. "I was nervous. But once the game starts, you lose all that. You're just ready to play. A few minutes into it, I was ready to go. All those butterflies were gone."

Donahue was pleased with the win and how well Gore and Hartford played. But the real test would come the next night against Syracuse, ranked No. 16 in the Associated Press poll. The players were eager play the Orange, but first they had to return to Ithaca for Wednesday classes. Two of the players had tests the next day. Any thoughts about Syracuse had to be pushed out of their minds, at least temporarily. Most coaches would have remained at the tournament rather than wear out their players with two bus trips within twenty-four hours, but this was the Ivy League. "The guys who run the tournament are surprised we're throwing the kids in a bus, bringing them back down, bringing them back up," Donahue said. "We've got class tomorrow. This is what we do at Cornell. The Ivy League education is the big leagues."

Syracuse and Cornell are familiar foes, having played each other fairly regularly since the 1900–1901 season. For many years, they enjoyed a home-and-away series before the Orange's trips to Ithaca ended in 1982. Despite only sixty miles separating them, it hasn't been much of a rivalry. The Big Red had lost twenty-eight consecutive games to Syracuse and hadn't beaten the Orange since 1968. Yet, Cornell longed to play Syracuse because the Big East power represented big-time college basketball. Coach Jim Boeheim's team won a national championship in 2003 and regularly appeared on ESPN. The Orange had sent dozens of players to the NBA, including Dave Bing, Billy Owens, Derrick Coleman, Sherman Douglas, and Carmelo Anthony. Realistically, Cornell didn't stand much of a chance. Syracuse is not supposed to lose to an Ivy League school on its home court. But the Big Red wasn't intimidated by the Orange. "You want to play the best every time you get the chance," Rourke said. "We definitely want the challenge. They have a good crowd. They're long. They're athletic. We've really got to be on top of our game. We've got to hit some big shots. We've got to take care of the ball. We've got to do a lot of things right to be in that game, but we want the challenge."

It took six and a half minutes before Cornell made its first basket against Syracuse. The Orange, however, wasn't playing much better. With just over six minutes remaining in the first half, the Big Red tied the score on a three-pointer by Gore, who didn't appear to notice the

17,000 fans rooting against him. In the second half, Cornell took its first lead on another three-pointer by Gore, one of six he made during the game. Then less than a minute later, Gore picked up his fourth foul guarding Gerry McNamara. Gore, who finished with twenty-two points, held McNamara in check throughout the game. McNamara had made more three-point shots than any player in Syracuse history, but he missed all ten of his shots from behind the arc against Cornell, ending his streak of fifty-three consecutive games with a three-pointer.

The Big Red clung to its lead over the next seven minutes, and then Cornell stopped making free throws. The Big Red missed five of its last ten foul shots. Syracuse forced a couple turnovers, and it wasn't long before the Orange was back in the lead. Syracuse went on to win, 67–62. "I really thought we were fortunate to beat them last year," Boeheim said after the game. "I think they're a better team this year."

Despite the loss, the Cornell players were overjoyed. They had come within five points of knocking off Syracuse. Collins described it as the most fun he has had playing a basketball game. "It was awesome to be out there," Collins said. "The guys on the bench were excited. We were getting after each other. It was just a fun experience out there. As the minutes wound down, and we were up a few points, we were right there. The thought starts creeping into your head, 'We could pull this off.' The motor gets running a bit more. You get charged up."

Donahue was no less enthusiastic about the team's performance. "I wish we could practice right now," Donahue said. "We've got great potential, I honest[ly] feel that. . . . We've arrived. We're in this. We're good. How good?" He shrugs his shoulders. "Now we can go to work. I'm going to be on them harder than ever."

Despite everything Cornell had to celebrate after its strong showing in the Coaches vs. Cancer classic, including Gore's breakout performance, highlights of which made *SportsCenter*, and the Big Red's near upset of Syracuse, the team did have reason to worry. Hartford, the junior college transfer who had a double-double in his first Division I game, fractured a small bone in his right wrist against Syracuse. The injury wasn't severe enough to keep him out of games, but it did limit him. Not having Hartford at full strength was a blow to Cornell's frontcourt.

The loss to Syracuse knocked the Big Red out of the tournament and meant the team didn't play again for ten days. Any momentum it had hoped to gain from its performance at Syracuse was lost. When Cornell finally returned to action, the Big Red fell, 66–54, at Penn State; beat Colgate, its intrastate rival, 70–56, at home; then lost to Hartford, one of the weaker teams in the America East Conference, 73–71.

Meanwhile, Jason Hartford's wrist injury wasn't getting any better. The six-foot-nine forward tried to play despite the broken bone, scoring in double figures in the last two games, but his discomfort increased. The medical staff decided several weeks' rest was the best remedy.

Cornell was scheduled to play Lafayette next, and Donahue was not looking forward to the game. Not only was he vexed about his team's recent erratic performances, but he also had to face one of his former mentors. Donahue's ties to Lafayette coach Fran O'Hanlon go back to the late 1980s when Donahue was O'Hanlon's assistant at Monsignor Bonner High School in Drexel Hill, Pennsylvania. They later served together as assistants to Dunphy at Penn. In the five times they had met as head coaches, O'Hanlon's teams had won three times.

Still searching for its first road win, Cornell was not going to pick up that victory in Easton, Pennsylvania. Lafayette's smothering defense made sure of it in its 57–43 victory. No Big Red player scored in double figures in Cornell's fourth loss in five games. "It's about as bad of execution since I've been at Cornell," Donahue said. "I take the blame. I'm not blaming my players. I take full responsibility for that. It's really disappointing."

A disturbing pattern was developing in Cornell's defeats. The Big Red kept losing focus during critical junctures in games, and these breakdowns were costly. Leads slipped away; deficits grew insurmountable. At Penn State, it was the big second-half run by the Nittany Lions. At Hartford, it was the eighteen-point lead the Hawks built. At Lafayette, it was the late first-half surge by the Leopards. These lapses were not what Donahue was expecting from his team. "I thought I knew our guys," he said. "I thought we would give a pretty consistent effort, but some of the veteran guys, the way they played tonight, it's just . . . there's a mental toughness that every coach looks for, and some kids have it. Other kids, they don't have it. The ones that do, they've got to lead your team. That's what disappoints me. I thought I had a couple guys who [would] straighten us out, keep us in the game. When the going got tough, they would figure out a way." Instead, the players Donahue thought would lead this team were disappearing when he needed them most. Few things are more frustrating for a coach than watching players underperform. The Big Red wasn't losing games because its opponents were superior; it was losing because the team wasn't playing up to its potential. "I think it's just maybe right now a mental thing," Lisle said. "At the start of the season, we had that poise and mental toughness throughout the game. . . . It just seems like the last week, these last couple games, we got off to slow starts."

Immediately following a loss, Donahue was usually at his most despondent. But even at this low moment, he remained optimistic about the season. "Like I said to these guys, I like this group so much I wish I was really angry," Donahue said. "I wish I could scream and yell. That feels good sometimes. Well, I'm just disappointed. I'm disappointed for them. I'm disappointed for us. I told them I don't have an answer. The thing I feel good about is I still feel good about this group. I had other teams here I'd walk into the locker room and I didn't even want to see them. I feel like grabbing this group and going back into the gym and working for two hours and figuring out what we want to do, and that's good. I know what I've got to do. I've got to come up with things that are going to be different in practice. We've got to keep changing stuff up. I thought we were over this. I thought we got off to a real good start. Gosh, we've had some ups and downs."

Returning home to Newman Arena didn't prove the antidote to Cornell's troubles. A sluggish second-half effort against Quinnipiac led to a 55–45 defeat. After another disappointing loss, Donahue decided to revamp the lineup in hopes of energizing the offense. He sent two of his captains—Rourke and Lisle—to the bench and replaced them with junior forward Jason Mitchell and Dow. Mitchell, the son of a turkey farmer in Saluda, South Carolina, was a surprising addition to the starting lineup. He hadn't played in four of the last five games and was making his first career start. But with Hartford sidelined with an injury, the six-foot-eight Mitchell was the tallest player available on the Big Red roster. Dow took over the point guard position from Gore, which would allow the freshman to focus less on running the offense and more on finding his shot.

It isn't often that the smartest student on campus is on the basketball team, but at Cornell that may be the case. Dow, a six-foot guard from Burlington, Ontario, had a 4.0 grade-point average in ecology and evolutionary biology. Recruited by Princeton and Harvard, he chose Cornell after taking one look at the school's science course catalog. "It was like pages and pages of courses I'd never even heard of before, and that was exciting to me," Dow said.

Dow wasn't fully healed from the nagging pelvic injury that had plagued him the previous season. When it was at its worst, he couldn't lift his leg to get out of bed. No one had been able to figure out what was causing him pain. Was it a sports hernia, a torn groin muscle, an inflammation of the pubic synthesis, or a problem in his lower abdomen? Whatever it was, it wasn't getting better and it was still hurting. "We're sort of to the point now where it's almost like a chronic condition where maybe three or four years down the road, when I stop playing, it will heal completely," Dow said. "But right now it's always fighting between healing itself and breaking down again. . . . I'm extremely thankful for the way [Donahue] has handled [the injury]. A lot of coaches could have said I don't want to deal with this. I'm not the most athletically gifted."

Dow, who had played for the Canadian junior national basketball team, may not be the speediest point guard, but he is steady. The Big Red was counting on him to lift the team out of its offensive doldrums. For the first twenty minutes against Lehigh, though, the lineup changes had little effect. Cornell's offensive futility continued. The Big Red failed to score twenty points in a half for the second game in a row and trailed the Mountain Hawks 29–16 at halftime. Early in the second half, Lehigh extended its lead to sixteen and Cornell appeared headed for another defeat. Then suddenly, the Big Red offense came alive. Andrew Naeve's layup sparked an 11–0 run, and Cornell ended its four-game losing streak by winning 57–53.

The victory was exactly what the Big Red needed heading into exam break. While the players turned their attention toward academics, Donahue went in search of answers for his team's inconsistency. He watched every game again, looking for clues to what caused the unexpected lapses that kept plaguing Cornell. He came away from the film session blaming himself for being too critical of the players for their poor execution. He realized instead of chastising the players for every mistake they made, he needed to let them play more freely. "These kids listen to every stinking thing you say," Donahue said. "I thought we could be different from past teams, but we're more of who we were in the past."

Cornell came out of exams and went right back on the road. The Big Red had played just three home games and would play only three more times at Newman Arena before February. Cornell's nonconference schedule featured twice as many away games, not because the Big Red enjoyed the travel—it's tough to win on an opponent's home court—but because Cornell had a hard time enticing teams to travel to Ithaca during the winter. As it was, the Big Red still was looking for its first road win of the season, and its prospects didn't look good as it headed to Bucknell. The Bison were the darling of the 2005 NCAA tournament, becoming the first Patriot League team to win a tournament game when they upset Kansas in the first round. Their momentum from that victory had carried forward into the 2005–2006 season. Bucknell had won its first five games before losing to No. 4 Villanova.

It was easy to tell which of the teams was feeling good about itself and which one wasn't. Bucknell dismantled Cornell. The Bison's 83–39 victory was Donahue's worst loss in his six-year career as a head coach. "The thing I'm most disappointed in is our level of competing," Donahue said. "I don't think we competed very well. . . . [The players are] trying. But it's one thing to try, and it's another to compete and get over that hump. I was embarrassed because I didn't think we competed."

"They kicked our butts for sure," Collins said. "I think we had a hand in it because we didn't respond to them well. I don't think we're mentally tough enough, mentally or physically tough enough right now to compete with a team like that."

No one could explain why the team was so mentally fragile. When things were going well, Cornell seemed capable of challenging any team in the country. But when tough times came, the Big Red appeared to lose confidence in its abilities. "I think we're still trying to find ourselves," Collins said. "We're still coming together as a team. We're still trying to find our identity. That just leads to inconsistency."

Considering the high expectations for this season, the mounting losses were beginning to sap the players. Heading into their tenth game, they had managed to win only three games. The Bucknell loss was particularly caustic. "It definitely takes a toll on you," Collins said. "We're sick of it. We think we can be a good basketball team. We believe in ourselves, and with each setback it gets tougher and tougher to get over. It's definitely frustrating, especially for [the seniors]. We fully expected to come out and be a very good basketball team. It's wearing on us a little bit."

Cornell hadn't scored more than forty-five points in three of its last four games, and it had lost all three. In an effort to generate more offense, Donahue decided to give Ugo Ihekweazu a spot in the starting lineup. Ihekweazu had played in only four games since transferring from Wofford, scoring his first points of the season against Bucknell. On a team of jump shooters, he was best at putting the ball on the floor and driving to the basket. Donahue hoped having him on the court would create opportunities for the others. Whether it was the lineup change or because the players were just tired of losing, Cornell turned in one of its better performances of the season against Army. The Big Red led the entire game, winning, 74–39.

Following a short break for the Christmas holiday, Cornell headed west to play Long Beach State and Washington. Donahue scheduled these games to give his West Coast players—Californian Collins, Washingtonians Rourke and Connor Mullen, and Oregonian Hartford—a chance to play in front of family and friends. Collins, bolstered by the friendly faces in the crowd at Long Beach State, sank six three-point shots to finish with a season-high twenty-seven points, which gave him 1,000 points for his career. Hartford returned to action after a five-game absence because of his injured wrist, but scored only two points in thirteen minutes. Neither Collins's performance nor Hartford's return helped

Cornell, which went into one of its trademark late-game swoons and lost, 79–65.

Everyone was baffled by why these lapses kept occurring. As it pondered ways to avoid future letdowns, Cornell headed north to face its toughest test of the season. Washington had dropped to No. 10 in the Associated Press poll after losing to Arizona in double overtime two days earlier but still would be the highest-ranked opponent the Big Red would face in the 2005–2006 season. The Huskies also were the biggest and most athletic team they would play. Although the outcome was never in doubt, this game didn't prove to be the embarrassment that the Bucknell contest did. Led by its West Coast contingent, the Big Red was respectable. Hartford, who grew up only ninety minutes away on the Oregon coast, paced Cornell with seventeen points. Rourke, playing in front of dozens of family and friends, scored in double figures for the first time since the season opener. But as well as it played, the Big Red failed to keep up with Washington's potent offense and lost, 87–71, its seventh consecutive road loss.

Rourke continued his strong play when Cornell returned home to play Keuka College, a Division III school. He scored twenty-two points and had a career-high fourteen rebounds in the Big Red's 78–52 victory. Rourke's resurgence seemed to be a result of Donahue switching him from power forward to small forward. "He's not as comfortable banging his body down low," Donahue said. "I think he likes to be away from the basket, attacking the basket."

With only one remaining nonconference game on its schedule, Cornell hadn't found its rhythm. Its season had gone in fits and starts. For every game the Big Red showed progress, it seemed to take a step back the next time out. With the Ivy League season approaching, this inconsistency and lack of cohesion troubled Donahue. He knew much of it had to do with the injuries to key players. Although Hartford finally returned from his broken wrist, Dow's injury continued to limit his contributions. Now Naeve was nursing a sprained ankle from the Washington game. Though none of these injuries were serious, they prevented Cornell from developing the cohesion that good teams have. "When you lose a kid, that can be disruptive because you're still trying to figure out a way to get better," Donahue said. "What we've done is we've moved guys around. Honestly, we've changed [personalities] offensively. We go inside more. I wasn't getting good guard play. The guards aren't really playing well and stepping up, so we just go big."

Besides the injuries, another concern for Cornell was its inability to win on the road. The Big Red was winless on its opponent's home court in the 2005–2006 season, a statistic it hoped to change at Albany. To that end, Donahue decided he was going to bus the team across the state on the day of the game rather than the day before. Coaches usually prefer to travel to away games at least a day ahead to give their teams a chance to rest. But Donahue thought it might be more beneficial to have the players sleep in their own beds. Plus, he was ready to try anything to get the Big Red out of its road funk.

Unfortunately for Cornell, Donahue's efforts were in vain. Doomed by another slow start, the Big Red fell behind by twenty points in the first half. They mounted a furious comeback in the second half, pulling within five points with just over three minutes remaining, but ultimately fell, 68–59. "You try to judge your team—at least I do—on how we're playing," Donahue said. "I can't say I'm totally satisfied, but I also think we're doing a lot of good things. . . . You don't feel great because you still need the wins. You need to feel good about yourself with wins, but I also think that we're [going to be okay]. The teams [in the Ivy League] aren't going to be as tough [as Cornell's nonconference opponents]."

Chapter 6

Roll
Crimson
Pride

The point guard often is the most important position on a basket-ball team. He calls the plays, makes sure everyone is in position, and finds the open shooter. Ideally, he knows when to shoot and when to pass. He has the savvy to forgo his own shot when his teammate is in a better position to score. A good frontcourt player can be ineffective if he doesn't have a point guard who can deliver him the ball in the right spot. The best point guards foster team unity, while poor ones can create divisiveness.

Because of these responsibilities, coaches typically are reluctant to allow freshmen to run the offense. Harvard coach Frank Sullivan had little choice. The Crimson's point guard from the previous season, David Giovacchini, had graduated. The player Sullivan thought would be his point guard of the future, Tyler Klunick, had left the team due to a situation, rare outside of the Ivy League but fairly common within it, involving how the conference awards financial aid. Basketball players at Ivy schools are admitted as students, not athletes, which means their financial aid is not tied to their participation in their sport. At most Division I schools, athletic scholarships are essentially one-year contracts renewed each season. In those cases, coaches can take away scholarships from players who are not performing up to expectations. In the Ivy League, athletes who opt out of playing their sports can remain in school without losing their financial aid.

Klunick, a heralded recruit out of Illinois, played only fourteen games as a freshman because of a hand injury. Then he tore ligaments in his ankle. If the injuries weren't bad enough, his course of study, computer science, was one of the more time-consuming at Harvard. Klunick found there weren't enough hours in the day to fit in both shooting drills and writing software. In the end, knowing his professional future lay with computers, not sports, he quit basketball, leaving Sullivan with a gaping void in his starting lineup.

With Sullivan forced to start a freshman, Drew Housman, at point guard, Harvard's season opener against Vermont became that much tougher. It already was seen as a troublesome first game, no matter who was starting at this crucial position. The Catamounts were coming off the best season in their school's history, highlighted by an NCAA tournament first-round upset of Syracuse. Although Vermont had undergone significant changes from the previous season—a new coach, Mike Lonergan, and the departure of four starters—the Catamounts were a formidable foe. Housman had watched Vermont knock off the Orange on national television only eight months ago. Now here he was making his college debut against the Catamounts.

The new point guard had a new look for the game. Housman's mom, who had traveled from California to watch her son play, took one look at his floppy curls and insisted on a visit to a barber that morning. The closely shorn Housman acquitted himself fairly well in the game, a 65–57 Harvard victory. He scored thirteen points and had more assists (three) than turnovers (two). Most important, Harvard won its season opener for the first time in three years. "It's actually huge for us," Brian Cusworth said. "Since my freshman year, we haven't started off a season with a winning record."

Three days later, Harvard traveled to Holy Cross and beat the Crusaders, 70–55. The Crimson made 50 percent of its shots in each half against its Patriot League opponent, a feat it hadn't accomplished the previous two seasons. It was Harvard's first win over its cross-state rival in six seasons, and even more significant, it was a road win. It took seven trips the previous season before the Crimson won an away game.

By the time Harvard won its third game, a 75–72 win at Sacred Heart—the nine-hundredth victory in the program's history—the Crimson was receiving a vote in the weekly Associated Press poll. Voted on by sportswriters across the country, the poll lists the top twenty-five Division I teams in the nation. Duke, which had won three national titles in its history, was ranked No. 1 that week. The fact that Harvard fell into the "also receiving votes" category didn't diminish the significance of being mentioned in this elite company. The Crimson also was the only Ivy League team on the list. After a 69–56 win against California-Davis gave Harvard its first 4–0 start since 1997, the Crimson closed out November with a 71–50 victory over New Hampshire. Harvard, which was 1–5 the previous two Novembers, was 5–0 for just the third time since 1947.

The most surprising aspect of the Crimson's strong start was the production of its backcourt. Housman was proving to be a capable point guard, and junior guard Jim Goffredo was providing the answer to Harvard's next greatest concern, perimeter shooting. Goffredo, an economics major and the son of a successful Southern California high school coach, had emerged as Harvard's best outside shooter and was leading the team in scoring. "I think going into the season it almost took a little bit of pressure off of [the backcourt] for [the frontcourt] to be hyped up so much," Goffredo said. "People weren't really expecting much from us. We didn't have to deal with what Cus and Matt had to deal with at the beginning of the season."

Harvard had beaten Central Connecticut State in its two previous meetings, and there was no reason to think the Crimson wouldn't make it 3–0 against the Blue Devils. But it was not to be. Central Connecticut State handed Harvard its first loss of the season, an 87–79 defeat. "The interesting thing was that we had a subpar practice the night before, and it continued into the Saturday morning shootaround," Sullivan said. "The guys knew it. It was good for them to acknowledge that had a part in the loss after the game. . . . It was a game we needed, a toughness game. I think we all feel we competed, but were out-toughed by Central Connecticut."

On top of the loss, Cusworth was injured again. He had fractured a bone in his left hand diving for a loose ball in the first half. He ended up playing thirty-three minutes, scoring thirteen points, grabbing six rebounds, and blocking three shots in that game, but now he could miss at least the next three weeks while his hand healed. It was a good thing Cusworth was a pre-med major, considering how often he was injured. Since he arrived at Harvard, Cusworth had missed games with an inflamed elbow (freshman season), a stress fracture in his foot (sophomore season), a thumb injury (the previous season), and now a broken hand. Because the Ivy League does not allow medical redshirts—athletes who continue to take classes but sit out a year of competition in order to preserve their eligibility—Cusworth chose to drop out of school his sophomore year after his foot injury so that he wouldn't lose any playing time. He was classified as a junior with three semesters remaining.

Cusworth's injury and the loss to Central Connecticut State began a downward spiral for the Crimson. It lost to crosstown rival Boston University, 72–63, then followed that defeat with a 67–56 setback against Lehigh. As happens with teams mired in losing streaks, the Crimson was trying so hard not to lose it had forgotten how to play to win. The players were pressing and trying to do too much. They were wound so tight that every mistake they made became magnified. And they were still adjusting to not having Cusworth on the court. Not only did Harvard miss having a seven-footer around the basket, but the players also were unfamiliar with playing alongside Cusworth's replacement, Brian Darcy, a six-foot-eight junior from Shrewsbury, Massachusetts. In basketball, it helps to have an intuitiveness among the five players on the court, each one knowing where and when to get another player the ball on the offense and trusting one another on defense. When a team changes personnel, it disrupts the rhythm and timing of the unit. "I think we all were a little disappointed [how the team played during the three-game losing streak] because we never felt like we were in control of anything," Sullivan said. "We got slapped in the face, and we needed to be slapped in the face. Everybody is giddy about the 5–0 start. Okay, that's over. We got slapped. Now, how are we going to move on?"

Harvard returned home to play Long Island in mid-December. Needing a victory to halt its slide, the Crimson won easily, 91–79. "All of us were kind of down after losing these past couple games," Goffredo said. "We knew we were a good basketball team. We just needed to get our confidence back. Losing takes that away. I think it was a big relief [to finally win]. . . . Not having Cusworth in the game definitely changes the way we play. I think we showed we were feeling a lot more comfortable playing with the lineup that we had."

Three days after snapping its losing streak, the Crimson traveled to Albany—or at least most of the team did. Harvard went into this game down not one but two starters. Cusworth was still out with a broken hand. Now Goffredo had developed a staph infection in his hip that required surgery. Even with its depleted lineup, Harvard defeated Albany, the preseason America East Conference favorite, 61–48. Next up was Colgate. Goffredo, back in the lineup after his short hospital stay, connected on three three-pointers to finish with thirteen points in Harvard's 68–59 win. Even more impressive, he took two charges against one of Colgate's top players, Alvin Reed, who eventually fouled out of the game.

For most of its nonconference schedule, Harvard had played teams similar to it—low- to mid-majors located along the Northeast Corridor. In its next game, the Crimson was stepping up in competition, taking on its familiar hockey rival, Boston College. Although Harvard plays Boston University nearly every year, it had played Boston College only four times during Sullivan's tenure. The last two times, BC barely escaped with a win, which is likely the reason the Crimson hadn't seen much of the Eagles recently, despite BC's 32–9 record against Harvard. No team outside the Ivy League had been more successful against the Crimson. Harvard knew it would have to play a perfect game to have a chance against the Eagles, who were ranked No. 14 in the Associated Press poll. The Crimson also was hoping Boston College might overlook it. After all, it was three days before Christmas. Maybe Harvard could catch the Eagles looking forward to their break. Or maybe not. From the tip, the Crimson was clearly overmatched. Boston College scored the first nine points and easily defeated Harvard, 89–55. Discouraged by their performance, the Harvard players parted for the holiday.

As bad as the loss to Boston College was, the one to Southern Methodist University was even worse. It had only been a six-day layoff. But the way the Crimson played, it looked as if it had taken six months off. SMU, not exactly a basketball power, clearly was more ready to play this game than Harvard was. The Mustangs used a 28–1 run in the first half to take a 40–9 lead. Instead of trying to find ways to get back into the game, the Crimson spent most of the first half complaining about the fouls being called against them.

During halftime, Sullivan had nothing to say to his team. Instead, he let the seniors do the talking. The three chastised their teammates for allowing the officiating to bother them. They reminded them that no referee is going to give a player wearing a Harvard jersey a break. If anything, they said, the guys with the whistles tended to view Harvard players as having had it easy all their lives and resented them for it. They were not going to get any calls, and they had better learn to deal with it.

"I say to the players when they whine to referees or appeal to referees: 'There is not one referee in the country that went to an Ivy League school. What do you think is going through their minds when an Ivy League player tries to tell them another alternative to the call or, specifically, a guy wearing a Harvard shirt tries to appeal the call? Do you think they're going to listen to you?'" Sullivan said.

Harvard outscored the Mustangs 34–26 after halftime, but its first-half deficit was too much to overcome. The Crimson lost, 76–55. If these last two games were a measure of where Harvard stood going into the Ivy League season, the Crimson came up short. Yet notwithstanding the back-to-back losses, Harvard still managed to tie the school record for wins against Division I non-Ivy opponents. The Crimson achieved this feat despite missing key players at times. With Cusworth's cast expected to come off any day now, Harvard hoped to have its full complement of players in time for the 2005–2006 Ivy League season opener. The next two months would decide whether the Crimson would become the first Harvard team to win an Ivy League title and go to the NCAA tournament or whether it would once again learn how difficult it is to wrest the title away from Penn and Princeton.

Chapter 7

Backdoor

Cuts

To the uninitiated, the Princeton offense appears to be a bunch of players running around the court passing the ball to each other until the shot clock reaches single digits. Then a player either lofts a three-point shot or throws a pass to a teammate cutting to the basket for a backdoor layup. In many ways, the offense is that simplistic but with a labyrinth of nuances. Pete Carril designed the offense—drawing heavily from the Boston Celtics' teams of the 1950s and 1960s—as a way of providing Princeton with a competitive advantage over stronger, faster teams. Its basic strategy involves all five players seeing and reacting to what the defense is doing. The offense eschews the traditional roles of each position and requires selfless and cerebral players—from point guards to centers—who are capable shooters, passers, and dribblers. "The best part about it is playing with other guys who are unselfish and who are very skilled," point guard Scott Greenman said. "They can shoot. They can pass. They can dribble. You don't have to throw some big meathead down on the low block and say 'Here, just stand here.' You get people who really know how to play."

When it is at its best, the Princeton offense is beautiful to behold. It creates a flow and movement on the court that at times resembles a heated chess match and at others a well-choreographed ballet. It is also antithetical to its core. Players have freedom within its structure and must think instinctively. A player doesn't have to be particularly athletic to flourish in this system, but he does have to be smart. That doesn't mean that only players with 4.0 GPAs can run the offense. Plenty of dumb players have succeeded in it. But a player must possess certain basketball knowledge.

"I know it's structured, but there's so many options within it," Greenman said. "Every time you catch the ball you can do four different things, and when you decide to do something, the guy who you're playing with can do four different things. Everyone has options." It is learning all these options that causes difficulty. Greenman figured it took him until his sophomore year until he fully understood the subtleties of the offense. The strategy doesn't work unless everyone is on the same page. It also needs a capable center because so much of Princeton's offense flows through that position.

"Learning the offense, first of all, is difficult," Greenman said. "While you're learning it, it's a ton of thinking. Ideally, you don't want to be thinking, 'What am I supposed to do? What do I do now?' You're kind of worried about what you have to do instead of relying on instinct. Once you learn the offense and you feel comfortable within it, then it's more of an instinctual thing. You catch the ball here; you know what your options are. Now I can do this, this, or this, depending on how the [defender is] playing me, depending on what [I] want to get when [I] do it. But I think once you learn the offense and you have it down, it's a great offense. When you can get guys who've been in the system for a while and really know what to look for and how to play it, it's unbelievable. It's so much fun to play in."

As the Princeton offense has evolved over the years, few teams run it in its purest form. Even within the Princeton family, it has its variations. Bill Carmody's version at Northwestern differs from John Thompson III's adaptation at Georgetown. Joe Scott's interpretation is said to more closely resemble Carril's rendition than the other two.

Heading into Princeton's first game of the 2005–2006 season, Scott fixed upon seven players who would receive the bulk of the playing time. What he was still trying to figure out was which combinations of those players he would use. He started his three most experienced players: Greenman at point guard and Luke Owings and Noah Savage at forward. He put six-foot-eight sophomore Harrison Schaen at center and freshman Geoff Kestler at shooting guard. Scott would have preferred a little more time to prepare his young squad for its first game. As it was, the Tigers' season opener was their earliest ever.

Fortunately for Princeton, the game was at home. The Tigers have enjoyed remarkable success at L. Stockwell Jadwin Gymnasium. Going into the 2005–2006 season, Princeton was 335–77 on its home court. That record, however, was more a tribute to the Tigers' prowess than to the arena's ambience. For a storied program, Jadwin is its least remarkable feature. Opened in 1969 as a multipurpose facility, Jadwin can hold four basketball courts and an indoor track comfortably. The main court of this domed building is dwarfed by the expansive surroundings and lacks the intimacy of other gyms. Aside from a few advertisements that hang above the benches, the antiseptic arena boasts no banners. Unlike at other schools where mere participation in the NCAA tournament merits a piece of cloth hung from the ceiling, Princeton doesn't even have its NIT championship banner dangling in the rafters. Scott wanted to see that changed and not just because it would make the court seem a little less like the local YMCA. He was concerned that too many of today's players didn't know Princeton's history. A visual reminder of the Tigers' past might help reinforce the expectation of success.

Princeton was invited to play in the Preseason NIT, and its first-round game was against Drexel, a member of the Colonial Athletic Association. Princeton had won all eight meetings with the Dragons and looked forward to continuing that streak. Drexel, however, had other ideas. The Dragons forced the Tigers into settling for jump shots, manhandled them underneath the basket, and won, 54–41. If this game was supposed to erase the bad memories of last season, it had the opposite effect. It confirmed many Princeton fans' worst fears.

Greenman was disconsolate afterward, saying he was "absolutely embarrassed" by the loss. "It's obvious. We're not physical at all," he said. "We got out-rebounded by twenty-nine, thirty. Probably nobody's ever won a game in the history of basketball being out-rebounded by that much. It's not acceptable to play like we played today. We can make all the excuses we want. We're young. We're inexperienced. But wherever you play basketball, no matter how old you are, how experienced, you should be able to keep guys off your back and show some physicality. . . . I realize that we're young, but I only have—it's a selfish way of looking at it—I only have twenty-six, twenty-seven games left. I have to do my hardest to make sure we get as good as we can by the end of the season."

The biggest concern coming out of the game, however, was not Princeton's lack of aggression but its poor play at the center position. Schaen, who had been a strong contributor off the bench his freshman year, seemed to have regressed during his time away. He finished with nine points—all on three-pointers—and three rebounds. Despite his height, Schaen seemed to want to play more on the perimeter than underneath the basket where the Tigers needed him. Worst of all, he looked tentative and unsure on the court. "I do think [Schaen] has ability," Scott said. "There needs to come along with that ability the sort of physical aspect of it too, of getting in there and throwing his body around and getting balls. . . . Schaen right now can't play forty minutes. He can't play thirty-five minutes. We have to find another center."

At the moment, the best candidates for the position were Owings and Patrick Ekeruo, a six-foot-eight junior enrolled in the Woodrow Wilson School of Public and International Affairs. Owings was better suited to playing forward than center, and Ekeruo had played in only three games last season. Scott hoped he could either bring Schaen around quickly or get the other two to produce. He didn't have many options at this critical position.

Since it didn't advance to the NIT quarterfinals, Princeton had nearly a week to prepare for its next opponent, Lehigh. The Tigers hadn't lost to the Mountain Hawks since 1930, winning twenty-two in a row. They kept the steak alive with their 64–54 victory. The road win evened Princeton's record and gave its fans hope that the Drexel loss had been a fluke. Yet when they returned home, the Tigers regressed against Lafayette, losing, 57–46. Going back to last season's loss to Penn, Princeton had lost three consecutive home games, its first three-game home losing streak in twenty-six years and only its second since Jadwin opened.

Princeton's maddening inconsistency, while typical of a young team, was frustrating for the players and coaches, not to mention its followers. The Internet message boards were inflamed with comments from peevish Princeton fans, blaming Scott for injecting fear in the players, which in turn made them hesitant and tight. By the time the Tigers went to Hamilton, New York, to play Colgate, Scott had decided to make personnel changes. The biggest move was starting Ekeruo in place of Schaen at center, but he also gave junior guard Edwin Buffmire and sophomore guard Kevin Steuerer opportunities to play. Neither had much experience. Buffmire, a Near Eastern studies major from Scottsdale, Arizona, had played in a total of fifteen games; and Steuerer, whose father Mickey was a two-year captain of the Tigers and helped lead them to their NIT title, appeared in one game the previous season.

It didn't seem to matter who was on the court, however, as the Tigers lost, 62–39, their lowest point total since a loss to Penn in 2002 and just three points short of the school record since the advent of the shot clock. Princeton was in an offensive funk, scoring only eleven first-half points. Alarmingly, the Tigers had only three assists to go along with fourteen field goals. Outside of Greenman and Savage, no one had an assist. For an offense rooted in sharing the ball, this was unsettling.

No team looks forward to playing Temple and its matchup zone defense, particularly one that's struggling offensively, like Princeton. Now the Tigers had to figure out a way to score against a team that had held UCLA to fifty-four points and was coming off a 50–46 win against Penn. These two proud programs—Temple and Princeton rank among the top fifteen in Division I all-time victories—had not seen much of each other over the years. Although the schools are only a one-hour trip away from each other, this was only their second meeting since 1975. It would not be one for the ages. Princeton scored fifteen points in the first half and finished with as many turnovers (fifteen) as field goals (fifteen) in its 60–47 loss. Only four of those baskets came from inside the three-point arc as the Tigers relied unsuccessfully on their outside shooting. Princeton, one of only three Division I teams to make a three-pointer in every game since the rule took effect in 1986, was becoming overly dependent on its perimeter scoring.

"We are who we are," Scott said. "We're not going to change who our players are. Our players have their certain strengths. Our players have their certain weaknesses. You just can't say to somebody, 'Hey, drive through there and throw it to somebody.' . . . That's not one of our strengths. That's not the makeup of our players right now." Schaen, who began the season as Princeton's starting center, didn't play a minute in the game, and it wasn't because he was sick or injured. Ekeruo was the Tigers' center for all forty minutes. "We're going to be changing some stuff around," Scott said. "I think I'm going to move [Schaen] to the forward spot instead of center. I don't think [center is] the right thing for him."

The center position wasn't the only personnel change Scott was dealing with. Greenman, who had taken a hard fall in the Colgate game, injured his back getting out of his car earlier in the day and played only seven minutes. Max Schaefer, who had the most experience at point guard, had taken a leave of absence from the team after the Colgate game. (He would quit the team three days later.) Sophomore Matt Sargeant, another possible backup, had a groin injury. That left Steuerer to run the offense. Steuerer, who until then had played six career minutes, was on the court for thirty-three minutes and finished with five assists and four turnovers. "Where he was when he got here as a freshman last September to where he is now is an unbelievable testament to Kevin Steuerer, solely to Kevin Steuerer," Scott said. "It's been a huge jump. That's why I'm happy. Those are the guys you want to do well because he's really done something about things he knew he had to get better at."

Regardless of the record-setting losing streak at Jadwin, Scott was surprisingly upbeat—at least with the media. He believed the team was making progress. Scott, effusive as ever, shared these thoughts during what was a typical postgame press conference for him. "I see us getting better as the games go along, and I'm glad we're starting to play more games now, because we get to play these guys and leave them out there," Scott said. "Tonight maybe we found a player [in Steuerer]. I hope we did. I think a lot of that kid Steuerer. I always have. . . . I know the more Pat Ekeruo goes out there and plays and plays and plays, he's going to continue to get better.

"I thought Noah Savage played very well. For a guy five games into his sophomore year, he's doing really well. It's not like there's veterans and leaders and guys who play who are making it easy to do well. He's doing this all on his own. To me, that's extreme improvement for a sophomore. He's worked extremely hard. I'm so happy to see him playing well. He will develop into a leader.

"Nobody is ever happy losing. But if you can see a Savage continue to play well, if you can see a Steuerer stick his neck out, start to do something, if you can see [Alex] Okafor get out there and do a little bit more of the things you're looking for, you can [be happy]. We've learned a lot about ourselves in these five games. The coaches are continuing to learn more about our individual players. For us right now, that's why the games are important. That's why we've got to play all these games, so we can continue to learn about Kyle Koncz. What's he going to do in the game? Can he get some game experience so that he can learn who he is and what he's good at? Can he then be in those experiences and make those things show up in a game? That's all our guys."

This lengthy discourse was not unusual for Scott. Win or lose, he loves to talk. Whereas most coaches assume a defensive crouch and become curt during losing streaks, Scott is chatty in a way that's almost therapeutic for him.

It didn't take long for Princeton's woes to become a topic of national attention. The day after the Temple loss, ESPN senior college basketball writer Andy Katz wrote an article about Scott and the Tigers titled "Ordinary Joe" that appeared on ESPN.com. In it, Katz quoted an unnamed rival coach who said: "There's no one on that team that scares you right now. I'm not sure they know who they are just yet." The day after the article appeared, the Web site ranked Princeton No. 2 in its Bottom 10 poll, just below 0–6 Savannah State.

Scott had seemed so sure of his lineup early in the season, yet it was turning out to be a work in progress. Greenman's back hadn't improved, which meant Steuerer would start at point guard against Wyoming.

Owings wasn't hurt, but he had scored a total of six points in the last three games combined. He was replaced by Koncz in the starting lineup. With these changes, Princeton started three sophomores, a freshman, and a junior—a lineup that featured only one player, Savage, who had played more than fifteen minutes in a college game prior to the 2005–2006 season.

With a depleted roster—particularly minus its only senior—Princeton slunk rather than swaggered into its game against Wyoming. There weren't many who thought the Tigers could beat the Cowboys, but they did, 59–50, as everything seemed to come together for Princeton. Led by Steuerer, who played all forty minutes, the offense ran smoothly. It wasn't so much what Steuerer did as what he didn't do. He was steady without trying to do too much.

The substitution of Koncz for Owings turned out better than expected. Coming into the game, Koncz had scored a total of nineteen points in his career. The six-foot-seven sophomore out of Strongsville, Ohio, had eighteen points on six-of-fourteen shooting. He also made five of Princeton's eleven three-point baskets. Owings, pushed into service at center, more than held his own as Ekeruo's backup. Even Schaen had a good game. Freed from the responsibilities of the center position, he flourished at the forward spot and had his first dunk of the season. Even more impressive, he played seventeen minutes and picked up only one foul. As Scott said after the game, "We beat a team named after a state. That's always good. Teams named after states are really good."

Monmouth wasn't just any school on the schedule for Scott. It was the place that gave him his start as a coach. Wayne Szoke, who coached the Hawks from 1987 to 1998, was Carril's assistant at Princeton during Scott's freshman year. Szoke, who had brought the Princeton offense with him to Monmouth, hired Scott as a volunteer assistant coach in 1991 after Scott decided to forgo a law career. It was a natural fit, but the alliance lasted only one year. Carril called Scott back to Princeton the following season. When Szoke resigned, his longtime assistant Dave Calloway took over and continued to run the Princeton offense. Monmouth was hardly the only team running the Princeton offense these days. The scheme had permeated nearly every level of basketball from elementary school to professional—including the NBA's Sacramento Kings, which employed Carril as an assistant coach. Once regarded as gimmicky, the Princeton offense gains converts seemingly daily.

The problem the Tigers ran into against the Hawks—a game that forever will be etched in the school's basketball lore—was that Monmouth was running the Princeton offense better than Princeton. Princeton's predicament was that the Tigers had few players on their roster with experience playing in the system. They had yet to find a player fit to handle the center's responsibilities. Their point guard was sidelined with a back injury. And the players' slowness to grasp the offense's key concepts made them appear disjointed on the court. At the moment, what the Tigers were running didn't resemble any Princeton offense anybody knew. Although the Tigers had shown a glimmer of understanding their offense against Wyoming, they remained a long way from being comfortable in it. The lengthy possessions the offense typically generates make for low-scoring games, but this was offensive futility to the extreme. Princeton was one of the worst scoring teams in the country, averaging forty-nine points per game.

In the end, Princeton would have been thrilled with forty-nine points against Monmouth. Considering how well they had played against Wyoming, the Tigers, playing at home, should have had no trouble beating the Hawks, a 1–7 team that had been plagued by injuries and suspensions.

The final score was Monmouth 41, Princeton 21. Most fans figured that had to be a halftime score. But no, Princeton really scored just twenty-one points. In their loss, the Tigers had only two assists on nine baskets. The Hawks had twelve assists on sixteen baskets. The sixty-two points was the lowest combined scoring total for Division I teams since the three-point shot came into existence in 1986. Princeton's twenty-one points tied the lowest score for a Division I team in that same span. The Tigers hadn't scored that few points in nearly seventy years. Princeton, which went scoreless for nearly fifteen minutes in the second half, was two of twenty from behind the three-point arc. Of the ten players who played, only five scored and just four made field goals. Had Okafor not made a layup with three seconds remaining—his only basket of the game—Princeton would have finished with as many points (nineteen) as turnovers (nineteen).

"There's only sixty possessions in our game, so that means every third possession you turn it over," Scott said. "That means sometimes you turn it over two possessions in a row. . . . When you're turning it over and then you get an open shot every third possession, that's usually when it doesn't go in. Nobody ever thinks they're going to get twenty-one, but that's the formula for it. Turn it over and miss every open shot."

The outcome drew national attention. Highlights (or lowlights) from the game ran on *SportsCenter*. "Where's Bill Bradley when you need him?" the anchor asked, then added "for the love of Pete Carril" when a Princeton player missed another shot. He closed with: "If this keeps up, no one will want to run the Princeton offense ever." The harshest attacks came not from the media but from Princeton fans. Calling the defeat "ignominious" and a "catastrophe," they wondered what "indignities" lay ahead. One said the program was about as low as it had ever been. Many railed against Scott, calling his courtside demeanor an "embarrassment." "I cannot fathom how things have gotten so bad so quickly," said another. Some questioned if the players had given up.

Three days after the Monmouth debacle, Princeton traveled to Winston-Salem, North Carolina, to play No. 16 Wake Forest in a game that would be televised nationally on ESPN2. The Demon Deacons were coming off their first home loss in twenty-one games and were averaging eighty-one points per game—more than Princeton had scored in its last two games combined. Even worse, neither Greenman nor Owings would play in this game. Greenman's back was still bothering him, and Owings came down with a 101-degree fever before the game.

Yet, the outcome didn't turn out as bad as many people expected. When Okafor's second free throw fell through the net to put Princeton ahead 21–20 with just over five minutes left in the first half, the Tigers had scored as many points as they did against Monmouth. They continued to keep the game close until the final ten minutes, when Wake Forest's speed and strength eventually wore them down. Although it wasn't nearly as embarrassing as the loss to Monmouth, the 61–42 defeat was still Princeton's sixth loss of the season by double digits. The Tigers were losing their games by an average of 16.5 points.

The result left many people scratching their heads trying to figure out how a team that lost by twenty to Monmouth could turn around and play nearly evenly with Wake Forest for thirty minutes. But consider that, unlike Monmouth, Wake Forest wasn't accustomed to playing against the Princeton offense. Also, Princeton's offense is designed to give the Tigers an advantage against Wake Forest–type teams (teams that are faster and stronger). Moreover, Wake Forest was an Atlantic Coast Conference opponent, and the game was on national television. Players are human. They will tell you they take every opponent seriously, but in truth, it is a much bigger deal to them to play Wake Forest than Monmouth, especially with the game on TV. All their friends and family could watch this game. They didn't want to embarrass themselves.

Chapter 8

A Tradition
Tarnished

Scott Greenman's back wasn't improving. Since his bad spill at Colgate, Greenman had played only twelve minutes in two games. He had missed two games completely and didn't appear ready to return to the lineup anytime soon. When traditional treatments failed, Greenman visited a chiropractor and tried acupuncture. Nothing worked. It seemed to be one of those injuries only time would heal. And Princeton was running short on time. The Tigers desperately needed their point guard. "It's extremely frustrating, especially since it's my senior year," Greenman said. "I've been doing therapy every day, trying a couple different things, anything to make it a little bit better. Hopefully, it will be sooner rather than later."

Even though a week had passed since the Monmouth game, Princeton was still hearing about it. It was like a mosquito bite that wouldn't stop itching. Not surprisingly, the players started to feel under attack and turned defensive. "We're all in this together," Greenman said. "We look at each other, and we're like it doesn't matter what anybody else is saying. No one else knows the work that we're putting into this. Everyone else can do and say what they want to say and make fun as much as they want, but we know how hard we're working. We know it's going to eventually pay off."

The players weren't the only ones suffering. The past month hadn't been easy on Princeton coach Joe Scott either. To look at him, one would have thought he was carrying around the weight of the Princeton legacy on his back. His eyes were hollow and rimmed with dark circles. Weariness seemed permanently etched in his face. Yet he was determined to turn the negativity that swirled around the program into a positive.

"I think it's been good for us," Scott said. "I think it's been good for our young team. It's been good for us from a coaching standpoint because we sort of are developing a coat of armor that you need to play this game. You need to be tough. You need to compete. You've got to learn who you are. You've got to learn your strengths. You've got to learn your weaknesses. Part of Princeton basketball, part of what I think Princeton basketball is, is we know who we are. We're trying to build that. We play the way we play for a reason. We've got to be proud of it. We've got to know it [inside] and out. We have to be disciplined in what we do. We have to know that's what makes us be as good as we can be. That's been a weakness of ours, [not] knowing who we are."

But for all this talk about toughness and a coat of armor, the players were beaten down by the losses. Their confidence ebbed. With his team battered emotionally, Scott began to soften his coaching style. He still rebuked players—"You don't open your mouth, Steuerer. You don't talk. You're a church mouse, Steuerer"—but his sarcasm wasn't as biting nor his tirades as long. Scott hadn't turned warm and fuzzy, but he was less caustic.

Just before Christmas, Princeton traveled across country for the Pete Newell Challenge, a four-team, one-night event held at the Arena in Oakland, California. Princeton would play Stanford in the early game, followed by DePaul and California in the second half of the doubleheader. The games were to honor Newell, a longtime coach who had won NIT and NCAA championships and now was best known for his "big man camps." Because Princeton was part of this year's field, former Tigers coach and current Sacramento Kings assistant Pete Carril would be given the Pete Newell career achievement award at halftime. It would be the first time Carril would watch one of Scott's teams play in person. "It will be good to see him," Scott said. "I talk to him all the time. We're very close. It will be good to have him see Princeton play. He's meant a lot to me personally. And to have him be here I know means a lot to me and means a lot to our program."

Carril was lucky. He didn't arrive at this game until a little more than fourteen minutes remained in the first half. By the time he took his courtside seat, the Tigers trailed, 14–3. His tardiness kept him from seeing Princeton turn the ball over on its first possession and shoot an air ball on its next. With the progenitor of its trademark offense looking on, Princeton was inept and disorganized against a mediocre Pac-10 squad. The Tigers were making Stanford, a team with a losing record, look like a national title contender. Princeton appeared completely bewildered against the Cardinal's zone defense. They missed layups and fumbled the ball away with regularity. No Princeton player scored in double figures, and the Tigers had more turnovers (eighteen) than field goals (thirteen). But that wasn't even the most remarkable statistic. Stanford, which led 35–14 at halftime before going on to win 58–34, did not even have to score in the second half to claim victory.

If Carril was dismayed by Princeton's play, he didn't show it, nor did he criticize Scott's coaching. He was well aware that plenty of others had. Even as he watched the rout unfold before him, Carril remained a staunch supporter. "The thing about it is, it doesn't matter whether [the criticism is] valid or not. It's there, and you just have to live with it," Carril said. "My own feeling is that they're going to get better. I can just see them getting better. . . . I think with time, things are going to be all right." Asked if he had spoken to Scott recently, given him any advice, Carril said he hadn't. "I don't like to bother him now, especially when things aren't going well," Carril said. "I never liked to have anybody bother me when I was suffering."

After a lengthy postgame discussion with the players, Scott emerged from the locker room, leaned back against the cement, and said, "This wall won't take my weight."

"Right now, we're at the point in time where when we get in a tough spot, we go to something we don't know," he said. "We press. We try to do something on our own. . . . You press when you don't have that inside you, that substance to fall back on. That's what veteran teams have. This is what we do. This is how we do it, good times, bad times. We do what we do. We don't have that yet. It's urgent that we learn it. It's urgent. I don't know any more urgent circumstances than under the ones we're in."

No one would fault Princeton for trying too hard. But in this case, it was to the Tigers' detriment. It was as if each player on his own wanted to save the season. Instead of working together as a team, they were splintering into a group of individuals with their own agendas. As Luke Owings put it: "We've got different guys doing different things. We've got to get over that hump. . . . I don't think you can really attribute it to merely being a young team because there are plenty of young teams out there that find it early. It's just a different growing process that each team has [its] own demons to face. We're trying to get through them. We have plenty of them."

Had Greenman been available, he likely would have brought a steadiness to the court and kept the Tigers from being anxious. But all Greenman could do was offer advice to Steuerer from the bench. "It obviously hurts not having Greenman out there in these games, a guy who has played, who knows what we do and has a good understanding," Scott said. "Kevin [Steuerer] is going to learn what we do, but he hasn't played. This is only his fourth, fifth game after never having played as a freshman, and he's out there forty minutes. Boy, would it be nice to have Greenman out there, knowing what to do against the zone. Maybe that would have given us a little bit of stability instead of going away from what we do."

The culmination of the losses had left many wondering if the players had quit on the season. No one who came to play for Princeton ever expected to be this bad. "We're not going to give up," Owings said. "But obviously, there's a frustration because we want to do better. You want to go out there and be better than we've been. It's frustration when you don't do as well as you think you should. . . . I think we all know there is something that can be built that takes things like this. Sometimes you've got to go through bad times to get into the good times. We all hope and are going to try to get to those good times. We hope they come, and we know they are not going to just come. We're going to have to make them come."

To Scott, it was no mystery what had to be done. He knew what it would take to turn this season around. It was just a matter of convincing the players they had to do it. "It's getting them to understand how important it is to have that discipline to do what you're supposed to do when you're supposed to do it," Scott said. "Because five guys relying on each other, that's the kind of team we have. We need to rely on each other, count on each other to be where you're supposed to be so I know what I'm supposed to be doing. That's breaking down. . . . The message is clear. That's all we want from them is [to] do what we do. If that means they're going to learn it the hard way, then they're learning it the hard way. But sometimes that's the necessary way to learn something."

Although he was troubled by the loss, Scott was more upset that he let his mentor down. It was one thing that Princeton had played poorly. It was quite another that they had played that way in front of Carril. This was not the first impression Scott had wanted Carril to have. "I know he's disappointed and he feels bad that we didn't play well," Scott said. "We didn't show what Princeton basketball is. I'm disappointed that he's disappointed. There's no reason why that guy should ever feel disappointed about Princeton. To do what he did for twenty-nine years, I just feel bad for that reason. There will be another day when he watches us play and we'll play well. Maybe that will be a more important day. That's why you can't really worry about that stuff."

As they headed their separate ways for the holidays, everyone was ready for the break. They were tired of losing and they were tired of each other. They needed some time away. "I think it will be pretty good for us to get a day or two away from the situation, get perspective, look in on ourselves," Owings said. "You can go out there, and every day you hear Coach Scott yelling at you [and] be like, 'Oh, Coach is killing you. He's killing you, killing you.' You can kind of look at yourself."

None of Princeton's players had been born the last time the Tigers started a season this poorly. In the 1979–1980 season, Princeton lost eleven of its first thirteen games but then went 13–3 and finished tied with Penn for the Ivy League championship. The Quakers won the playoff game, 50–49, to earn the NCAA bid. As bad as things stood now, at least the Tigers could take solace in knowing that their predecessors had been able to turn their season around. Maybe they could too.

Princeton returned from its holiday break to play Carnegie Mellon, a Division III school in Pittsburgh. The Tigers have played a Division III school every year for the last twenty years, usually immediately following their final exam break in January. Princeton is hardly ever challenged in these games. The Tigers were 27–0 against Division III opponents in the past twenty-two years, winning by an average of 27.5 points per game. But Carnegie Mellon, at 9–0, was one of the better Division III teams in the 2005–2006 season and was ranked No. 22 nationally. The Tartans averaged 91.6 points per game. Princeton had scored a total of ninety-seven points in its last three games.

This was Princeton's first meeting with Carnegie Mellon in seventy-three years. It might be that long until the Tigers see the Tartans again, after Carnegie Mellon shocked Princeton by winning, 51–46, at Jadwin. The Tigers, who held the Tartans forty points below their average, were undone again by their anemic offense. Princeton scored just fourteen second-half points. "It's a humbling loss, probably one of the worst losses in Princeton history," said Greenman, who watched from the bench because of his sore back. "I think it was a reality check for guys who think just coming to Princeton you're automatically good without putting in extra time or work or really listening to what Coach says. It was a reality check for those people and us as a team. If we don't do the stuff we're supposed to do and we don't really concentrate on it, we can lose to anybody in the country."

First Monmouth. Now Carnegie Mellon.

"It couldn't be any worse," Scott said. It was the most discouraged he had been all season. "We're in a constant state of making changes," Scott said. "I don't know how much we've gotten better because we're changing so much stuff."

Conventional wisdom held that Scott needed to stop tinkering so that Princeton could develop continuity. When it was disclosed that freshman center Noah Levine—one of Scott's recruits—had left the program earlier in the week, the departure caused increased speculation that Scott was creating a toxic environment for the players. The loss of Levine—who hadn't played a minute this season—wasn't a major blow to the team, but it did give fans another opportunity to criticize Scott.

As if his critics needed it. Scott's shortcomings were being zealously dissected on the message boards. If the Princeton boosters were restless before, they were downright militant now. Many expressed outrage at how far the program had fallen.

- "It's not a rebuilding. It's a demolition."
- "Frankly, I am embarrassed to be a Princeton fan."
- "There's no excuse losing to a Division III team. Joe Scott should be ashamed."
- "I've never been this depressed about a Princeton basketball team."
- "I am ready to see the Joe Scott era come to an end."
- "Scott seems like he wants to constantly 'prove' that he's the man in control. The players seem intimidated, fearful."
- "Does Scott get to last thru next year or does his cord get cut at the end of this season? . . . I'm curious as to how far we're willing to let the team slide downhill."
- "If the poor performance continues, I think we should cut our losses and wish Coach Scott well elsewhere."

There were a few voices of support for Scott against these waves of criticism.

- "What I find so interesting . . . is that no one ever says the players should be ashamed, only the head coach. The players should be ashamed for the turnovers, missed shots, not holding on to rebounds, being beaten one-on-one by [Carnegie Mellon] players. . . . I don't think any coach would do a whole lot better under the current circumstances. Why aren't we ripping JTIII for leaving the cupboard so bare?"
- "Let's see what he does when he gets more of his own players, and let's see what happens when these freshmen and sophomores gain experience. It's way too early to give up."

• "Joe will some day get huge credit for doing to Princeton what he did at Air Force and he will probably win coach of the year honors when that happens. The only question is why did he have to destroy a winning tradition to get there."

Nearly everyone was predicting at best a 4–10 finish in the Ivy League. A few optimistic souls claimed 7–7 was possible. Others lamented how Princeton's misfortune would influence Penn's recruiting efforts positively. It was becoming very difficult to be a Princeton fan.

It wasn't any easier being a Princeton coach or player. In some ways, Joe Scott had brought this censure upon himself. Had he not made such audacious predictions in his first season, then failed monstrously to meet them, Scott likely would not have been subject to such condemnation. Even if Princeton had won the Ivy League and then flamed out spectacularly in the first round of the NCAA tournament, the fans would not have been happy but they probably would not have been as harsh in the 2005–2006 season. After winning the Ivy League his first season, John Thompson III began his second year 2–6. There were grumblings then too, but not nearly to the extent Scott was experiencing now. Yet, in spite of the vitriol that was being directed at him, Scott wasn't suffering as much this season as he had his first year.

"Well, I mean, I would say nothing's worse. Everything is what it is," Scott said. "I can only look back at last year and blame myself for everything that happened. That's why last year was worse. I wish I would have done things better and done things differently. This year, I don't think that." Scott may not be as dispirited as a year earlier, but that didn't mean he was immune to the attacks. Some coaches avoid reading what is written about them or their programs in times of trouble. Not Scott. He read everything and dissected every detail. Nearly everywhere Scott or the players went, people asked them what was wrong with the team, why they had become so bad. At first, they chafed at the criticism. But now the rampant negativity was gnawing at the players' self-esteem.

"Hey, when you score twenty-one, attacks come," Scott said. "Truth be told, there's tons of negativity. It's totally unfair to these players. Those days are over. The negativity can continue to exist, but it's not going to affect us because our team is our team." He admitted that although he had tried to remain strong and not let the negativity affect him, it had. "And if it was affecting me, I know it's affecting [the players] because they respond to me," Scott said. "I've coached them differently. . . . Negativity can do that to you. I let it happen to me."

Still, as bad as things had gotten, Scott was finding ways to look at the situation positively. He had convinced himself this was another step in rebuilding the program. "Everybody's tradition and history gets stronger when you go through times like this," Scott said. "That's what makes tradition—seasons and times like this—because it fortifies the program. It makes you stronger. Good times over time just chip away, wear away. You need crisis. You need conflict so that you can make it as strong as you can make it."

Hungering for good news, Princeton finally received some. Greenman's back had improved, and he returned to practice the day after the Carnegie Mellon loss. Greenman termed his back "80 percent" recovered, which was good enough for him to play in the Rutgers game. No team was more ready to leave 2005 behind than Princeton, which was scheduled to play the Scarlet Knights at Louis Brown Athletic Center on New Year's Eve.

Everyone expected Greenman's calming presence would help Princeton's offense run smoother than it had recently. But after only two practices, no one knew if Greenman would make much of a difference. He did. With Greenman playing all but one minute, Princeton looked nothing like the team that had lost to Carnegie Mellon three days earlier. That's not to say they played a perfect game, far from it. The Tigers turned the ball over a season-high twenty-three times. But they made 47 percent of their shots—their second-best field-goal percentage of the season—and had thirteen assists on sixteen baskets.

Noah Savage was the biggest beneficiary of Greenman's return. Savage had made only six of his last twenty-five three-point attempts coming into the game, but with Greenman directing the offense, he got the ball at the right times and in the right places. Savage, who had scored in double figures only once during Greenman's absence, made five three-point baskets to lead the team with seventeen points. "Nobody's wanted to make a big deal over the last month that the senior point guard has not been playing for us," Joe Scott said. "It's a world of difference. The weight of the world is off Noah Savage's shoulders. The weight of the world is off these young guys' shoulders because we've got a guy out there that's going to take some pressure away from them having to do things, things that they shouldn't even be asked to be doing when you're freshmen and sophomores."

Rutgers used a 12–2 run to close out the 54–44 victory, handing Princeton its fifth straight loss. It was the Tigers' first five-game losing streak in more than a quarter century. Yet despite another defeat, the mood after the game was upbeat. Savage joked about how switching his sneakers to the new LeBron James shoes helped his shooting touch. "I was, like, channeling LeBron," he said. Greenman teased Savage about his new haircut. "Guys had a lot more fun playing," Greenman said. "I really noticed it [against Carnegie Mellon]. I said a couple things to Noah during the game. 'You look like you're dying out there. What's wrong? Have fun. Play. Talk to guys.'"

"Everybody was just real down and in a perpetual state of being down," Savage said. "We just kind of got back to why we play basketball: to have fun no matter what is going on. Competing is fun. Playing basketball with a bunch of your friends, that's fun. There's no reason to walk around with your head down all the time."

In what was becoming a common occurrence, Princeton debuted a new starting lineup against Rutgers, its fifth in eleven games. Michael Strittmatter, a six-foot-eight freshman out of Brophy Prep in Phoenix, Arizona, became the latest to start at center for the Tigers. Strittmatter, who had played only three games prior to his promotion, finished with a typical stat line for a Princeton center—more assists than rebounds. Scott acknowledged after the game that Strittmatter wasn't the answer to the Tigers' woes at this position, just their latest solution. "He can't be out there the whole time," Scott said. "We've got to get Harrison [Schaen] to help so that Mike can help more."

Scott also decided to move Schaen back to center after trying him at forward. Scott hoped Schaen could provide a presence underneath the basket that the Tigers sorely lacked. Schaen would back up Strittmatter, and Patrick Ekeruo, who had started the last seven games but did not play against Rutgers, would also be in the mix. "It's Harrison's turn to see if he can help us, and then we'll go from there," Scott said. "To be honest with you, we're probably going to have games where they're all going to have to play."

Only one game remained before Princeton embarked on its Ivy League season, a last chance to solve its problems. Greenman's return had given the Tigers' offense a boost, but it wasn't a cure-all. They still ranked last among Division I schools in scoring, at 43.9 points per game. No other school averaged fewer than fifty points. It would take more than one game to heal Princeton. As their 52–41 loss to Rice in Houston showed, the Tigers had a long way to go before they overcame their offensive limitations.

Having won only two of its first twelve games, Princeton seemed no closer to becoming the team Scott envisioned than it had at the beginning of the season. And the Tigers' 2005–2006 Ivy League opener was only eight days away.

Chapter 9

Bright
Lights,
Big Stages

P enn typically plays one of the stronger nonconference schedules in the Ivy League, and this year was no exception. Besides their games against Colorado and Temple, the Quakers scheduled games against two teams ranked in the top five in the preseason Associated Press poll, No. 1 Duke and No. 5 Villanova. They were one of only three mid-major programs scheduled to play two top five teams in the 2005–2006 season. (Bucknell and Stony Brook were the others.) Penn also planned to take a trip to Hawaii to play the Rainbow Warriors in late December. "That schedule just got a whole lot tougher now that Hawaii beat [2005 Final Four participant] Michigan State," Steve Danley said. "We want to play everybody. . . . I think that's how you get better. That really helped us last year when we got into the league."

While Ivy football teams would never consider playing a Bowl Championship Series team such as the University of Southern California,

Florida, or Texas, Ivy basketball teams routinely schedule games against the top teams in the country, and often they are competitive with them. It is not uncommon to see Penn play Duke, Princeton play North Carolina, or Yale play Kansas. What made Penn's schedule especially challenging in the 2005–2006 season was that the Duke and Villanova games came less than a week apart, and the Blue Devils were the top-ranked team in the country. Duke set the standard for college basketball most of the last two decades. The Blue Devils have won three national titles, made fourteen Final Four appearances and claimed fifteen Atlantic Coast Conference championships. They have produced nine national players of the year and thirty-one all-Americans. The 2005–2006 season's team featured player-of-the-year candidate J. J. Redick and likely all-American Shelden Williams.

The Penn players had the Duke game circled on their calendars since the schedule was announced. Not only would they be playing on national television and in one of the more storied college basketball venues in the country, but next to the NCAA tournament, it would be the biggest stage they would compete on in their basketball careers. "We want to play the best players, the best teams that are out there," Eric Osmundson said. "I think Coach does a great job facilitating that, especially for my senior year. I couldn't imagine, I mean, it's the greatest feeling getting to go down to Durham and play in front of the "Cameron Crazies" [Duke fans]. It's going to be a dream come true for me."

While the Duke game lay tantalizingly ahead, Penn had plenty of basketball to play before its showdown with the Blue Devils. The Quakers finally opened the 2005–2006 season in late November, the last of the Ivy League teams to do so and nearly two weeks after Cornell. Given that they had the most time to prepare, they should have been the most ready for their first game. Instead, injuries got in the way. With starters David Whitehurst and Mark Zoller still hobbled, Penn coach Fran Dunphy was forced to cobble together a patchwork lineup.

Zoller, a junior forward out of St. Joseph's Prep in Philadelphia, could not play. After severely spraining his ankle three weeks before the game, he aggravated the injury by stepping awkwardly on a teammate's foot during practice a week ago. Not having Zoller on the court hurt the Quakers the most underneath the basket. At six foot six, Zoller was a shooting guard trapped in an undersized power forward's body. But in spite of his height deficiency, he was the team's best rebounder. Whitehurst might play limited minutes, depending on how the game went. His ankle had improved, but Dunphy didn't want to risk reinjury to the two-sport standout from Tinton Falls, New Jersey.

These injuries meant Brian Grandieri and Friedrich Ebede would make their first career starts. Grandieri, a sophomore guard out of Malvern Prep, Dunphy's alma mater, had yet to play in a game for Penn after sitting out his freshman year with a torn anterior cruciate ligament. Ebede had waited not so patiently for three years to break into the starting lineup. Since coming to Penn, the strong-willed senior swingman from Cameroon had clashed with Dunphy over his playing time. Ebede wanted to play more; Dunphy wanted Ebede to practice harder and become better skilled. Now both players were getting their chances to make up for lost time.

Penn's opponent, Siena, was making its first trip to the Palestra, but it was not a first for the Saints' coach. Fran McCaffery was quite familiar with the building. A 1982 Penn graduate, McCaffery had helped the Quakers win three consecutive Ivy titles. Needless to say, Penn fans were hoping to ruin his homecoming. Given that the Saints had lost, 89–62, to Penn a year earlier and had five new starters on a team that went 6–24 the previous season, the Saints weren't expected to put up much of a challenge.

But Siena ended up being better than advertised. The Saints were loose, while Penn looked out of sorts. Aside from the sloppiness that is typical in first games, the Quakers were suffering from a lack of cohesion. Players weren't anticipating passes, which led to turnovers, or they were out of position, which led to fouls. Their confusion was a big reason they squandered a thirteen-point second-half lead before escaping with an 82–77 victory.

"It looked like we were a little bit disorganized, and that's something we will work on," Dunphy said. Most coaches—and players—would prefer to win every game by twenty points. But in lieu of a rout, coaches don't mind a close victory. It gets their players' attention. Practices usually are more focused and intense after narrow wins.

Dunphy wasn't the only one who realized that Penn had plenty to improve on before its next game. "A test is good for us," Eric Osmundson said. "It shows us where we stand as a team, and it also shows where you stand as an individual. Now we can take the film and go over it the next couple days, see what we can improve on both offensively and defensively. If it's a blowout, you tend to get lackadaisical. It was good that they came back on us and forced us to group together. That's part of the game—when things start getting tough, whoever is going to stick with it and not make big turnovers."

The Siena game began a stretch of five games in thirteen days for Penn. The Quakers' next opponent was their neighbor, Drexel. The

Dragons, whose campus abuts Penn's, were coming off an impressive Preseason NIT run. After an opening win at Princeton, Drexel advanced to the semifinals at Madison Square Garden where it lost, 78–68, to No. 1 Duke. The night before their game against Penn, the Dragons came up short against No. 16 UCLA, 57–56, in the NIT consolation game. This would be their fourth game in six days and their second in less than twenty-four hours. Any confidence Drexel gained from closely playing two top twenty-five teams would be offset by the Dragons' fatigue.

Penn had beaten Drexel by thirty-one points a year ago and had every reason to believe, especially given the Dragons' weariness, that it would win this game handily. And for a while, it appeared the Quakers would. Penn went up by nineteen early in the second half only to have that lead dwindle to four with ninety seconds remaining. In the end, Drexel's legs were too tired to make a final push. The Dragons missed three of their final four shots and Penn held on for a 68–60 win.

Although they hadn't played particularly well in their first two games, the Quakers were 2–0 for the first time in eight years and only the second time in Dunphy's tenure at the school. Getting to 3–0—something no Penn team under Dunphy had ever done—wouldn't be easy. Up next was Colorado, a strong, athletic team from the Big 12 Conference. Teams from power conferences usually won't agree to play on an Ivy League home court. But to Coach Ricardo Patton's credit, he accepted a home-and-home series with Penn. The Buffaloes had beaten the Quakers, 80–57, in Colorado in 2003. Now they were coming to Philadelphia.

Penn would go into the game with one fewer player. Junior guard Lorenz Manthey had left the team. It wasn't a surprise. Manthey had played in only eight games in his career at Penn, and he had been hurt in the preseason. Faced with the likelihood he would not play much this season and the demands of his major—the Hamburg, Germany, native was enrolled in the Wharton School concentrating in management—Manthey realized he couldn't afford the enormous time commitment that basketball required. "He said he was down to the point where he couldn't get four hours of sleep a night and still do his academic stuff," Steve Danley said. "You can't live on less than four every night."

Penn held its own against Colorado and went into halftime tied with the Buffaloes. But the Quakers couldn't overcome their poor second-half shooting and lost, 78–60, snapping their ten-game home winning streak that dated back to last season. The Quakers didn't have much time to brood. They had just two days to prepare for back-to-back games against Navy and Temple. The Friday night meeting with the Midshipmen was scheduled to coincide with the Army-Navy football game being played in Philadelphia on Saturday. Navy hoped to draw fans in town for the football game to the Palestra to cheer for the Midshipmen.

For a team looking for its first win of the season, Navy proved a formidable opponent, though the scrappy Midshipmen were aided by Penn's generosity. Dunphy had rearranged his starting lineup, inserting Whitehurst in place of Grandieri, but the move didn't seem to explain the Quakers' poor performance. Penn opened the game with three consecutive turnovers, and that shoddy start seemed to doom the Quakers. Had it not been for the first-half efforts of Ibrahim Jaaber, who scored twenty-three of Penn's first thirty-seven points, Penn would have been in trouble. The Quakers eventually pulled away, scoring thirty-nine points on free throws to win, 86–73.

Penn is accustomed to quick turnarounds during the Ivy League season, so it hardly mattered to the Quakers that they had less than twenty-four hours to prepare for their Big 5 rival, Temple. The Big 5 is a round-robin tournament to determine a city champion among five of Philadelphia's six Division I schools: Penn, LaSalle, Saint Joseph's, Temple, and Villanova. (Drexel was left out of the mix.) Originally conceived to help pay for the Palestra's upkeep, the Big 5 is what makes Philadelphia college basketball special. No other city pits its teams against one another, and as a result, few cities rival Philadelphia's passion for the sport. There was a time when a Big 5 doubleheader was *the* social event in Philadelphia, when crowds squeezed into the Palestra to watch Temple's Guy Rodgers, La Salle's Lionel Simmons, Villanova's Ed Pinckney, Penn's Corky Calhoun, and Saint Joseph's Mike Bantom. These fiercely contested games were and continue to be all about bragging rights—the right to say your team is the best in the city. Temple had done more bragging than any other Philadelphia team. With their twenty-three Big 5 titles, the Owls were usually the team to beat.

Penn trailed, 36–18, in its series with Temple, but lately the Quakers had been very competitive with the Owls. The last two games between the schools had been decided by a total of five points. In six of their last eight meetings, the margin of victory had been fewer than ten points. It was no surprise that this game was also close. Temple escaped with a 50–46 victory.

The loss capped an especially tough week for Osmundson. Penn had hoped Osmundson would be one of its more dependable outside shooting threats in the 2005–2006 season, but so far that hadn't been the case. Osmundson made only one of his seven shot attempts against Temple. In the Quakers' three games that week, he was five for twenty-nine (17 percent), including three for twenty-three (13 percent) from three-point range. Clearly, he was in a slump. "I think young people go through that," Dunphy said. "That is what Oz is working through. When we get him in a timeout or during the course of a game, the instructions are always the same. 'If you're open, you've got to shoot the ball. That's what you do.' In order for us to be successful, he has to make some of those shots. . . . Hopefully, he'll work out of it."

Penn hoped Osmundson would find his shooting touch, and soon. The Quakers had a tough slate of games coming up, beginning with No. 1 Duke. For most teams, the biggest obstacle to overcome when playing the top-ranked team in the country is getting past the ranking. Too many teams are intimidated by it. They unravel mentally before they take the court and are brought down by the awe they have for the No. 1 team. Although this would be only the second time in school history that Penn would play a top-ranked team, the Quakers had shown in the past they were up to the task when it comes to playing top competition. "Any time you're an underdog, you want to get out there and try to knock off the main guy," Osmundson said. "They're No. 1 in the nation. If we have an opportunity to do that, it's going to be awesome. It's all about creating memories that will last a lifetime. I can tell my kids that I played against the No. 1 team in the nation at Cameron Indoor. We're going to go down there with the mind-set that we're going to beat them."

For Dunphy, this game would be a special experience not only for his players but also for him. It would mean a reunion with a former teammate. In 1971, when they were both in the Army, Dunphy and Duke coach Mike Krzyzewski played together on the U.S. squad in the Conseil International du Sport Militaire, a tournament for armed-forces teams held throughout the Middle East and in Germany. Dunphy had brought along a team picture taken in Syria to show Krzyzewski. Although the men had known each other for years, this would be the first time they would coach against one another. "We see each other a lot obviously at Final Fours and those kind of things, through our Coaches vs. Cancer work," Dunphy said. "I just have so much respect for him and how successful he's been. It's pretty remarkable, that record that he has."

Although Duke has a history of success against the Ivy League—the Blue Devils are 43–9 overall against Ivy teams—they are just 7–6 against Penn. The Quakers are the only Ivy team to have more than one win against the Blue Devils. Their last win at Cameron Indoor, a 50–49 overtime victory, came in 1971—the same year Dunphy and Krzyzewski were teammates. Since then, Duke has won four in a row against Penn. The teams last met in December 1980 when the Blue Devils pulled off an 88–82 victory. Duke came into the game undefeated at 7–0 after narrowly escaping with a 77–75 win in its ACC opener against Virginia Tech.

The game was being televised on ESPN2, one of the Blue Devils' twenty regular-season appearances on the ESPN network. Every Duke game is televised, either nationally or on a regional network. On the other hand, the Quakers had eleven games televised in the 2005–2006 season, mostly on regional networks. Their only other appearance on the ESPN network would be their final regular-season game against Princeton, which would be shown on the fledgling ESPNU.

At most college campuses, the students show up for a game around tip-off time. Not at Duke. The Duke students—or Cameron Crazies, as they are sometimes known—take their spots well in advance of game time. Many of them are positioned in bleachers near the floor opposite the scorer's table. This proximity to the court maximizes the effect of their heckling. The Cameron Crazies consider it their duty to help rattle the opponent. It's a role they take very seriously. They scrutinize media guides for information that can be used to unnerve opposing players. Their chants are usually clever, sometimes bordering on salacious, but their efforts have made Cameron Indoor one of the more forbidding environments for road teams in college basketball. In Krzyzewski's twenty-six seasons at Duke, the Blue Devils are 326–48 at home.

As the Penn players began to warm up, the Cameron Crazies were ready for them. They chanted "Quaker oatmeal" and "safety school" in general toward the team and taunted specific players. Few escaped their scorn. "It was funny," Whitehurst said. "They say some crazy things, those guys. Stuff about my socks; this, that, and the other. They clearly looked up some of the players, because they were shouting about people transferring and all types of things. It was great. . . . I feed off every fan no matter if they're for me or against me. I just love the action."

Far from being daunted by the jeers, Whitehurst was in his element. He clearly was enjoying the atmosphere. He did not acknowledge the students but soaked in their energy. When it came time for the Penn players to finish their stretching, they usually spread out around the court. But no one seemed to want to go near the Duke student section—except Whitehurst, Danley, and Jaaber. The three walked over to the low press table that separates the students from the court. As the three stretched their calf muscles and quadriceps, the Cameron Crazies stood with their arms extended in front of them, waving their fingers frenetically in the players' faces and droning "AAAAaaaaaahhhhhhhhhh." Barely inches separated the players from the students. Had she been so inclined, the girl in the front row easily could have planted a kiss on Whitehurst's cheek without having to move. Through it all, the impassive expression on the players' faces never changed.

"I didn't understand why everyone [went to the opposite side of the court]," Whitehurst said. "Usually we split up. I don't know. That crowd kind of intimidated some people. Me and Steve looked at each other and we wondered, 'Why did everyone go over there?' So we're like, 'Well, we might as well go over here. See what they're going to do.' Because I'm not afraid of the crowd, no less the players. I wanted to see what they were going to do. It was good fun. It was a good time."

Having only seen Cameron Indoor Stadium on television, the Penn players were surprised by its size. "I would have thought this gym was a lot bigger," Osmundson said of the 9,314-seat venue. What made this arena seem larger than it truly was—both in person and on television—was the sellout crowd. A sea of Duke fans engulfed the court, leaving just enough room for a small collection of Penn fans to squeeze into a tiny space behind the Quakers' bench. It was mostly parents and family members—including Dunphy's mother and brother—and a few die-hard students. Mark Zoller's contingent came dressed in T-shirts that read: "Holler for Zoller, Grow the Fro," a reference to the forward's decision to shear his shaggy mop of hair into a neater, though less distinctive coif. Outnumbered but undeterred, the Penn fans tried to blunt the effects of Duke's boisterous crowd. It was a losing battle.

Although they tried to show composure as the game got under way, the Penn players were jumpy. Adrenaline coursed through their veins, causing them to play erratically. Duke's Sean Dockery stole the ball from Jaaber twice to open the game—two of the three turnovers by the Quakers in the first minute and a half. Usually it was Jaaber stealing the ball away from an opponent to set the tone. Instead, the Blue Devils served notice that they planned on making it a long night for Penn. The Quakers weren't easily cowed, however. They shook off those early miscues to go on a 6–0 run that put Penn ahead, 6–3, at the first scheduled time-out.

Under withering defensive pressure from Duke, Penn rushed its offense. The Quakers were launching shots hastily rather than patiently waiting for a clean look at the basket. They were throwing ill-advised passes. They were playing much faster than they wanted. Yet Duke failed to pull away from the Quakers. The Blue Devils held just a 10-point lead at halftime. Even more remarkably, the Quakers grabbed five more rebounds than Duke did in the first half. "I was real proud of our guys that we didn't allow that separation to get too much greater," Dunphy said.

It was a physical game, particularly underneath the basket. Zoller and Ebede picked up five first-half fouls between them trying to contain Shelden Williams. With less than a minute remaining until halftime, Danley caught an elbow from Williams as the two went for a rebound and had to leave the game with a bloody gash on his forehead. He needed fourteen stitches to close the wound. When the second half began, Danley was still in the locker room receiving treatment. Dunphy couldn't risk having Ebede pick up his fourth foul quickly, so he sent the spindly Tommy McMahon, a six-foot-seven freshman from Hillsboro, California, to start in Danley's place.

Duke, undoubtedly motivated by Krzyzewski's halftime talk, surged to a nineteen-point lead. Danley returned to the lineup less than three minutes into the half but neither his nor his teammates' shots fell. Then, just as it appeared the game was starting to slip away, Jaaber came through for the Quakers. Jaaber, known more as a slasher than a shooter, launched a three-pointer from in front of the Penn bench that energized the Quakers' spirits. "He hadn't made [that shot] in his three-year career," Dunphy said. "He kind of drove with one dribble, rose up, and shot a jumper. It was probably a twenty-two- or twenty-three-footer. That was a pretty impressive shot."

With Duke's defense now preoccupied with Jaaber's outside shooting, David Whitehurst found room to shoot. The sophomore guard began a three-point barrage, making three shots from behind the arc in a two-minute span. "David is a very confident kid," Dunphy said. "He stroked it very well in the second half. He's got a beautiful jump shot." After Ebede converted a three-point play by sinking his free throw, the Quakers were within ten points of Duke's lead with just over six minutes remaining. Plenty of time remained to pull off the upset. Penn had seized the momentum away from the Blue Devils. A few more three-point baskets, and this game belonged to the Quakers.

It was not to be. Williams and Redick were not about to let their team lose to a bunch of Ivy Leaguers. Duke regained control and held on for a 72–59 victory. "Give credit to [Penn]," said Williams, who finished with twenty points. "They played good defense, and whenever I touched the ball, they were clamping down on me. They had a really good defensive plan, just trying to take me out of the game. Fortunately, J. J. started driving toward the end of the game. They were collapsing down on him and leaving me open, and I got a few free touches there."

In the end, Penn was simply overmatched. The Quakers didn't have enough answers for Duke's two all-Americans. Still, Penn hadn't embarrassed itself on this grand stage. Instead, the Quakers proved they were comfortable playing there. "I was pleased," Dunphy said. "We talked a little bit before the game that we would have this tremendous respect for this program and we cannot let that become a fear factor. I thought our guys did a pretty good job of understanding that concept."

Osmundson was more blunt. "I think we showed we can play with these guys," he said. "We couldn't get over the hill a couple times, but I think all the guys did a good job. A lot of guys stepped up."

Games like these are always dangerous. Had it been a rout, Penn's psyche could have been destroyed. The players might have lost confidence in themselves and their teammates. But by playing well against the top team in the country, the Quakers didn't feel bad about their 3–3 record. "We're not upset about [the losses] at all," Whitehurst said. "We've just got to take them in stride. I'm looking forward to Villanova because I feel we'll play even better. We're gelling very well, also. We're learning who can play and who can't play."

Danley didn't know it at the time, but the elbow to his face in the Duke game had given him more than just fourteen stitches. He had a concussion. He also had an exam scheduled for the morning after the team returned from Durham. "They told me I could have waited," Danley said. "But I would have had to take it at a bad time, and they would have had to write a different exam. Basically, it was going to be a big hassle, and I wasn't thinking too clearly at the time anyway. I was like, 'Take it and get it over with.'"

Danley's exam was in his game theory class, which sounds like a breeze, the kind of class an athlete takes for the easy A. Only *this* game theory referred to economics, not athletics. Game theory is used to understand patterns of behavior in several fields of study. Two economists, one from the Hebrew University of Jerusalem, and the other from the University of Maryland, were awarded the Nobel Prize in Economic Sciences for their work in this area earlier in 2005. Now Danley had to tackle the subject with not only a massive headache but also an inability to think straight. "I couldn't read for more than twenty seconds at a time," Danley said. "I couldn't actually get through the problems on the exam at one time. I had to keep skipping from problem to problem, doing about thirty seconds' worth of work. I was lucky it was a topic I understood pretty well." Apparently, Danley understood game theory quite well. He received an A-plus on the exam. "Sam [athletic trainer Phil Samko] tells me he's going to knock me out for every test," Danley said.

Danley may have felt well enough to take his exam, but he wasn't cleared to play against Villanova. Danley's absence meant that Ebede would return to the starting lineup—Penn's fourth starting lineup in seven games. Because of injuries, only Jaaber and Osmundson had started every game for the Quakers. By the time these two Big 5 rivals met, Villanova was 6–0 and had moved up to No. 3 in the Associated Press poll. The Wildcats had won their previous two games by an average of twenty points and were looking pretty invincible. Penn, having just gone toe-to-toe with Duke, was feeling pretty plucky itself.

The only problem was that the Quakers somehow misplaced their shooting touch on the way back from Durham. Had they been able to make their shots, this might have been a different game. As it was, they were colder than the Schuylkill River in January. Penn missed its first eighteen shots from behind the arc and trailed Villanova by twenty-one midway through the second half. But just as Villanova appeared to be on its way to an easy victory, the Wildcats couldn't make a basket either. Eventually, Villanova prevailed, 62–55, though not before Penn gave the Wildcats a scare.

"These [Big 5] games are crazy," said Villanova coach Jay Wright, who appeared relieved to escape with the win. For as poorly as it had shot the ball, Penn showed remarkable resiliency in rallying from a double-digit second-half deficit. The Quakers could have easily given up after falling so far behind. But to their credit, they didn't. "I'm proud of the guys for coming back, but obviously we've got to look at things and make sure we don't get down that much," Dunphy said. "We obviously need to learn from this and build on this, but you never know how these tough games in the early part of the year [affect a team]. . . . Hopefully, that's the sign of things to come that when we do play teams that aren't quite as athletic and as talented maybe we'll have our opportunities to win a game."

With two exams the next day—sociology and ancient Greece—Jaaber didn't have much time to dwell on the loss or to consider how these last two games might benefit Penn for the rest of the season. There were lessons to be learned from the losses to Duke and Villanova, but right now, the Quakers had more pressing concerns. They had to get through final exams. Once those ended, they would fly to Hawaii for their game against the Rainbow Warriors. But that was more than two weeks away, a long time to carry forward the momentum from their recent games. "Any time you have a long break, it's like you haven't played," Jaaber said. "It's like the summer off. You don't know until you step out on the court if it benefits you or not. Personally, when I don't have my best game, I want to be right back on the court."

After exams and a short break for the Christmas holiday, Penn went on its longest trip of the season. The Quakers left the continental United States for Hawaii, making the program's first trip to the fiftieth state since 1974. They would play two games during their stay on the island of Oahu, one against the University of Hawaii and the other against BYU-Hawaii, a Division II school. It was their first meeting with a Division II team since 1993 and only the second in Dunphy's tenure at Penn.

Hawaii is typically one of the stronger teams in the Western Athletic Conference. The Rainbow Warriors had been to the postseason four of the last five years and, in their first game of the 2005–2006 season, knocked off Michigan State, a Final Four participant the previous season, by a whopping twenty-two points. Lately, though, Hawaii had been struggling. Part of the reason for Hawaii's poor showings was its schedule. The Rainbow Warriors were playing their fifth game in ten days. They were tired. By contrast, Penn was well rested—perhaps too well rested. The Quakers hadn't played in sixteen days, the longest in-season layoff for a Dunphy-coached team at Penn. It was almost as if they were starting their season all over again. Throw in a long plane ride, a time change— the tip-off would be at midnight Philadelphia time—and weather that made the players long for the beach instead of the basketball court, and Penn's chances of winning this game appeared slim. But considering it had been nearly a month since the Quakers had won, they didn't want to become too accustomed to playing teams tough yet falling short as they had against Duke and Villanova.

Penn seemed determined not to let this one slip away. The Quakers' offensive execution was nearly flawless and their defense was stingy. Hawaii kept the score close, but the Quakers exploited the Rainbow Warriors' ball-handling problems to eke out a 58–55 victory. The win not only ended Penn's three-game skid, but it was also the best nonconference road victory by an Ivy team in the 2005–2006 season. The Quakers had cemented their designation as Ivy League favorite.

With only one day between games, there was no time to celebrate the team's biggest win to date. But before they headed across the island to play BYU-Hawaii, the Quakers stopped for a tour of Pearl Harbor. Dunphy likes to make these trips as educational as possible and he knew that to his players, this World War II site was just a page from their history books. The dramatic and poignant memorial had a sobering effect on the team.

On New Year's Eve, Penn appeared on its way to an easy win against BYU-Hawaii. Then the Quakers' eleven-point first-half lead disappeared, and the Seasiders made a 17–5 second-half run to go ahead by six. But just as it appeared that Penn was going to follow its impressive win against Hawaii with an ignominious loss to a Division II school, the Quakers found their footing and pulled out a 72–62 win. Penn's 2–0 road trip pushed their overall record above .500 with two games remaining before the Ivy League season began. "I think coming away with a win, particularly [against] Hawaii, was a boost to our confidence," Dunphy said. "The fact was we weren't ready to win against Temple, Duke, and Villanova. Sometimes, you're just not ready to win."

Four days later, Penn put on a jump-shooting clinic in its 84–49 win at the Citadel. Led by Osmundson, who seemed to regain his shooting touch on the return trip across the Pacific, the Quakers made a season-high twelve three-point baskets in recording their largest margin of victory in three years. Osmundson went four for six from behind the arc to finish with sixteen points.

For its final tune-up before the Ivy League season, Penn headed to New York to play Fordham. The Rams started the season losing six of their first seven games but seemed to turn things around after beating the University of Virginia in early December. Given how well the Quakers had been playing, they should have had little trouble dispatching Fordham. Instead, they found themselves in a closer-than-expected game. After taking a 35–32 lead into halftime, Penn allowed the Rams to shoot 67 percent from the floor in the second half and lost, 78–63.

Fordham exposed Penn's most glaring failing—its tendency to lose focus. When the Quakers are on their game and playing to their potential, they can beat just about any team. But when they aren't, they can lose to any team. Dunphy recognized that this flaw could be a problem for his team heading into league play, but he also knew the players tended to find ways to compensate for that shortcoming. "This is not the most mature team we've had," Dunphy said. "[But] they are more timely than any team we've had in a while in terms of making shots."

Part II

THE HEART
OF THE SEASON

Chapter 10

Harvardization

January means two things at Harvard: the start of the Ivy League season and the start of final exams. Before exams, though, is reading period. This nearly two-week session is designed to give students time to study and write term papers. It is an intense, pressure-filled time that causes stress for even the most well-prepared bookworm. Some students use reading period to catch up on what they put off during the semester. And for this reason, Zach Martin views it as an enormous waste of time. "I feel it's a huge disadvantage to someone like me who has done the reading throughout the semester, because then I have to reread the stuff," Martin said. "I actually have to do double the work. That's why I really frown on the reading period. One of the reasons that the college justifies it is there's more time for the classes to assign papers."

"It's called reading period, but you're on call around here," Coach Frank Sullivan said. "It's almost like you're a doctor with a beeper. You can have a class called at any time, a section called at any time." Not surprisingly, in the midst of this roiling academic cauldron, the players feel pulled in several directions. On the one hand, it is important to them to do well academically. On the other, the same competitiveness that drives them in the classroom also fuels them on the basketball court. As a result, many spend their afternoons at practice—while their peers are in the library studying—and their nights cramming for their exams. Eventually, these all-nighters take a toll not only on their minds but on their bodies, and the lack of sleep is manifested in the practices during this time. It is especially tough on the freshmen who aren't accustomed to having this many demands placed on them.

Sullivan often spoke to his players about what he termed the "Harvardization" process. When they arrived in Cambridge, the players thought of themselves as basketball players first, students second. In time, though, their priorities were reversed, and they started spending more time studying than working on their game. "You go to Harvard, you're expected to be academic," Martin said. "Scholarship basketball players are paid to play basketball. If I was in school on a basketball scholarship, I would be more pressed to go down to the gym more."

At the same time that the academic calendar is reaching its climax, the basketball season is shifting into its defining stage. It's a predicament for coaches. While they are sympathetic to the players' academic loads during this time, they also have to prepare for the Ivy League season. Ideally, they want the players getting plenty of rest, working hard in practice, and studying game films. Of course, that is next to impossible during reading period. Instead, the coaches accomplish what they can, hoping it will be enough and still not strain the players mentally or physically. It is a delicate balancing act. Harvard's upcoming opponent, Dartmouth, didn't have to worry about exams. The Big Green, which is on a quarter rather than a semester schedule, took its exams nearly a month earlier.

Since the Crimson returned from Texas, practices had taken on a more serious tone. The seniors, in particular, had become more purposeful and less patient with their teammates' foibles. They knew what was at stake. Only seven opponents remained on the schedule. Each one stood between them and an Ivy League championship. If they were going to win the title this year, they couldn't afford any lapses. At the practice before the Dartmouth game, the coaches hardly had to say a word. The seniors made sure their teammates got the message. "Today, Zach and I were on the sideline yelling at Cus and Drew [Brian Cusworth and Drew Housman] because they screwed up two consecutive plays," Matt Stehle said. "They weren't big things, but that can mean a three-point shot, six points here or there."

"That's the problem," Michael Beal added. "When we were playing other games, if you mess up [on defense], it usually leads to layups. If you mess up [in Ivy League games], it leads to an open three-pointer. In our conference, a three-point shot that's open is good. [Dartmouth senior guard Mike] Lang and all these people, they are not going to miss threes."

Harvard's preparation for Ivy League games was much more specific than its scouting of nonleague opponents. No detail was too small to consider. In its nonleague games, the Crimson concentrated on a few key players on the opposing team and their tendencies. For its Ivy opponents, it scrutinized every player on the team from the starters to the last man on the bench. The players knew if an opponent preferred to go to his right rather than his left, where and how he liked to get his shot, and how good an outside shooter he was. They knew each team's favorite plays: who curled, who cut, and who slipped behind the screen. They studied game film and stat sheets, looking for anything that might give them an edge. "It's really every minute detail," Stehle said. "You know your matchup or you don't. That foul you commit because the guy went the other way—it could mean the game, it could mean a loss, it could mean the whole season."

No one could question the Harvard seniors' desire or their commitment, which isn't always in the case in the Ivy League. This is usually the time of year when the league's coaches start to worry that their seniors will lose interest in basketball. With everything else going on in their lives—waiting to hear from graduate, medical, or law schools; going on job interviews—seniors are often distracted. They become less passionate about playing, especially since most of them know their future won't be on the basketball court. While the rest of Division I basketball contends with players leaving early for the NBA, the Ivy League grapples with seniors whose minds drift to their postcollege careers while their desire to play basketball dwindles.

Brady Merchant, captain of the 2003 Harvard team, recalled how his priorities shifted from his freshman season to senior season. "One of the lessons I learned was that basketball is not the most important thing in life," Merchant said. "You see, oh, there's only forty-four people at our game, and that's including both teams and the refs. You learn that basketball might not be the most important thing in life. I thought it was a good thing. It's tough because you are pouring all your time and your energy into it. You just kind of reevaluate your relationship with the sport. I found I enjoyed [basketball] more after I discovered that."

Sullivan didn't have to worry about his seniors losing interest. Instead, he had a different concern. "I'm just worried they don't put too much pressure on themselves, actually," Sullivan said. "You hope they don't try too hard. You want them to relax and play."

Dartmouth was an important game not just because it was the start of the league season, but it was also Harvard's travel partner. In the Ivy

League, the teams are divided into four pairs: Dartmouth and Harvard, Brown and Yale, Columbia and Cornell, and Penn and Princeton. For the most part, the teams are linked geographically with the exception of Cornell, which given its location in Ithaca, New York, isn't near any of the other schools. The purpose of this division is to make scheduling easier. Each twosome plays another the same weekend. For example, Penn and Princeton go on the road to play Brown and Yale the same weekend that Dartmouth and Harvard go on the road to play Columbia and Cornell. Dartmouth plays at Columbia on Friday and at Cornell on Saturday, while Harvard plays at Cornell on Friday and at Columbia on Saturday. It is a simple formula, but one that is not without controversy. Because Penn and Princeton—typically the top two teams in the league—are paired, the other schools often have to play the league's better teams on back-to-back nights. In the last seventeen years, only two teams have managed to knock off both Penn and Princeton in a single weekend: Columbia in 2001 and Yale in 2005.

Each school also plays a home-and-home series with its travel partner. Harvard and Dartmouth choose to play their games against each other before playing the rest of the teams in the league, while Penn and Princeton space their games a month apart. "I think your travel-partner games are extremely important," Sullivan said. "It is the two games you have time to prepare for, you can prepare longer. They are the one time that you are playing an Ivy League game that's like a nonleague game in rest, preparation. You don't get that [with] the other ones. You get three days to prepare for two opponents."

"I also think that a lot of it has to do with the fact that we play them our first two games," Stehle added. "It really sets the tone for the rest of the season. The last two years, we dropped the second game both times, and that just set us back immensely. . . . It's not an option to lose. It's not the Pac-10, where you can lose to UCLA and then go back and beat them in the conference tournament. You have to be the best from the first game to the fourteenth game. That's what Penn was last year. That's what Princeton was the year before. They didn't let anybody touch them."

Although Harvard trailed Dartmouth in the overall series, 91–69, the Crimson had fared better against the Big Green recently. Harvard had won ten of its last twelve against Dartmouth and had beaten the Big Green six straight at Lavietes. The teams had split their meetings the last two years, each team winning on its home court. "We always heard, 'The guys before you never lost. The guys who wore the shirts never lost to Dartmouth,'" Beal said. "I think that I have a chip on my shoulder, [because] hey, we've lost twice to these guys. We can't go out our last season losing to these guys. We have to start establishing that [winning streak] again, because that was a big thing. That was the thing that kept Harvard in the hunt. We need to get that tradition back. There's a lot of things we've kind of taken upon ourselves to try to get back into this program, and I think that has to be as big . . . as any."

It had been eighteen days since Harvard had last played a home game, and it was good to back at Lavietes, where the Crimson was 5–1 in the 2005–2006 season. Despite its disappointing end to the nonconference season, it still was considered among the favorites for the Ivy title. Harvard had fallen out of the Associated Press poll but remained in the Mid-Major Top 25, a poll for programs outside the major conferences run by CollegeInsider.com and voted on by thirty coaches. The Crimson had more wins than any other Ivy team at this point in the season; had the second- and third-leading scorers in the league, Stehle and Jim Goffredo; and was getting back Brian Cusworth, who had missed seven games with a broken hand.

Cusworth had his cast removed the Monday before Saturday's game. The return of a player can be as disruptive as his departure, but Sullivan knew there wasn't time to ease the seven-footer back into the lineup. "We're just going to put him in right away," Sullivan said. "We're just going to start him. He has to get going. . . . Who knows what his stamina will be? It's an important game. It's an important series. I talked to Matt [Stehle] specifically [after Cusworth got hurt], 'Let's not make a big deal out of it. Let's just keep moving forward.' I think the fact that we won in his absence made the transition a little easier. The guys weren't waiting for him to come back [to save them]. It wasn't like we were in a situation where we lost a lot of games and hadn't been playing well."

Like Harvard, Dartmouth is known more for hockey than for basketball these days, but the Indians—as the Big Green was called during less politically correct times—were once among the top teams in the country. Dartmouth made seven NCAA tournament appearances between 1941 and 1959. Lately, however, the Big Green's luster had faded. Dartmouth had posted a winning record only twice in the last ten years. In the 2005–2006 season, Dartmouth was again having trouble competing. The Big Green's season had all the smoothness of a sixteen-year-old learning to drive a stick shift, lurching forward and stalling out on several occasions—a not-unexpected development for a team featuring eleven freshmen and sophomores on its sixteen-man roster.

Yet, not all of the Big Green's lack of success could be attributed to its youth. Its schedule also had done the team no favors. Unlike Harvard, which had evenly spaced games, Dartmouth played in fits and starts. The Big Green opened the season playing three games in an eleven-day period then took a two-week break for exams. When it resumed playing in mid-December, Dartmouth had four games in nine days followed by a one-week layoff for the holidays. The Big Green next went out West, playing three games in four days—two at New Mexico's tournament and one in Colorado. With few teams wanting to visit charming, but frigid, Hanover, New Hampshire, during the winter months, Dartmouth was forced to go on the road to play fifteen of its first nineteen games. The Big Green had played one home game in November and one in December and would play only twice at home in January.

With all its traveling, Dartmouth was bound to run into problems. The Big Green's flight home from Colorado was canceled, resulting in an extra day of travel. Then their bus trip to Army was prolonged by a snowstorm. By the time Dartmouth traveled to Harvard, the Big Green was worn down and beat up. "If they were seniors, it would be different," Dartmouth coach Terry Dunn said of the rigorous schedule. "The younger kids—they're so fragile. It's a fine line."

Dartmouth, which had managed only two wins in its first eleven games, was looking for a fresh start with the advent of the 2005–2006 Ivy League season. A year earlier, the Big Green turned around a dismal season by winning five of its last seven league games to finish 7–7 and tied for third place. The players and coaches were hoping for a similar improvement this year, and they had reason to be optimistic. Dartmouth had snapped its eight-game losing streak with a 55–42 win at Army. Before that victory, it had played well against New Mexico, putting itself in a position to win with two minutes left, and had a strong first half against Colorado.

Mike Lang, a senior guard out of Gordon Tech High School in Chicago, had been trying his best to keep his young teammates upbeat about the season. "I think we're in striking distance of being the team we want to be," Lang said. "This last couple weeks, we are a new team. We're having fun again. During the losing streak, we were down. You tend to point fingers at someone, not take responsibility. A lot of problems happen once you're losing. As soon as you get a win, it seems like all that goes out the window. . . . We're a team that started off bad, but we're starting to turn it around right now, and I honestly think you do not want to play us."

Dartmouth's optimism didn't last long. Harvard was clearly the better, more experienced team in this contest and won easily, 78–65. The Crimson's strategy going into the game was to capitalize on its height advantage by scoring around the rim, getting fouled, and making free throws, because the Harvard coaches didn't think their shooters could match the Big Green three-pointer for three-pointer. Harvard not only dominated underneath the basket—Stehle nearly had a triple-double with fourteen points, eight rebounds, and eight assists, while Brian Cusworth added fifteen points in his return—but the Crimson also was remarkably productive from the perimeter. Jim Goffredo scored a career-high thirty-three points, making seven three-point attempts. He had nearly as many threes as the entire Dartmouth team.

"For us, it's just a relief," Sullivan said. "Any time we play during reading period, you just don't know what you're going to get." He was particularly pleased with how often the players passed the ball to Goffredo and Cusworth during the game. It was important that Cusworth touched the ball early and often to make sure he felt involved in the offense. If he didn't, he might think his teammates had lost confidence in him. Goffredo just happened to find himself in one of those rhythms that shooters can fall into. "We didn't have to tell them, and some teams you've got to tell them," Sullivan said. "I think it shows the character of the team. We didn't have to tell them that Jimmy was having a great day today. We didn't have to tell them that we have a guy who's seven feet. We didn't make a big deal. They just kind of did it on their own."

After two bad losses, Harvard was glad to win again. Even more important, the Crimson was thrilled to open Ivy play with a victory. Because Harvard-Dartmouth was the first league game played, the Crimson stood atop the standings at 1–0. It was a spot it hoped to occupy throughout the season. "We look at this as a fourteen-game single-elimination tournament," said Cusworth, who along with shedding his cast had shaved off his goatee for this game. "Obviously, you don't have to go undefeated, but you've got to aspire to be. The way we look at it, we advanced to the second round."

Round two for Harvard was another game against Dartmouth six days later. Meanwhile, the Big Green would play a nonconference game against Stony Brook on Tuesday before hosting the Crimson on Friday. The second game in this series is always more difficult for both teams. Having thoroughly prepared for the first game and having played once already, each team becomes nearly as familiar with the other as it is with itself. "It's a lot harder to score because they know everything we do," Beal said. "In the second game, we call a play, they're saying, 'All right, he's coming here. Twenty-three is coming here. Screen here.' They're calling out every play, just like us. We know everything that they're about to do. They know what you're going to do just from your eye signals because that's Ivy League coaching."

Dartmouth was just glad to be returning to Hanover and looked forward to back-to-back home games for the first time in the 2005–2006 season. The Big Green would play two consecutive games at Leede Arena just twice more this season. Not once would the team play three in a row at home. Unfortunately for Dartmouth, its return to friendly surround-ings didn't help it against Stony Brook. The Seawolves defeated the Big Green, 51–48, sending it to its tenth loss in eleven games. This string of setbacks left Dartmouth reeling. The Big Green needed to beat Harvard, not only to exact revenge for the lopsided loss at Cambridge but also to avoid falling into an 0–2 hole in the league standings.

The Crimson, however, wasn't about to let this game slip away. After a second-half surge by Dartmouth to pull within three points, Harvard resolutely held off the Big Green and prevailed, 65–53. As was the case in its previous meeting with Harvard, Dartmouth couldn't find enough scorers to counter Stehle and Cusworth. The win sent Harvard into its fourteen-day exam break on a high note. It was exactly the wrong time for an extended layoff, but there was nothing the Crimson could do except hope that the momentum it had generated would carry through to its game against Yale in two weeks.

Chapter 11

Conference

Calls

A week after the Harvard-Dartmouth series concluded, the rest of the Ivy League teams began their quests for a championship. Yale and Brown would play the first of their travel partner games, and Cornell and Columbia would travel to Penn and Princeton. Everyone was ready to leave behind the nonconference season—not to mention those disappointing losses—and make a fresh start. As league play got under way, half the teams had records below .500 and three of the other four were barely above it. Columbia (7–6), Harvard (8–5), Penn (6–5), and Yale (8–7) were the only teams with winning records. With just five nonconference games remaining among its teams, Ivies were 42–62 against nonleague opponents. Penn's victory over Hawaii notwithstanding, notable wins by Ivy teams were few.

Aside from wanting a few more wins to boost its confidence, an Ivy team doesn't pay too much attention to its record outside the league, because its nonconference wins and losses have little effect on its NCAA aspirations. Other teams in Division I worry about the RPI—or Rating Percentage Index, a mathematical formula that ranks teams based on wins and losses and strength of schedule—but not Ivies. Because of the league's lightly regarded reputation, no Ivy team is going to receive an at-large bid to the NCAA tournament. At best, a team that misses out on the league championship can hope to be invited to the less-heralded National Invitational Tournament (NIT).

In 2002, a banner year for the league, three teams tied for the league title—Penn, Princeton, and Yale—and the conference recorded its highest RPI in the preceding ten years, ranking No. 14 out of thirty-one conferences. Yale had wins over Penn State and Clemson that year; Penn beat Georgia Tech, Villanova, and Temple; Brown knocked off Providence. Yet only one Ivy team, Penn, went to the NCAA tournament. Princeton and Yale played in the NIT. In the nonconference season, the goal for Ivy teams is not to pick up RPI points in hopes of boosting their chances of making the NCAA tournament but rather to play teams that will help them get ready for the league season.

Based how they had fared so far, some Ivy teams appeared better prepared than others for the 2005–2006 league season. Penn was showing some vulnerability after its loss to Fordham but was looking to build on its performances against Duke, Villanova, and Hawaii. Harvard appeared in the hunt for its first league title. Yale was emerging as a contender after adding Dominick Martin, a six-foot-ten senior center from Asheville, North Carolina, to the lineup in mid-December. The Bulldogs were 5–3 with him and had played Kansas evenly for much of the first half earlier in the month. Cornell was an enigma, but if the Big Red could put it all together, it too could challenge for the title. Penn continued to be the favorite to win the championship; however, many observers felt that the league was up for grabs, and this would not be one of those years that one team ran away with the title.

"I just honestly believe it's going to be a four-loss season" for the league champion, Cornell coach Steve Donahue predicted. "The teams in the league are too good. Everyone is too balanced. Penn is the best team by far right now, but I also think our teams match up better with them than teams they play outside the league."

As the defending champion, Penn was the team to beat. Meanwhile, the rest of the league was just waiting for the Quakers to slip up, and the players knew it. "My freshman year, we got picked No. 1," Steve Danley said. "We went out and lost those first two Ivy League weekends, and I haven't looked at too many prognostications since then. . . . [Losing early] pretty much ruined our season. I talk about that with those guys every day. You can't lose the first two because you're done."

Penn's first Ivy opponent was Cornell. For the Big Red, it was not an ideal start to league play—going against the two traditionally strongest teams, especially on the road. Cornell was still looking for its first road win of the season and had lost fourteen in a row to the Quakers and eleven of its last thirteen to the Tigers. Ever the optimist, Donahue found something positive in the scheduling misfortune. "When we were first looking at this, I think: if you lose to two of the better teams, you're losing at their place. That's what you're telling your guys—that you're going to get them back at your place, and now you've got the hardest trip of the season over with," Donahue said. "We've had that season where we start out pretty well in the league, we go 5–1, 5–2, 5–0, and we still have to play Penn and Princeton once let alone four times. If we go in there and do a great job, no matter what, I think we're still around because it's the hardest weekend and it's done with."

Donahue should have known Friday the thirteenth wouldn't be his lucky day. Penn, eager to put its bad loss to Fordham behind it, broke the game open early in the second half with a 19–0 run. Cornell, which trailed by nine at halftime, suffered another of its dreaded lulls. When Adam Gore finally ended the Big Red's five-minute forty-second scoring drought with a three-pointer, it was too little too late. Penn's 84–44 win was its largest margin of victory over Cornell in eleven years. The Big Red's starting five combined for only three more points than Ibrahim Jaaber, who led the Quakers with twenty points.

After its resounding win over Cornell, Penn had little trouble dispatching Columbia the next night. The Quakers went to the locker room ahead by fifteen at halftime, then blew the game open by scoring sixteen consecutive points to start the second half. Their 87–55 victory was Penn's 1,600th win as a program, making it the eighth Division I team to reach the milestone. The Quakers had won their first two league games by a combined seventy-two points, their largest margin of victory in an Ivy League weekend since 1974.

"I don't think it was our intention" to send a message, Eric Osmundson said. But "I think it definitely sends a message that we're not going to let down at any moment. Remember, last year Princeton was picked to win the league, and Coach does a good job of reminding us [of what happened] because he doesn't want us to let our guard down. Anything can happen."

Cornell and Columbia also had the misfortune of playing Penn following its bad loss to Fordham. The practices between Monday night's setback and Friday night's Ivy opener had been some of the more rigorous of the season. "We came into [the league season] with a chip on our shoulder more than anything else," Danley said. "We were pretty upset about that Fordham game. We didn't feel like we played particularly well. Even more embarrassing, we didn't feel like we did things, hustle things, very well. We didn't get a lot of stops. It's not just hitting shots. Sometimes you have games where you miss shots. We didn't do a lot of the little things. Coach got on us. We got back to focusing. It showed. It showed up."

Yale's season seemed stuck in neutral. The Bulldogs, who hadn't won more than two in a row but also hadn't lost more than two in a row, weren't going forward, but they weren't sliding back either. Some of the inertia stemmed from biding their time while awaiting Dominick Martin's return. Martin had started twenty-one games for Princeton as a freshman before deciding to transfer to Yale because he felt it was a better program for him. After sitting out the 2002–2003 season because of NCAA transfer rules, he played two seasons for the Bulldogs and was the team's top returning scorer and rebounder. With only one semester of eligibility remaining under Ivy League rules, Martin chose to drop out of school the first semester. He rejoined the team in mid-December. In his first game, after only one practice, Martin scored fourteen points on seven-of-eleven shooting. Still, missing the first part of the season had set him back. "Gelling with the team is tough," Martin said. "Coming back midseason is not the same as going though preseason individual workouts. The first seven games I wasn't there. I wasn't at any practices. It's hard to come back and jump right in and be able to play."

It can be quite disruptive adding a player to a team at this late date. But in Yale's case, the Bulldogs were able to easily assimilate Martin into their lineup because most of the players had played with him in the past. The shooters in particular were thrilled to welcome him back. Martin's presence underneath the basket drew defenders away from the perimeter. "He takes a lot of attention," senior guard Josh Greenberg said. "He just has the ability, when things break down, you can give him the ball and you can pretty much count on it to go in the hoop."

Greenberg was one of the more unlikely members of a Division I roster. Generously listed at five feet eight inches, Greenberg can sink a shot from just about anywhere in the gym. What he lacked in height and athleticism he made up for with his boundless energy and enthusiasm. Yet those qualities weren't enough at first to earn him a spot on Yale's roster, not even as a walk-on. "My whole life goal was to play Division I basketball," Greenberg said. "I wanted to go to Duke. I wanted to be the next Bobby Hurley. My freshman year in high school I was still real small. I realized I'm probably not going to play Division I basketball. So I decided to do the next best thing, go to an Ivy League school."

When he arrived at Yale, the Fayetteville, New York, native found he couldn't leave basketball behind. He pestered the coaches for a walk-on spot, but they refused. They did, however, allow him to be a manager.

And after one season as a manager, they relented and gave him a jersey. Greenberg didn't play much his sophomore and junior seasons, only getting into games when the Bulldogs were up by twenty or down by twenty. In two years, he had played in fourteen games and made only two baskets—both three-pointers. "You know, [former NBA coach] Jeff Van Gundy went to Yale, transferred out and went to a junior college," Greenberg said. "There would be days when I'd be practicing, not getting to play a lot, I just really wanted to go play somewhere. It's a pretty ballsy move to leave Yale, I guess."

Despite his desire to play more, Greenberg didn't leave Yale. He stuck it out and had a job lined up with the investment-banking firm Merrill Lynch after graduation. Basketball had worked out pretty well for him, too. His teammates, impressed by his perseverance and determination to be a part of the team, voted him captain his senior season. Greenberg had gone from manager to walk-on to captain. "I think basketball is one of the most important things in the world," Greenberg said. "I think the guys that suck it up [and stay with it]—that really says something about you, how you are going to be in life."

By the Brown game, Yale had played more games with Martin than without him and appeared to be hitting its stride. The Bulldogs had won three of their last four, the only setback an 87–46 defeat at Kansas. They appeared confident heading into the Ivy season and ready to challenge for the title. Above all, they were looking forward to returning to New Haven. Yale's last six games had been away from home, a journey that included stops in Providence, Rhode Island; Corpus Christi and Houston, Texas; Lawrence, Kansas; and Washington, D.C. The Bulldogs' nomadic odyssey was due to the school's policy of closing down its dorms during the holiday break, which meant winter athletes were forced to move into a nearby hotel. Figuring that if they had to be living in a hotel they might as well be on the road playing a game, the teams usually scheduled as many away contests as possible during this time. Yale's Ivy opener would be its first home game in twenty-five days.

Meanwhile, Brown's season had a déjà-vu feel to it. In the 2004–2005 season, with one senior and one junior on the roster, making them the youngest team in Division I, the Bears labored to a seventh-place finish in the Ivy League. This season, again with one senior on the roster, they weren't faring much better. Brown had only four wins entering Ivy play. This slide was discouraging for the players and coaches who had grown accustomed to being one of the top teams in the league. Under Coach Glen Miller, who took over in 1999, the Bears recorded four consecutive winning seasons. They had twice finished second in the league, most recently in 2003 when they won a school-record twelve Ivy games and became the first Ivy team other than Penn or Princeton to win that many games in a season since 1968. Although Brown lost out on the league championship and subsequent NCAA tournament berth to Penn, which went 14–0, the Bears were invited to play in the NIT that year.

Those good times now seemed very far away. Brown's most experienced player, senior swingman Luke Ruscoe, had missed five games with an ankle injury. Ruscoe who comes from a basketball family in New Zealand—his parents and sisters all played for its national team—was one of the Bears' better all-around players. His absence had a significant effect on the younger players. "A lot of guys had been role players, valuable role players, but they've had other guys with experience in previous years to help them along," Miller said. "Now all of a sudden, they have to step up, play a larger role, be consistent players, put some points on the board. It's an adjustment for them. Some of them aren't quite there yet with their self-confidence. . . . They're still thinking a little bit too much out there, insecure with their games. As soon as we can get to the point where we can relax and execute offensively and defensively and just play the game, I think we'll start to make progress."

One of the players struggling with his larger role was sophomore guard Damon Huffman, who had been the Ivy League rookie of the year. As a freshman, Huffman was the team's most efficient and second-most prolific three-point shooter. This season, although the Petoskey, Michigan, native led the team in scoring at 10.2 points per game, his shot wasn't falling as easily. Huffman had made only 25 percent of his shots from behind the arc, more than twenty percentage points below his three-point shooting average the previous season. It isn't unusual for a player who had a breakout year as a freshman to struggle the following year. Opponents have more film to study and learn the player's tendencies, making it easier to defend him. The term for it is "sophomore slump," but Huffman wasn't about to apply that label to his shooting woes. "These terms bother me; hearing 'sophomore slump' absolutely bothers me," Huffman said. "Because I played basketball my whole life. I know, when I shoot the ball, what it feels like exactly—the path of the ball, the flight of the ball. When it's not going in but everything feels right? That's kind of what it felt like to me. . . . [The coaches say] 'You've got to change this. You've got to tweak this. You're not doing this. You're not doing that.' That starts to wear on me too, and then it becomes a mental thing."

With Ruscoe out and Huffman struggling, Brown looked to its younger players to assert themselves. Most recently, freshman Scott Friske had emerged as a reliable scorer. Miller had been trying to take the undersized power forward from Charlevoix, Michigan, and make him into more of a perimeter player, and Friske seemed to be developing a comfort level playing farther away from the basket. His scoring and rebounding averages had increased significantly in the four games leading up to the Ivy League opener. The Bears hoped Friske would become another scoring option, because they urgently needed to put more points on the scoreboard. Brown was averaging 57.1 points per game and had scored seventy or more points only twice. Fortunately, the Bears were holding their opponents to 63.4 points per game. "We're playing good defense by necessity," Miller said. "We led the Ivy League in scoring the last two years, but we couldn't stop a chair. This year we have to play good defense because we have trouble scoring."

Brown didn't have a lot of advantages going into its game with Yale—except one. The Bears had dominated the Bulldogs the last seven years, winning ten of the last fourteen meetings. Although Yale leads the overall series, 89–46, Brown had won six in a row against the Bulldogs. Even last season, the Bears' worst Ivy showing in five years, Brown swept the Bulldogs. Of all the setbacks to Brown, the one that stung the most came in 2002. The Bulldogs lost at home, 87–82, to the Bears then traveled to Providence the next week and won there, 80–77. Yale went on to finish tied with Penn and Princeton for the Ivy League championship. That Brown loss kept the Bulldogs from their first outright Ivy title and first NCAA tournament appearance in forty years.

Yale wanted nothing more than to end this streak of futility against Brown, and at long last, it did. Led by Dominick Martin, the Bulldogs overpowered Brown underneath the basket. Martin was one of four post players to score in double figures for Yale, finishing with thirteen points in the 75–61 victory. Brown's 21–6 run during the final five minutes made the outcome appear more competitive than it was. Even the return of Ruscoe couldn't help the Bears, who surrendered the most points they had all season.

For a team searching for continuity, Princeton received no favors from its January schedule. The Tigers began the month with a loss to Rice and then had eight days to prepare for their first Ivy League weekend. After a fifteen-day break for exams, Princeton would return to action against Davidson on the final Sunday of the month. The Tigers, who would play only four times in January, wouldn't resume their Ivy League schedule until the following weekend—a nearly three-week intermission between conference games. The rest of the league—with the exception of Harvard—would play nearly double the amount of games during this month.

At this point in the season, Princeton needed to play more games, not fewer. The Tigers were no closer to achieving cohesiveness or forging an identity than they were at the start of the season. While it is unusual for a team this late in the season not to have its rotation set, it was not unprecedented, especially for a team this inexperienced. Heading into Ivy League play, Princeton (2–10) was near the bottom of the overall standings with Dartmouth. If the Tigers could win the Ivy League—not unrealistic considering what the 1979–1980 team had accomplished—then those early losses wouldn't matter. But in order to win the championship, Princeton first had to end its six-game losing streak and beat Columbia at Jadwin.

It had been more than a month since the Tigers won a game—the victory over Wyoming on December 10. Usually, because of Princeton's historical superiority in the league and its longtime mastery over Columbia, the Tigers would be heavily favored. Few teams are as familiar with one another as Princeton and Columbia, which have played every year since 1901 for a total of 213 games. The Tigers were 23–1 against the Lions over the last twelve seasons and had won twenty-two of the last twenty-three at Jadwin. But given the events of the past month, no one knew what to expect. Columbia certainly felt it had a shot at upending the Tigers. The Lions started the season strong, winning their first five games, but had struggled lately because of injuries. Four players had missed Columbia's 82–42 victory over CCNY a week ago, including starters Dalen Cuff and Ben Nwachukwu and key reserve Justin Armstrong. But those three were expected to return for the Princeton game.

In order to accommodate television, the tip-off was changed from 7:30 P.M. to 9:00 P.M. Joe Scott and Joe Jones agreed to the time change, recognizing how immeasurably important it is to kids to play on television —even a network with limited viewership, like ESPNU. But it is a good thing that ESPNU does not reach many households because it is doubtful that either team wanted this game seen by a large audience. It took nearly four minutes before the first basket was scored, and the teams combined for fifty fouls, fifty-seven free throws, and thirty-two turnovers. As the game wore on, it became clear how evenly matched Columbia and Princeton were.

With eight seconds remaining, Nwachukwu scored to put Columbia ahead by two points. The Lions appeared on their way to their first victory at Jadwin in thirteen years. All they had to do was prevent Princeton from scoring. But Mack Montgomery fouled Edwin Buffmire with 0.8 seconds left on the clock, sending Buffmire to the free-throw line with Princeton down two. Scott couldn't bear to watch. Then again, Scott never watches his players shoot free throws. Instead, his habit is to stand next to the bench with his back to the shooter, sipping water while waiting to hear the crowd's reaction. When the fans roared for the second time, Scott knew the game was going to overtime. Princeton, which hadn't made a basket in the final ten minutes and fifty-two seconds of regulation, managed to send the game to an extra period by making ten of ten foul shots in the final three minutes. Freshman Michael Strittmatter made six in a row.

The Tigers finally made a basket in the opening minute of over-time when Alex Okafor scored and was fouled. His three-point play gave Princeton the early lead. The Tigers wouldn't make another basket, but they would keep the score close by making ten of thirteen foul shots in the extra period.

With twelve seconds remaining, Dragutin Kravic sank his first free throw to pull Columbia to 64–62. The senior forward from Zrenjanin, Serbia, who was majoring in European history, missed his second foul shot, but the ball bounced off a Princeton player and fell out of bounds. The Lions had possession underneath their own basket with a chance to tie or win the game. Cuff, the senior captain, tried to inbound the ball; however, Princeton had every Columbia player covered. Worried that he was going to be whistled for a five-second violation, Cuff called for a time-out. Unfortunately, the Lions had no more time-outs, and Colum-bia was assessed a technical foul. Scott Greenman made both foul shots to put Princeton up by four. John Baumann answered with a layup to pull Columbia within two. The Lions were forced to foul to stop the clock, sending Princeton's Kyle Koncz to the free-throw line. Koncz made a pair of foul shots to seal the 68–64 win.

Even though it won, finally ending its six-game losing streak, Prince-ton didn't feel good about the victory. The Tigers needed a herculean effort—not to mention some lucky breaks—to beat a team they had lorded over the past decade. If it took this much effort to beat Columbia, how would Princeton fare against the rest of the league? It might have been one of the more fretful wins in Princeton history.

Columbia didn't feel much better about the loss. Though the Lions were encouraged by how close they came to winning their first game at Jadwin since 1993, that they had victory in their grasp and let it slip away was disheartening. It was the kind of defeat that can shatter a team's confidence.

By the time the game ended, it was nearly midnight, and both teams had to play the next night. Whatever long-term benefits the teams had gained from playing on television, the short-term consequences were severe. Princeton, exhausted from the effort it expended winning its first Ivy League game, failed once again to put together back-to-back wins. Cornell jumped out to a 31–16 halftime lead against the Tigers, then went on to win, 57–49. It was the Big Red's first road win of the season and its second in a row at Jadwin.

Chapter 12

We Interrupt
This
Season . . .

Harvard began the Ivy League season exactly how it wanted. The Crimson swept its games against its travel partner, Dartmouth, and was atop the league standings at 2–0. As a bonus, everybody was finally healthy. Then the season came to an abrupt halt. It was exam time. "The worst part about Harvard, hands down," Zach Martin said. "The whole thing with exams being after Christmas is, hands down, the worst thing about Harvard. You can't relax and focus on basketball, because the semester is not over."

Almost as soon as Harvard stepped off the bus from its trip back from Dartmouth, basketball ceased to be a priority. Some of the players had tests the next morning. For the next ten days, exams would consume the players, taking them away from everything else in their lives. During this pressure-packed time, coaches at Harvard are forbidden from holding practices. They can arrange voluntary sessions, but they can't require the players to attend. "We try to organize it so each day at 1 P.M., we have a workout," Coach Frank Sullivan said. "Whoever comes, comes. If there's two guys there or twelve guys there, we'll do something. We never go more than sixty minutes. We won't let it become like a practice. They can't get fatigued. They've got to have stamina for the exam period."

In Division I basketball, every team takes a break for exams at some point. Outside the Ivy League, however, few teams take as much time off. Just as with the reading period, the coaches are put in a difficult situation. They want their players to do well academically—ultimately, that is why they are in college—but at the same time, even Ivy League coaches are pushed out the door when their teams don't win enough games. Dave Faucher spent thirteen seasons at Dartmouth, leading the Big Green to two runner-up finishes in the league. He resigned in 2004 after going 3–25 in his final season. Dick Kuchen stepped down in 1999 after thirteen seasons at Yale, winning the second most games of any Bulldogs coach. He went 4–22 in his final season. "The thing about athletics, and of course I played a lot of sports in my time as well," said Hunter R. Rawlings III, the president of Cornell from 1995 to 2003 and its interim president from 2005 to 2006, "is that somebody's always keeping score. There are winners and losers in every single contest. You can't help but pay attention when you see those wins and losses."

Taking a hiatus during a crucial part of the season isn't the best way to ensure victories, especially when most of the league is practicing and getting better. Sullivan is 6–8 in the game following exams during his tenure at Harvard. "You try to talk about it," Sullivan said. "It's definitely disruptive to developing continuity to the season. If you [say to] any coach, 'Hey, we're going to pull ten to fourteen days away from you during the middle of January,' I think any coach would say, 'Wait, are you crazy?' Yes, it's disruptive, but we all know it, and we have to live with it. It's one of the X factors of coaching men's and women's basketball and men's and women's ice hockey at Harvard."

Harvard, which wouldn't play for fourteen days, isn't alone in its predicament. Princeton has a similar academic calendar. The Tigers, who had fifteen days between games, followed much the same schedule as the Crimson during this time. "Basically, what we do is give guys off when they have exams," Coach Joe Scott said. "We look at schedules and see what days do the majority of guys not have exams. We would only go for an hour and fifteen minutes [on those days]. What you do is you go one day, give them off two days. Over the whole exam period, we probably have seven days off."

While Harvard and Princeton were mired in exams, the rest of the league was put on hold. Brown and Yale finished out their travel-partner series. Columbia and Cornell began theirs. Penn played Lafayette and its final Big 5 contests, and Dartmouth traveled to New Hampshire. Even with these games, there would be long gaps of inactivity. As a result of this fractured schedule, the coaches were left searching for ways to prevent their teams from atrophying. "Amazing, isn't it?" Cornell coach Steve Donahue said. "No other league does this."

Before it resumed its Big 5 competition, Penn played Lafayette, a team coached by former Fran Dunphy assistant Fran O'Hanlon. The two men have been friends since high school, and O'Hanlon spent six years with Dunphy at Penn before taking over Lafayette. The game was scheduled for the Monday following the Quakers' Ivy League opening weekend, leaving them not much time to prepare. They hardly needed it. Playing its third game in four nights, Penn used a 15–0 run to go up 53–34 at halftime before sailing to a 105–73 victory. At this rate, Dunphy wasn't going to get many future games with his former assistants. The Quakers hadn't scored that many points against a Division I opponent since February 11, 1978, and it was their first one-hundred-point game in nearly two years. All five starters scored in double figures—also a first in the 2005–2006 season.

Penn had won six of its last seven games, with an average margin of victory of 34.7 points in their previous three contests. Yet with no games for the next nine days, Penn had no way to build on its momentum. Dunphy made the best of it. He gave his players three days off to let them concentrate on their studies as well as give their bodies a rest before the final push to win the league championship.

When they finally returned from the interruption to their schedule, the Quakers played La Salle. In many ways, Dunphy had been dreading this game, and not because his team was coming off such a long break and could be rusty against its Big 5 opponent. For Dunphy, it was another in what had been a month full of emotionally wrenching games. He already had gone up against two of his former assistants this month—Cornell's Donahue and Lafayette's O'Hanlon. Now he had to face his alma mater. Dunphy's deep feelings toward the school nearly tempted him two years ago to leave Penn for La Salle. Now, in a remarkable coincidence, if Penn were to beat the Explorers, the victory would give Dunphy his three-hundredth career win.

Dunphy, the dean of the Ivy League coaches, has more wins than any men's basketball coach in school history and the second-most wins of any Ivy League coach. (Former Princeton coach Pete Carril has 514 victories.) In his sixteen seasons at the school, Penn has recorded only four losing seasons and never finished worse than fourth in the league.

Dunphy's teams have won nine Ivy League titles and gone undefeated in league play five times. He has guided Penn to eight NCAA appearances and three Big 5 titles. And if you ask him, he had nothing to do with any of it. "You walk in the locker room, [and] you've got all these pictures [of former teams] on the wall," Dunphy said. "[Those are] the things that are meaningful. The number three hundred, I can tell you, I could care less. It doesn't mean one stinking thing. . . . I think those things, those milestones, are for guys who are retired. You look back and you say, 'You know what? I had a great group of guys who helped me greatly through my career,' and that's how I will look at it."

Next to revealing his strategy for beating an opponent, the topic Dunphy likes to discuss the least is himself. This modesty may be one of the reasons he doesn't get enough credit for his coaching. For all his success, he is rarely mentioned as a candidate for the top job openings. Too often, his accomplishments are dismissed because it is assumed that anyone can succeed at Penn, given the talented players the school tends to attract, or because his success has come in the lightly regarded Ivy League. Yet, you don't win three hundred games without having some idea of how to draw Xs and Os on a dry-erase board and get the most out of your players.

Dunphy wanted nothing more than to put the La Salle game behind him. He was tired of being asked about achieving three hundred wins, and he dreaded having to face his alma mater. It was like having a root canal and a tax audit on the same day. Fortunately, the game wasn't nearly as painful as either, although it was close. Penn held off the scrappy Explorers to win, 73–65, the Quakers' first Big 5 victory of the season. Besides his career milestone, Dunphy improved to 13–4 against his alma mater. Lost amid the celebration of Dunphy's accomplishment was Ibrahim Jaaber's achievement. The junior guard became the school's all-time steals leader. His five steals against La Salle gave him 167 for his career.

"It feels good just to get it over with, to be honest with you," Dunphy said. "Way too many people asking way too many questions about [three hundred wins]. Again, the longer you are in this stuff, if you have a degree of success, you're going to get some numbers, and I'm appreciative of it. Don't get me wrong. But I'd just as soon not ever have to talk about it again."

After the game, team captain Eric Osmundson presented Dunphy with the game ball. "It's cool to be a part of it, because he's a great coach," Osmundson said. "He's been doing this for so long. He played in the Palestra. He played for La Salle. He's been around Big 5 basketball and Philly basketball for so long. I think it was awesome to get it against La Salle. He's deserving of it, and we're thankful for getting an opportunity to play for him and be a part of it."

Yale had every reason to believe it would sweep its series with Brown, a feat it hadn't accomplished in eight years. Putting aside their recent troubles against the Bears, the Bulldogs appeared to have plenty in their favor. They had won four of their last five games; they had beaten Brown handily in the first meeting, and the Bears had yet to win a home game in the 2005–2006 season. This should have been another easy victory for Yale. Unfortunately for the Bulldogs, it wasn't.

Brown was celebrating its one hundredth season of basketball, and it had picked this night to welcome some of its greatest players back to the Pizzitola Center. The school gave special recognition to its two NCAA tournament teams, the 1938–1939 and 1985–1986 squads. Most of the 1986 team was present, including Rhode Island attorney general Patrick Lynch. There was no way the Bears were going to let themselves be embarrassed again by Yale in front of such a distinguished crowd. Fueled by this additional motivation, Brown used a 14–0 run to go ahead 39–30 at halftime. The Bears increased their lead to 18 points in the second half before holding on for a 67–62 victory. It was a huge win for Brown and one of the more stunning turnarounds in Ivy League play. One week after losing by fourteen, the Bears surprised the Bulldogs by winning their third in five games.

As the outcome between Yale and Brown showed, travel-partner games are unpredictable, especially when they fall so close together. The coaches try, when the league schedule allows it, to put as much distance as they can between these games, but it rarely works out. More often than not, the teams play each other twice within a two-week period. "It's hard to sweep," Cornell coach Donahue said. "You spend fourteen straight days thinking about one opponent. We have to look at each other's film, dissect it. . . . It's extremely difficult. I hate it."

Despite his apprehension over the upcoming games against Columbia, Donahue was feeling pretty good about his team. The Big Red had returned home from their most challenging league road trip of the season with a split and would play three of their next four games at Newman Arena, where they were 4–1. If Cornell could win these next four games—especially the two against Columbia—the victories would bring some much-needed stability to what had been a roller-coaster season. Meanwhile, Columbia just needed to start winning again. The Lions had lost eight of their last ten, hadn't beaten a Division I team in more than a month, and were still reeling from their calamitous loss at Princeton the previous weekend.

As expected, Cornell took control early and was ahead most of the game. Then, inexplicably, the Big Red fell victim to another of its lapses. In less than a five-and-a-half-minute span in the second half, Cornell went from leading by eleven points to clinging to a one-point advantage. The more Columbia's deficit shrunk, the tighter and more tentatively the Big Red played. Still, when Lenny Collins sank a three-point basket with 8.5 seconds remaining to put the Big Red ahead, 57–55, it appeared that Cornell was going to escape with a victory. But Dragutin Kravic, who had missed a pair of free throws on the Lions' previous possession, atoned for his errant foul shots by making a three-point basket with 2.5 seconds left to lift Columbia to a 58–57 victory. "We played pretty well for the first thirty minutes," Collins said. "They just started making all the hustle plays throughout the last ten minutes that really kept the momentum in their favor. . . . On the offensive end for us, I think we started panicking."

Cornell was stunned by the loss. The Big Red couldn't understand how it let this game slip away. The team had suffered yet another ruinous collapse in the waning moments of a game. Donahue termed it "the toughest loss of his career at Cornell." He was so troubled by the defeat that he didn't sleep that Saturday night. It would have been a short night for him anyway. He had to leave his house at 3 A.M. to catch a 6 A.M. flight to the West Coast for a recruiting trip. He took the red-eye back Monday night, arriving in Ithaca around noon on Tuesday.

The time away had given him a chance to gain some perspective on the situation. The season wasn't turning out as he or anyone else had hoped. Nonetheless, all was not lost. He felt the need to remind the players that they still could accomplish great things. So before practice that afternoon, he brought the team together. "You get judged," Donahue told the players. "You judge guys on wins and losses, and when we're at a place like Cornell, it's just a shame that it has to be that way. I know that you guys are high-achieving people who care for each other. I almost wish we had headaches, discipline problems, so that I can get angry at you. But you're great guys. When I was your age I didn't accomplish anywhere near what you have accomplished. You got into this school. You're a Division I athlete. You're achieving great things already. It's hard sometimes to keep it in perspective. These losses are an aspect of life that has nothing to do with how successful you guys are."

Donahue didn't want the players to become so discouraged by the Columbia setback that they gave up on the rest of the season. He knew each of them had an inner drive to succeed and he wanted them to tap into it. Losing two of the first three Ivy games wasn't a great way to start the league season. The Big Red had dug itself into a hole, but all was not lost.

Practice that day was fierce. The players were throwing themselves into their work, going all out on defense and playing aggressively on offense. About an hour into the session, during a rebounding drill, there was a scramble for a loose ball underneath the basket. Ryan Rourke and Khaliq Gant dove for it with Brian Kreefer coming in late. The three collided hard. Graham Dow who was watching on the sidelines was worried about Rourke and Kreefer because it appeared their heads had hit the floor hard. "I was immediately looking at them because they were woozy and stuff," Dow said. "They're getting up, walking around slowly, and then you look back and see Khaliq still on the floor. Just the way he was lying, you could just sense it was different from a normal injury."

Gant wasn't moving. The sophomore guard from Norcross, Georgia, had no sensation in his arms or legs. "When I dove for the ball, I heard a loud scream, but I didn't realize initially that was me," Gant said. "I just remember laying there, my body feeling a little bit weird. I was about to get up and I realized I couldn't get up at all." He was paralyzed. Fortunately, trainer Marc Chamberlain was only steps away and recognized the seriousness of the injury immediately. A call was made to 911. As the players and coaches stood watching in uneasy silence, Chamberlain kept telling Gant to relax and not panic. "I guess by nature I'm more of a calm person," Gant said. "I was kind of trying to take it in stride. I knew it was pretty serious from the get-go, but I wasn't going to freak out. I knew those kinds of injuries you want to stay relaxed and not add the adrenaline to the injury. . . . I wasn't really thinking about, 'Oh I can't move.'"

The paramedics arrived. They put a neck brace on Gant and began administering steroids to reduce the swelling. A helicopter landed on the field behind the gym to airlift him to Arnot Ogden Medical Center in Elmira, New York, the closest hospital equipped to handle this type of traumatic injury. At the hospital with the help of a nurse, Gant spoke to his mom. "Khaliq said to me in his very calm voice, 'Mom, I'm going to be okay,'" Dana Gant said. "Something about the way Khaliq said it, it hit me in a way. It was a knowing that Khaliq felt and knew within the deepest part of his being that he was going to be okay, and I felt that."

Gant may have sensed things were going to turn out fine, but everyone else was panicked. Later that evening, after spending several hours waiting in the emergency room for news, the team was told that Gant had dislocated vertebrae in his neck. "Initially, we knew he couldn't move anything. Is it that bad?" Dow said. "And then we got some pretty optimistic news right away. That it wasn't a complete break, but I didn't really know what that meant. I'm a biology major, and I don't know what that means. We were all just hoping for the best." Bolstered by the news, the players left the hospital and returned to campus while Donahue remained with Gant. What Donahue had not told the players was that the doctors feared the worst. Although no one would know for certain until the swelling went down, there was a chance that Gant would be paralyzed for life. There was nothing to do but wait.

Donahue was disconsolate. He couldn't understand how this could happen to one of his players. It had been such a routine play, the kind that happens countless times during practices and games. Yet this one play had taken a vibrant young man and rendered him helpless. One minute Gant, all six feet three, 175 pounds of him, was racing up and down the court with abandon, the next he was lying eerily still in a hospital bed, unable to even wiggle his toes. Donahue, who had spent a lifetime devoted to basketball, now wanted nothing to do with the sport. "I didn't ever want to be in a gym again," Donahue said. "I never wanted to see a young kid play basketball."

Gant's parents, Dana and Dean Gant, arrived from Georgia on Thursday. Had it not been for their fortitude, Donahue might not have been able to cope with this tragedy. They didn't blame anyone or feel sorry for their son's predicament. They wasted no time on pity. Instead, they focused on what it was going to take for their son to recover. "They're unbelievable people," Donahue said. "That's when it hit me. My job is to coach. We have responsibilities as players, coaches."

Up until that point, Donahue had given no further thought to the season. He had all but abandoned his players and his family to be with Gant. Now he had to start thinking about life outside the hospital, and he was unsure what was appropriate. Should he go forward with the game against Columbia on Saturday? Or would that be perceived as unfeeling toward Gant? If they did play, would Gant and his family think that he was placing a higher importance on a basketball game than on Gant's welfare? Could the team even be ready to play, given the circumstances of this week? Donahue decided to ask Gant and his parents what they thought. They told him to play the game. "I said to the guys, 'We really don't have a choice whether we want to play or not. He wants us to play. That's our responsibility,'" Donahue said.

Although the team had gone through a light workout led by assistant coaches Izzi Metz and Nat Graham on Wednesday, Cornell really hadn't practiced since Gant's injury. And Thursday was the Big Red's only chance to prepare for the game because they would be traveling on the bus Friday. Donahue decided to meet with the players in the locker room before practice. This time, he didn't hold anything back about Gant's condition. "That was the first time we had a real meeting about it," Dow said. "Coach just kind of laid on the table the information that we had at the time. They said he's going to need surgery. They didn't know what his long-term prognosis was. They didn't know what was going to happen. They seemed to think there were some good signs going in Khaliq's favor. Then, I think the big transition we made with the team was Coach talked to Khaliq. Coach was struggling with whether or not we should even play. We [the players] didn't know [how bad the situation was] so I think we were all kind of assuming that we would play. Coach was like, 'I talked to him and Khaliq said he wanted us to play as a team.' I think for all of us that was kind of a confirmation, what we were supposed to do as a team to help him get through it. If us playing on Saturday and winning is going to help his spirits, then that was what we were going to do."

After days of uncertainty and waiting around, the players finally were given something tangible they could do for their teammate. They took the court with a sense of purpose. For the players, getting back to the routine of practice was a welcome diversion from all they had gone through the past week. For the coaches, it was an unsettling experience. "It didn't hit me until I started coaching again," Donahue said. "There was a loose ball, and my heart just dropped. I said, 'Holy shit.' I almost fainted." No one was hurt. Everyone got up off the court and moved onto the next play. None of the players gave it a second thought. The coaches, however, cringed every time there was a collision.

"I asked the players [later]," Donahue said. "They didn't feel that [fear], they told me. As athletes, they don't feel they'll get hurt. People warned me about that. We've been in contact with Penn State people. [Penn State football player Adam Taliaferro shattered his fifth cervical vertebra during a game in September 2000 and was temporarily paralyzed from the neck down.] They warned us. They said their players were not as aggressive the next three years. That accident on the field was a big reason why."

Practice didn't go by without incident. Freshman guard Jason Battle badly sprained his left ankle. But if the coaches were fearful of another serious injury, the players were not. "It was such a freak thing that you can't go out and play basketball tentatively like that," Collins said. "You can't think if I do this there's a possibility that I could get hurt. To be successful, you can't have that sort of attitude."

On Friday, Gant underwent a seven-hour operation. The doctors took a bone graft from his hip and used it to fuse the C4 and C5 vertebrae, then inserted titanium screws and plates for stability. Before leaving for Columbia, several players went to the hospital to wish him luck. Gant, in turn, wished them luck against the Lions and told them to play hard. Because the game was not being televised, he planned to listen to it via an Internet broadcast. "They were pretty tentative," Gant said. "They didn't know what to say, what to do. I was trying to make them feel at ease. I felt at that point I was more comfortable than they were, just because I knew in the back of my mind I was going to be okay eventually."

This game mattered more to the Big Red players than any game they had ever played. They wanted to win more than they ever had. Yet, given all they had been through, it would not have been surprising if they lost. They had spent more time worrying about their teammate than preparing for the game. "It's been the hardest week of my life in a lot of ways," Donahue said.

Donahue tends to be an emotional guy. On the sidelines, he bounces up and down, waves his arms, gets in a defensive stance, whistles, and has more facial expressions than a stand-up comic. He wants his players to feed off his energy. But on this day, he was doing all he could to keep his emotions in check. He didn't want to lose it. He didn't want his players to lose it. Easier said than done. Even as the team tried to focus on basketball, reminders of Gant were everywhere. Each player wore a patch with the number 21—Gant's number—on the upper left part of his uniform, close to his heart. Donahue wore a bright red tie with the number 21 embroidered on it. "Coach told us that the outcome of the game, win or lose, didn't matter to him as long as we went out and gave everything we could on the court for Khaliq," Collins said. "If we played as hard as we could, he told us good things would happen. If we did that, then it didn't matter to him if we won or lost."

Not long after the game got under way—a mere minute into the contest—Andrew Naeve went down hard. The crowd gasped. It was clear what was on everyone's mind. Donahue sprinted across the court to the injured player before the trainer even left the bench. Fortunately, it was just a bloody nose. Fueled by adrenaline and emotion, Cornell surged to an 8–0 lead. Columbia wisely maintained its poise, weathering the onrush before slowly chipping away at the lead. The Lions went into halftime ahead, 37–34. In the second half, Cornell's guards took over. Graham Dow played his best game of the season, scoring a career-best nineteen points. Adam Gore broke out of his midseason slump, finishing with a career-high twenty-eight points. Cornell went on to win, 81–59.

As the final seconds on the clock wound down, it became impossible for the players and coaches to stifle their feelings any longer. They embraced each other and sobbed on one another's shoulders. They wiped away their tears long enough to shake hands with the Columbia players before heading to the locker room to shed some more. This game had been more trying than they expected. They were exhausted, but relieved to have won.

"In all honesty, I didn't care what the score was going to be today because that's not what this is about," Donahue said. "It's not what Khaliq has to face. It's about trying your best, no matter what. I thought we did that to the nth degree when things could have easily collapsed. . . . I just can't be more proud of a group of guys than I am now."

"The way we were able to go out there, despite everything that had happened, still handle our business, to be able to play like that for Khaliq is something that will stick with me for the rest of my life," Collins said.

"I don't think there was anything more [Gant] wanted to hear today than Cornell wins," Dow said. "He was in the back of our heads all day. We just wanted to go out and play as hard as we possibly could in his honor."

On the way back to Ithaca from the game, Cornell's bus made a detour. The team went to visit Gant in the hospital. The surgery had gone well. After days of pessimistic prognoses, the doctors were beginning to talk optimistically about Gant's recovery. Everyone was in good spirits, especially Gant. He joked with his teammates, teasing Dow about his turnaround jumper. He clearly shared the team's elation over the win. "I remember them being in pretty good spirits after that game, which helped raise my spirits as well," Gant said.

No one knew for certain what lay ahead for Gant. Five days after his operation, he was flown by a medical plane to Georgia and taken to Shepherd Center, a spinal-cord-injury hospital in Atlanta, to begin his rehabilitation closer to his home. It was still too early to know how much movement, if any, Gant would regain. He would have to endure months of arduous physical therapy. Not wanting him to feel cut off from the team during his time away, a videoconferencing system was set up in Donahue's office. It allowed the players and coaches to see and speak with Gant daily. Several players were making plans to visit him during spring break.

As he reflected on what the team had been through this past week, Dow realized it was times like this that he was glad he chose to attend Cornell. "That's the biggest thing with Khaliq and what happened, was how as a team, everybody was there for him," Dow said. "He is like a brother. We wanted to help him as much as we could, help each other try to get through it."

In the course of a week, Cornell had suffered a devastating loss to Columbia, endured a life-altering injury to a teammate, and celebrated an emotionally charged victory. There was never a dull moment with the

Big Red. "I believe this season, it's not the worst season ever and it's not the best but it's been, for some reason, it's been very trying," Donahue said. "We've had injuries. We've had Graham's [injury] situation, and we're not playing like I thought we would. And now this happens [to Gant]. . . . What I'm worried about is Khaliq and my team. I've got a family that I've ignored for a week now. I've got four children and my wife, and they need me too because I haven't been around. I think we're going to get better if we stay healthy, if we figure some stuff out. I always thought this group could be really good."

Chapter 13

The Road
Is the
Thing

H arvard squeezed in three practices after exam period ended and before Ivy League play resumed. It wasn't really adequate preparation for the crucial stretch ahead. Coming out of its exam break, the Crimson had back-to-back road weekends, including the dreaded trip to Columbia and Cornell, considered by many the worst trip of the Ivy League season because of its arduous bus ride. Coach Frank Sullivan believed it would be this road swing that would determine the course of the team's fate. "To me personally, the road is the thing," Sullivan said. "It's not winning early in the league. It's not winning late, although winning late is certainly important in any league. You've got to win on the road. You've got to find a way." Certainly the previous Ivy League season bore out Sullivan's theory. Penn, the defending champion, was the only team to finish with a winning record on the road.

Yale was a tough first opponent for Harvard. The Bulldogs had played two games during the Crimson's two-week layoff, including a dis-

couraging 67–62 loss to their travel partner, Brown. They would be motivated by that setback and likely in better game shape than Harvard.
They also were the second-best scoring team in the league (behind Penn
and just ahead of Harvard). And the game was at their home court, the
John J. Lee Amphitheater, where Yale was 4–1 in the 2005–2006 season.

Other than the Palestra, there isn't a better place to watch an Ivy
League game than Lee Amphitheater in Payne Whitney Gymnasium.
The building's soaring facade brings to mind a gothic cathedral with its
spires and ornate stone carvings. Once inside the lobby, it is easy to
understand why this structure, built in 1931, is often referred to as "the
church." The dark wood and masonry almost compel you to speak in a
reverent, hushed tone. Off to the right, past the heavy doors, lies the basketball court, sunk into the bowels of the building. Hanging high above
the court are the banners of the eight schools, arranged not alphabeti-
cally as they are in most gyms but in order of each school's founding—
Harvard first, Cornell last.

This sacrosanct feeling lasts only until the students—some inexplicably dressed in baseball uniforms—and the band arrive and fill the
bleachers near the court. Then Lee Amphitheater loses a bit of its gran-
deur and becomes a rowdy bandbox. Yale boasts one of the more enthusiastic student cheering sections in the league. Lately, as the Bulldogs
have enjoyed increased success, the students have become more involved
in the games, giving Yale a significant home-court advantage. The Bulldogs had won twelve of their previous fifteen Ivy League home games
and only three Ivy teams had won at Lee Amphitheater in the previous
five seasons: Brown, Penn, and Princeton. The Bears were the only ones
with a winning record (4–1). The Quakers and the Tigers were a combined 3–5, while the rest of the league was 0–18. Harvard had lost six in
a row at Lee Amphitheater.

When Harvard comes to town, the students ramp up their enthusiasm. Next to Penn and Princeton—which the rest of the league despises
because those two win so often—Harvard is the team the others love to
hate. Harvard tends to be *the* brand name in the league, and therefore
whenever an Ivy school can score a victory over Harvard, it is a source of
great pride. Because Yale and Harvard are two of the oldest and most prestigious universities in the country, their rivalry is deep rooted. Although
the Harvard-Yale basketball rivalry hasn't achieved the same level of intensity as the schools' football rivalry, it isn't lacking in passion.

Adding to the hoopla surrounding this contest was that it was being
televised. YES, a regional network that is carried in New York, Connecticut, New Jersey, and Pennsylvania, was broadcasting the game, one
of five Ivy men's games it would air during the 2005–2006 season. The

audience for this broadcast would be limited, but that didn't mean that the players weren't excited about the prospect of playing on television.

Yale had played more recently than Harvard so it wasn't surprising to see the Bulldogs more relaxed at the start. The Holmes twins, Nick and Caleb, made back-to-back three-pointers to open the game, a foreshadowing of Harvard's poor perimeter defense. Their baskets incited the crowd, which was into the game from the start. With less than five minutes off the clock and the Bulldogs leading 13–7, the students began chanting "overrated" at Harvard.

In this hostile atmosphere, Drew Housman came undone. The Yale fans mocked the freshman point guard every chance they got, and the more they chanted, the more rattled Housman became. The students could sense they were having an effect on him, which only encouraged their taunts. Between the students' heckling and Yale's pressure defense, Housman was out of sorts and the Crimson wasn't getting into a rhythm offensively. Besides Housman's struggles, Yale's defense around the basket was preventing Harvard from establishing its post players, Matt Stehle and Brian Cusworth. Somehow, despite an erratic point guard, a limited inside game, and four players with two fouls apiece, Harvard only trailed 33–30 at halftime.

In the second half, the game spiraled downhill for Harvard. Yale continued to shoot well from behind the three-point arc, and the Crimson's foul troubles mounted. The Bulldogs would go on to make nine three-point baskets, shooting 69 percent from three-point range. Stehle and Cusworth would foul out. The more likely a Yale victory became the more rowdy the crowd became. During one boisterous time-out in the second half, with his team clearly rattled, Sullivan pulled his players into a nearby hallway to try to settle them down, only to be chased back onto the court by the referees. Yale handed Harvard its first Ivy loss of the season, an 82–74 defeat that quashed the Crimson's first 3–0 league start under Sullivan.

The win resurrected the Bulldogs' hopes for an Ivy League title and diminished the pain from the Brown loss. They were particularly pleased to have limited the effectiveness of Stehle and Cusworth. "Myself, Dominick [Martin], Ross [Morin], and [Matt] Kyle, we've all been looking forward to this matchup because they've gotten a lot of publicity, papers talking about how they're the best front court in the league, how they're both first-team all-Ivy players," said Sam Kaplan, one of six players to score in double figures for Yale. "It felt good to get a big 'W' against them tonight."

Harvard had plenty of excuses it could have made for its poor performance—exams, playing on the road, lack of preparation time, et cetera. But Stehle wasn't about to cut himself or his teammates any slack. "We really got smacked in the face, embarrassed on TV in front of our rivals," Stehle said. "It started with me. I played an awful game. I kind of hung my guards out to dry on a bunch of plays. [Yale] hit a bunch of threes. If you look at the stat sheet, you think it's the guards' fault, but it was really more the big men, in particular me, not helping them out, kind of left them out on an island. There was a little rust but not enough to have this happen. It was us getting out-toughed, us not playing good-enough defense, them making shots. . . . Universally, as a team, we got out-toughed. We didn't come ready to win."

The Crimson had only the bus ride from New Haven to Providence to wallow in its disappointment and less than twenty-four hours to prepare for its game against Brown. "It's hard to put a game like this behind you, especially with the expectations we set for ourselves, kind of the hype about our team," Stehle said. "But you've got to have a short memory."

Fortunately for Harvard, it was getting a team that was tired and shorthanded. Brown was coming off a 73–70 double-overtime victory over Dartmouth on Friday. Kennan Jeppesen scored a career-high twenty-five points and Damon Huffman sank two three-pointers in the second overtime to lift the Bears to their fourth win in six games. The victory did not come without a price. Luke Ruscoe, Brown's only senior and most experienced player, would not play against Harvard because of a lingering ankle injury. Neither would junior Sam Manhanga, Brown's beefy six-foot-six, 250-pound forward, who was sidelined with a foot injury. Their absences left the Bears with a lineup of three sophomores, a freshman, and a junior.

Brown was overmatched from the start. Jim Goffredo sank five three-point baskets during a three-minute span, part of the Crimson's 16–3 run that turned a seven-point game into a twenty-point blowout in the first half. Brown failed to get within fifteen points of Harvard's lead the rest of the way, and the Crimson won easily, 75–58.

Yale had little trouble dispatching a road-weary Dartmouth team to cap its successful weekend. The Big Green, fatigued from a double-overtime loss and a bus trip, shot just 36 percent from the floor in their 72–55 loss to the Bulldogs. The win left Yale (3–1) and Harvard (3–1) tied in the league standings, with Penn (2–0) as the only undefeated Ivy team.

As a tribute to the Big 5's fiftieth anniversary, a tradition was revived at the game between Penn and Saint Joseph's. After their team's first basket, the students tossed streamers in their school's colors onto the court. Such an action had been banned since 1985, but on this occasion an exception was made. It created a festive start to an otherwise ugly game that Saint Joseph's coach Phil Martelli would describe later as "listening to somebody scratch their fingernails on a blackboard."

Because these games are for bragging rights, Big 5 contests often resemble neighborhood brawls—hard-fought and scrappy, less about skill than survival. The tussle between Penn and Saint Joseph's was not a game for basketball purists. Those at the Palestra on this day saw two evenly matched teams slug it out like heavyweight boxers. Each blow sent the other reeling, and yet both refused to drop to the mat. Both teams checked finesse—and their offense—at the door.

Saint Joseph's went nearly thirteen-and-a-half minutes without a field goal and yet won the game. Penn's sloppy play—too many turnovers, too many fouls—cost them. The Hawks closed out the game on an 8–0 run to come away with a 47–44 victory. The Quakers ended their Big 5 season 2–2, while Saint Joseph's improved to 3–0. The Hawks' game against Villanova (3–0) in February, commonly referred to as the "Holy War," would determine the city title winner. Unable to claim the Big 5 championship, Penn turned its attention to the Ivy League, where its title hopes remained intact.

The discouraging start to Princeton's Ivy League season left many wondering if the Tigers would or could turn their season around. They had barely escaped with a victory over Columbia, then played poorly in the loss to Cornell—both home games. What would happen once they went on the road? The outlook appeared very grim. But with finals looming, the players had more important things to worry about than where their season was headed.

It was during this two-week break that Coach Joe Scott made the bold decision to start former walk-on Justin Conway at center. After watching Conway score thirty-three points in a junior varsity game, Scott realized he needed to make room for him on the varsity roster. Here was a guy who scored more than thirty points by himself, while Princeton had scored fifty points as a team only three times this season. "Plus, he was killing everybody in practice every day," Scott said. "He might be doing the other team's stuff [on the scout team], but he's the best guy every day. Every day in practice, Conway is doing well. Then he played in that JV game, and he played extremely well. I just said, 'Whoa, what are we doing? Why not try him?' The only problem was where."

Conway's ascension to center was by far the most radical of Scott's lineup changes. Until his promotion, Conway had played one minute of college basketball and nearly had been cut from the team at the beginning of the season. In addition to his lack of experience, Conway stood a mere six feet four inches, making him the shortest starter, with the exception of point guard Scott Greenman. At best, Conway's muscular body made him an undersized power forward. Now he was being asked to play one of the most important positions on the court for Princeton.

His limitations aside, Conway's best attribute was his ability to make those around him better. He had a firm grasp of the Princeton offense and knew where and when to get his teammates the ball. Conway—a Santa Fe, New Mexico, native who the previous spring had received the Paul Richard Friedman Memorial Award given to the member of the team "who does his very best every day in every way"—also invigorated the Tigers with his energy and feistiness. His height would be a liability on defense, but the coaches felt his athleticism and toughness could make him effective in the matchup zone.

The center position wasn't the only change that occurred during the break. Scott, once and for all, settled on the players in his rotation. Conway would start at center, Kyle Koncz and Luke Owings at forward, and Noah Savage and Scott Greenman at guard. Edwin Buffmire would be the first of the bench at guard and Michael Strittmatter at center/forward. Kevin Steuerer would back up Greenman at point guard. Scott had decided on his eight guys, and he was sticking with them, come what may.

"We gave everybody a chance during the first half of the year, playing different guys, trying different combinations, because we were pretty young," Greenman said. "You had to give some of those guys shots. Some guys, for whatever reason, it didn't work out. . . . We are starting and playing guys who are doing everything the right way. It's guys whose attitudes are great. We're concentrating on doing things that we're good at and know what Coach wants. Nobody has anything to say back to Coach. Nobody has any comments, and those are the guys who are playing. We're going to need more guys to become like that. Look at Buffmire's career. He just works so hard. It's not like you immediately get rewarded. He wasn't playing earlier in the year. Maybe he should have been, but he stuck with it."

After taking heat for his inflexibility the previous season, Scott had spent much of this season adapting the offense to accommodate the weaknesses of certain players. But considering how many lineup changes had taken place, Scott's fiddling had only led to mass confusion for the players. From this point forward, he was not going to modify the offense to fit every personnel change. "We were experimenting early," Scott said. "Trying to find out: Is this guy going to help us? Is that guy going to help us? This combination, that combination, changing offenses to see if that guy can help us, then making the decision that, hey, nobody can help us so let's get good at what we do. Go back to the drawing board.

Go back to what we do. . . . I was fighting myself, trying this guy, trying that guy, trying this guy. Again, that's what the nonconference schedule is for: to find those things out about a young team, to find these things out about guys who have never played before, to find these things out about guys you haven't coached before. The exam break probably came at the right time, from a rest standpoint, from a mental rest standpoint, from sort of a start-anew standpoint. We also started a whole new team, not a whole new way of playing but sort of going back to 'This is our way.' There's no other way. It's going to be this way. Our guys were either going to be able to do it or not do it."

Scott unveiled his sixth and what he hoped would be his last starting lineup of the season at Davidson. The Wildcats were a tough first opponent out of the exam break for Princeton, which usually plays a Division III team before resuming its Ivy League schedule. Davidson (12–7), a perennially strong team from the Southern Conference, had won eighteen consecutive home games. The Tigers managed to keep the game close, trailing 39–32 early in the second half, before the Wildcats went on a pair of backbreaking runs that put them ahead by twenty points with seven minutes to go. Davidson eventually won, 65–50, which left Princeton, one year removed from its worst Ivy League season ever, with its worst nonleague record (2–11) since the creation of the league.

Aside from the loss, there were some good things to come out of this game. For just the fourth time in the 2005–2006 season, the Tigers scored fifty points. They shot 46 percent for the game, only the sixth time they had done so this season. Their nineteen field goals were the most baskets in a game since their win over Wyoming. Scott's changes hadn't worked miracles, but at least things seemed to be moving in the right direction. Conway, the eleventh player to start a game for Princeton this season, was impressive in his debut, scoring seven points in the first twelve minutes of the game. He played nearly the entire game (thirty-three minutes), tying for the team high with three assists.

Now it was back to the Ivy League for Princeton. Unless something dramatic happened, only six weeks remained in the season. No one was more aware of how little time remained than Greenman, who was frustrated not only by the Tigers' losses but also by how poorly he was playing. The senior guard had struggled lately. Since returning from his injury, Greenman had scored in double figures only twice. He was making only 23 percent of his three-point shots and his scoring average had plummeted to 5.7 points per game. As captain and the team's only senior, Greenman did not want his legacy to be that he led Princeton to its worst season in recent memory. He had to start playing better, beginning with the Yale game on Friday night.

Chapter 14

Everyone Onto the Court

The first weekend in February brought a full slate of Ivy League games, with all eight teams playing on the same weekend for the first time in the 2005–2006 season. Dartmouth and Harvard would make the dreaded road trip to Columbia and Cornell. Brown and Yale would travel to Penn and Princeton. Only five weeks remained in the fourteen-game tournament to decide the league champion, and time was running out for some teams. Slow starts by Dartmouth (0–4) and Columbia (1–3) seemed to have doomed their chances for a title. Brown (2–2), Cornell (2–2), and Princeton (1–1) remained in the race but couldn't afford any slipups. Only Harvard (3–1) and Yale (3–1) appeared likely to keep Penn (2–0) from defending its championship.

Following practice on a Thursday afternoon in February, the Harvard players and coaches boarded a bus that would take them on their penultimate road trip of the season. For the seniors, the trip was bittersweet.

They were thrilled this was the last time they would be making the lengthy Columbia-Cornell bus trip, but it was also a reminder that the season was winding down. In the Ivy League, the Columbia-Cornell weekend is the most unpopular of all the trips. It involves a Friday night game at one school followed by a Saturday night game at the other school with a bus trip across the state of New York sandwiched between the two. Cornell will argue, with some merit, that its Harvard-Dartmouth trip is no picnic either. But at least the distance between games is much shorter.

If, as usually is the case in late January and throughout February, winter is raging, the trip can turn into an ordeal. On this trip, it wasn't snow or ice that slowed the Harvard bus—it was traffic. This year, because the Crimson would be playing Columbia before Cornell, the team was headed south rather than west. As the bus made its way toward Stamford, Connecticut, Interstate 95 became choked with vehicles. It was rush hour on one of the busiest corridors along the northeastern seaboard. No one was going anywhere fast. When the team finally arrived at its hotel in northern New Jersey, it was after 7 P.M., much later than planned.

The next morning, before shootaround, there was bad news. Matt Stehle had a stomach virus, a bug he apparently caught from his roommate, who had gone to the hospital recently because of persistent vomiting. During the night, Stehle made so many trips to the bathroom that at one point he fell asleep there. Suddenly, the coaches had more to worry about than Columbia's two big men, John Baumann and Ben Nwachukwu. They discussed having trainer Stacie Barlow rent a car and drive Stehle back to Boston. Not only did they think it would help Stehle recover quicker—being on the road is no place to be sick—but they also worried that he might infect the other players. They decided to wait and see how Stehle responded to the medication Barlow gave him.

As the players gathered in the hotel lobby before boarding the bus for the game, a pale and drawn Stehle came down from his room clutching a package of saltine crackers. The medicine seemed to be working. His nausea had abated, but all he'd eaten were seven crackers. Most people in his condition wouldn't think of leaving their beds let alone playing in a basketball game. Not Stehle. He wanted to play. There was no way he was missing this game.

This wasn't Willis Reed in game 7 of the 1970 NBA Finals hobbling onto the court with an injured knee or Michael Jordan shaking off the effects of the flu in game 5 of the 1997 NBA Finals. This was Matt Stehle, playing in a seemingly meaningless Harvard-Columbia game in early February. Outside the family and friends of the players involved and those associated with the Ivy League, almost nobody was paying any attention to the outcome. Yet, no game is insignificant in the Ivy race. In a league in which every game matters, Stehle knew his team couldn't afford to have him sit this one out. An Ivy player really thinks twice before taking himself out of a game because he knows how damaging it can be to his team's fortunes. Those who favor a postseason tournament in the Ivy League point to situations such as Stehle's as a reason for having one. If a player is injured or sick—particularly a player as important as Stehle—it can significantly affect a team's fortunes. A team that loses two games in one weekend because a player is ill or injured can be out of the Ivy race all together.

Not only was Stehle playing, he was starting. Then less than four minutes into the game, he was sitting. He had picked up two fouls by the first scheduled time-out. Stehle is prone to bad fouls, but in his weakened condition, he was a step slower on defense. Stehle didn't sit on the bench long, though. He came back into the game and scored on his team's next possession.

Columbia didn't look like a team with only one league win. With two of the better, albeit younger, frontcourt players in the league—Baumann and Nwachukwu—the Lions proved a tough matchup. Baumann, a six-foot-seven sophomore from Westport, Connecticut, also pitched for the baseball team, and Nwachukwu, a six-eight sophomore from Enugu, Nigeria, spent his summer working in a stem-cell research lab. They were a handful underneath the basket. Columbia capitalized on the Crimson's limited depth by rotating fresh bodies into the game and held Jim Goffredo in check by not allowing him open looks at the basket. After leading most of the first half, the Lions went into halftime ahead, 34–33.

The game continued to be tight early in the second half. Then after eleven lead changes and eight ties, Harvard pulled away for a 69–59 victory. Stehle played only twenty-eight minutes because of foul trouble and illness, yet he still finished with eighteen points, six rebounds, three assists, and two steals. Baumann and Nwachukwu combined for thirty-one points and nineteen rebounds but didn't get much help from their teammates.

Facing a long bus ride to Ithaca, New York, Harvard didn't linger to savor its win. The players dressed quickly and then boarded the bus. By 9:40 P.M., they were on their way. Fortunately, the trip was much easier than the one between Boston and northern New Jersey. The bus made good time and rolled into the Ithaca Holiday Inn parking lot at 1:40 A.M. It had been a short night, but the players didn't seem exhausted by their journey. Stehle wasn't at full strength, but at least he was keeping food down.

The Big Game in Ithaca this weekend wasn't being played on a basketball court but rather on an ice rink. Cornell's hockey team, ranked No. 5 in the country, was hosting No. 17 Colgate in a televised matchup between the top two teams in the Eastern College Athletic Conference standings. That game made the basketball contest between Cornell and Harvard an afterthought in the minds of many Big Red fans. But that didn't mean this game didn't have huge implications for both teams. Cornell, trying to move past the emotional aftermath of Khaliq Gant's neck injury, and Harvard, trying to prove that its loss to Yale was a mere misstep on the way to its first Ivy title, were still in the thick of the Ivy race. Neither could afford a loss.

Cornell had followed up last weekend's stirring win against Columbia with a 63–47 victory over Dartmouth on Friday night. The easy win against the Big Green—which was missing one of its top players, Leon Pattman, because of an ankle injury—meant that Cornell coach Steve Donahue could rest his starters for the game against Harvard.

As expected, the Cornell-Harvard game was tense, hard fought, and punctuated with dramatic momentum swings. With ten minutes left to play, the score had been tied ten times and the lead had changed eight times. Neither team could gain an edge on the other. Overtime seemed inevitable. Then the fouls began to mount. Stehle fouled out with three minutes remaining. Despite his lingering illness, he scored twenty-seven points and grabbed twelve rebounds. Brian Cusworth fouled out seventeen seconds later.

After a three-point basket by Goffredo put Harvard ahead 73–69, point guard Drew Housman fouled out, leaving the Crimson without three of its starters for the remaining two-plus minutes of the game. With thirty-six seconds remaining and the score tied at 77, Goffredo tried to hand off the ball to Michael Beal in front of the Crimson bench, and the ball went out of bounds. The Harvard players and coaches contended that Cornell's Graham Dow slapped the ball out of Goffredo's hands and it went out of bounds off him. Their pleas fell on deaf ears. It was the Big Red's ball. "The official who made the call certainly did a sprint fifty yards," Harvard coach Frank Sullivan said. "I thought he was running out the door. Usually when people run away from the scene of the crime like that, something's up."

Referees have a difficult job. They must make judgment calls on the spur of the moment with thousands of eyes watching their every move. No matter what call they make, somebody is going to be upset with it. They are cursed, maligned, and taunted for their efforts. Coaches and players blame them for costing them the game. Fans rain invectives on them. Good referees are barely noticeable. Bad ones, however, are like

Matt Stehle, with the ball, goes against Princeton's Luke Owings. Stehle was the first Massachusetts native to be voted Harvard's basketball captain in more than fifty years. © *DSPics.com/David Silverman. Photograph courtesy of Harvard University Athletics.*

Though he didn't want to be defined simply as a basketball player, Michael Beal was one of three seniors who hoped to lead Harvard to its first Ivy League championship. © *DSPics.com/David Silverman. Photograph courtesy of Harvard University Athletics.*

Ibrahim Jaaber was a two-time Ivy League player of the year known for his preternatural instincts and agile reflexes. Jaaber broke the league record for career steals with 303. © *Drew Hallowell. Photograph courtesy of University of Pennsylvania Athletics.*

Scott Greenman doing what he does best: setting up the Princeton offense. In the Tigers' seesaw season, Greenman, the team's lone senior, tried to be a steadying influence. *© Beverly Schaefer. Photograph courtesy of Princeton University Athletics.*

Brown's Damon Huffman went on to become one of the most prolific three-point shooters in Ivy League history. Huffman set the school record for career three-point baskets with 223. *© DSPics.com/David Silverman. Photograph courtesy of Brown University Athletics.*

As Harrison Schaen and Kevin Steuerer look on, Princeton coach Joe Scott implores his team to play better. Scott wanted the Tigers to be one of the top teams not only in the Ivy League but also in the country. © *Beverly Schaefer. Photograph courtesy of Princeton University Athletics.*

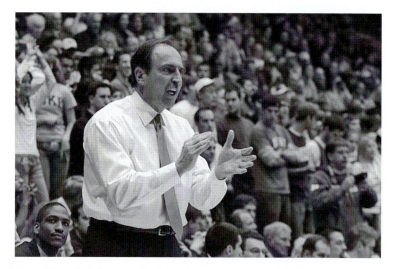

Coach Fran Dunphy's long and successful career at Penn includes the second-most wins of any Ivy League men's basketball coach, ten league titles, and five undefeated Ivy seasons. © *Sean Meyers/Photogator.com. Photograph courtesy of University of Pennsylvania Athletics.*

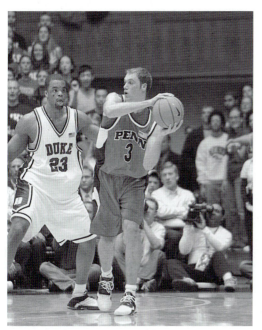

Penn's Steve Danley looks to pass against Duke's Shelden Williams. Danley ended up with a concussion and fourteen stitches in the game against the Blue Devils. © *Sean Meyers/ Photogator.com. Photography courtesy of University of Pennsylvania Athletics.*

When things looked bleak for Dartmouth, senior guard Mike Lang tried his best to keep his young teammates upbeat about the season. © *Mark Washburn. Photograph courtesy of Dartmouth College Athletics.*

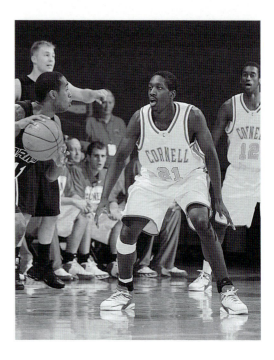

Cornell guard Khaliq Gant's basketball career was unexpectedly cut short. Gant's devastating injury shook the Big Red. © *Patrick Shanahan. Photography courtesy of Cornell University Athletics.*

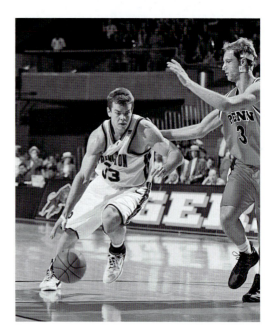

Justin Conway drives on Penn's Steve Danley. Conway, who made the game-winning shot against the Quakers, went from junior varsity player to Princeton demigod in a few short months. © *Beverly Schaefer. Photography courtesy of Princeton University Athletics.*

When Joe Jones (bottom photo) became Columbia's head coach, he didn't fully appreciate what it meant to coach against his older brother, Yale coach James Jones (top photo). The Joneses were the first brothers to coach teams in the same league since Hank and Clarence Iba coached against each other in the Missouri Valley Conference during the 1950s. *Top photo: © Gene Boyars. Photograph courtesy of Yale University Athletics. Bottom photo: © Woody Lee. Photograph courtesy of Columbia University Athletics.*

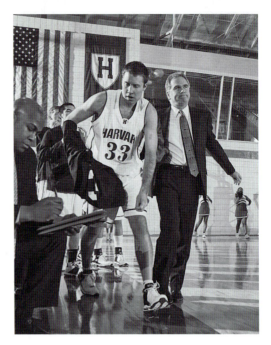

Harvard coach Frank Sullivan puts Zach Martin into the game. Martin's future involved a court, just not a basketball one. The Harvard senior would attend law school after his playing days were done. © *DSPics.com/David Silverman. Photograph courtesy of Harvard University Athletics.*

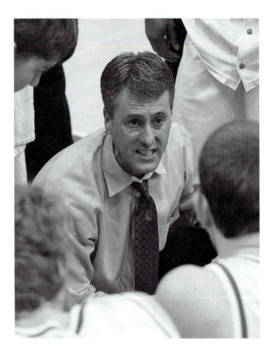

Cornell coach Steve Donahue gives his team instructions during a time-out. Donahue said immediately after Khaliq Gant's injury he didn't want to be in a gym again. © *Patrick Shanahan. Photograph courtesy of Cornell University Athletics.*

spinach stuck on your front tooth. Because the Ivy League is not considered one of the premier conferences in the country, in general, the officials assigned to work its games often are inexperienced or lightly regarded. The officiating tends to be better on Friday nights because Big East officials often work a game that night before their game the next day. It is on Saturday nights that Ivy League teams usually suffer from the worst officiating—and few teams suffer more than Cornell. Because of its out-of-the-way location, it isn't easy convincing referees to travel to Ithaca during the winter months. Those that do usually had few other choices.

This crew was not having a good night. There seemed to be no uniformity in their calls. Sometimes a hand check would result in a foul, sometimes not. Other times, a player would drive to the basket with a defender draped all over him and no foul would be called. But inadvertent contact in the lane that gave no advantage to either player would result in a whistle. The only consistency was that the calls didn't favor either team.

Coaches are fined, reprimanded or, worse yet, face retribution from fellow officials in their next game if they speak out against referees. As a result, they are very careful how they word their comments about officiating. But it was obvious both coaches felt the referees were not at their best on this night. "I think Frank and I would agree, the officiating—not negative—it was a crazy game to officiate," Donahue said. "Both benches, I think, were frustrated by the officiating," Sullivan said. "Both benches felt, not that it was fair or unfair, [but] that there were a lot of whistles called; there were a lot of whistles not called. I think the players had a difficult time adjusting to the game. At the end of the day, I think there might have been some calling of fouls to make it even, if you will. It was a frustrating game for everybody in that respect."

The players had learned to be philosophical about the referees. "We knew coming into it there was going to be bad officiating," Beal said. "It just sucks. That really annoys us to have that kind of stuff come down to that type of play. It's something you just have to fight through."

Certainly the fouls affected Harvard more than Cornell. The Crimson lost its starting frontcourt and its point guard to fouls, and its reserves contributed only two points. No one from Cornell fouled out of the game.

With thirteen seconds remaining, Donahue drew up a play during a time-out to get Graham Dow the ball and have him score the final basket. Harvard, though, had other ideas. When the Crimson prevented Dow from getting an open look, he threw a pass to Lenny Collins who was standing in the right corner near the baseline in front of the Cornell bench. Collins launched a shot that missed the rim. Jason Hartford, doing his best Lorenzo Charles impression, collected the rebound and tipped the ball in the basket with 2.4 seconds on the clock. Harvard had one last chance to win the game, but Ko Yada's desperation three-point heave fell short at the buzzer. Cornell won, 79–77.

"I didn't shoot a very good shot, but we got the rebound and it went in," Collins said. "The past two weeks have been pretty unbelievable. An emotional win like this against one of the top teams in the league, the way we did it, is something I'll remember for a long time." Hartford anticipated that the first shot might not go in the basket and was ready when the ball came his way. "Me and Andrew [Naeve] talked right before we came out on the court" out of the time-out, Hartford said. "We told each other if they get it up on the rim, we've got to be there if they miss, to get that board. He crashed one side. I had the other. It just came off on my side. I got it back up there, got it in. It had that dramatic pause" on the rim before it fell through the net.

After the buzzer sounded, the Cornell players leaped up and down for joy. Dow raced around the court, his arms spread wide like he was an airplane about to take off. It was not only a huge win; it was another stirring victory for Cornell. "I'm starting to feel like Dick Vermeil," said Donahue, referring to the NFL coach known for his teary news conferences. "I've got to stop being emotional after all these [games]. I don't know if I'm coaching different, but I feel different. The guys are playing with no worries about making mistakes. Tonight, everything went against us for so long. They were making every foul shot. We were missing. Calls going back and forth against both teams. It seems like we're not getting the calls. . . . Games like this, honestly, I feel bad for [Sullivan] and his guys. They just played the game the right way. That was a great college basketball game. I hate to see someone lose."

In the end, it may not have been foul trouble that doomed Harvard. The Crimson starters each average thirty-plus minutes per game. By comparison, Cornell only had two players—Lenny Collins and Adam Gore—averaging that many minutes a game. Harvard's downfall may have had more to do with its limited rotation than sluggishness from the most grueling road trip of the season. "It's a weird team to go play five guys that aggressively," said Donahue, still wearing a red tie with the number 21 in honor of Gant. "They're going to run into those nights. Especially this trip for them is very difficult. Going to Columbia, who plays hard, then they come in here and it's a war again. I thought that played to our advantage."

Unlike at Columbia, where Harvard was in a hurry to get on the bus, it took a long time for the coaches and players to emerge from the locker room after such a disheartening loss. It was almost a half hour after the game ended before Sullivan came out to speak to the media. He called the loss the toughest of the season. Beal echoed his coach, saying, "It is actually the toughest [loss] of my career, especially with the significance of it."

"Coach has done a good job of making us realize that [the season] is not over," Beal said. "That's the main difference from our freshman year. We lost a couple games, and everybody just gave up. We're a lot stronger than that. We're not going to allow that to happen. We can go one of two ways: either we're going to pull together and win out the rest of the season and win the championship, which is what we're going to do, or we can have the type of stuff that happened freshman year come, where people started pointing fingers. I already see that that is not going to happen. We are taking responsibility for what we did wrong. We just have to get back to work and get ready for Princeton-Penn. If we sweep them, we're right back where we need to be. As Coach was saying, 4–2 isn't bad considering the difficulty of our opening schedule. It's definitely not where we wanted to be, but we're still in there.

"We have to come together starting Monday, really work hard and get this thing back on track. Just like we did when we lost to Yale, when we lost those three straight, BU, whoever else was in that thing, we've always bounced back. I think that's the main difference with this team versus teams in the past, that we'll bounce back and we'll stay together and that we're not going to let it fall apart, because this means too much to us."

A steady rain fell as the Harvard players and coaches silently filed into the bus for their journey home. No one would sleep much during the five-hour ride through the middle of the night, the heartbreaking loss remaining fresh in everyone's mind. The bus finally rolled into the parking lot next to Lavietes around 4 A.M. on Sunday, disgorging its sleepy-eyed passengers, who hoped the worst was behind them. "I felt going into the season that this was a very ugly part of the schedule," Sullivan said. "When we looked at it in the fall, I think we all winced because we knew in our case we were coming out of exams. We're not happy we couldn't sweep either weekend, but I think a split is still good enough for us right now."

A split was more than good enough for Harvard's travel partner, Dartmouth, which concluded a brutal five-game road trip at Columbia on Saturday. The Big Green finally won its first Ivy League game, a 78–68 victory over the Lions. Columbia, which had upset Cornell for its only Ivy win, had yet to win a league home game.

Yale had lost twelve in a row at Princeton, with ten of those twelve losses by double digits, and even though the Bulldogs had not fared well on the road over the last five seasons—Yale was 24–7 at Lee Amphithe-ater but 12–17 away from home during that period—they were sure they would beat the Tigers this year. After all, Yale was coming off a sweep of Harvard and Dartmouth, and the Bulldogs (11–8) were one of only three Ivy teams with overall records above .500. Princeton, with its 3–12 record, 1–1 in the league, hardly appeared dangerous.

But this was not the same Princeton team that barely beat Colum-bia three weeks earlier. The Tigers had undergone a transformation. Princeton didn't look lost on the court any more. Gone was the tenta-tiveness and confusion that had plagued the Tigers for so long. They moved the ball with purpose. They ran to the right spots. They took smart shots. Simply put, Princeton was in sync, and Justin Conway was a big reason for this metamorphosis. His presence on the court helped the offense flow. All of a sudden, everyone was getting better looks at the basket. "He's really good at helping other guys get shots," Scott Green-man said. "I think we needed somebody like that in there, because we weren't getting great looks before. He dribbles hard at a guy and really sets a good pick so you can get open. The ball just moves crisply when he's in there, and that's very important in our offense."

Greenman, who had been consumed with making sure the offense ran properly, now was free to find his own shot. He made his first seven baskets against Yale, including four from three-point range. Princeton, which shot fifty-three percent from the floor in the second half, posted its fourth victory of the season, a 66–49 win. It was the Tigers' second-highest scoring output of the year. Greenman led the way with a career-high twenty-seven points—one fewer point than he had scored in the last four games combined. He also had five of Princeton's sixteen assists on nineteen field goals. Conway, despite giving up six inches to Yale counterpart and onetime Princeton player Dominick Martin, grabbed six rebounds and helped the Tigers out-rebound the Bulldogs, 28–23.

Brown, meanwhile, was one of the few teams to have had success recently at Jadwin. The Bears, who were 2–3 in the league after losing, 68–51, to Penn on Friday night, had beaten Princeton at home in two of the last three years. And since Princeton hadn't won back-to-back games this season, Brown stood a pretty good chance of making it three out of four. Except Princeton's defense was as good as its offense was the pre-vious night against Yale. It took Brown more than eleven-and-a-half min-utes to make its first basket of the game. By the time the Bears scored, the Tigers held a double-digit lead. They would go up 30–12 at halftime before winning, 52–37. Princeton held Brown, which shot just 26 per-cent from the floor, to its lowest scoring output of the season.

   With two minutes left in the game, Princeton coach Joe Scott did something he hadn't done all year—he emptied his bench. Freshman Jason Briggs and sophomore Zach Woolridge played for the first time in their careers. "Everybody who is playing now are the people who deserve to play and have shown throughout the year that they're willing to do what the coach wants us to do and what's necessary for our team to win," Greenman said. "The other guys on the floor feel comfortable with who we're playing with. I feel great with the other four guys on the court. We have a single-mindedness of what we want to get done when we're out there."

   Princeton's first Ivy League sweep of the season—a feat the Tigers accomplished only once the previous year—vaulted them into sole possession of second place in the league, trailing only Penn. In one weekend, Princeton's season had seemingly turned around. But now the Tigers had to go on the road. The next five games would be away from Jadwin, including a trip to the Palestra to play the Quakers. Even with back-to-back wins, Princeton had yet to show any consistency this season. No one knew how the Tigers would perform on the road. If this really was a turnaround, Princeton had to play well at Harvard and Dartmouth the coming weekend.

   Despite its seventeen-point victory over Brown on Friday night, Penn was not playing well. The Quakers' offensive performance, particularly their shooting, left much to be desired. Penn made only 38 percent of its shots, just the second time this season it had made less than 40 percent of its field goal attempts and won. Had it not been for the Quakers' stingy defense against the inexperienced and undermanned Brown—holding the Bears to fifteen first-half points and 35 percent shooting overall—Friday's outcome might have been a little less decisive. This lackluster offensive performance came on the heels of Penn's poor showing against Saint Joseph's, indicating that the Quakers were perhaps slipping into an offensive funk.

   That funk turned into a full-fledged slump against Yale. Penn missed its first nine shots as the Bulldogs raced to a 16–1 lead. Eric Osmundson finally ended the Quakers' field-goal drought with a three-pointer that pulled Penn within twelve. The Quakers, flailing on offense and ineffective on defense, were struggling to stay in the game. Meanwhile, Yale, which hadn't won at the Palestra since 1997, shot 60 percent from the floor in the first half—nearly doubling the Quakers' shooting percentage. Dominick Martin, the catalyst for the Bulldogs' impressive surge, dominated underneath the basket, making six of his first ten shots in the half.

Then, inexplicably, Yale deviated from its successful strategy. The Bulldogs began lofting jump shots rather than working the ball inside to Martin. Over the next ten minutes, which spanned the first and second halves, Penn capitalized on Yale's unproductive outside shooting by going on a 25–3 run. This twenty-two-point swing—the Quakers went from trailing by twelve to leading by ten—completely deflated the Bulldogs. Yale was outscored 44–19 after halftime and lost, 74–52.

Anyone seeing only the final score would never have suspected how close this game had been for twenty minutes. Before its second-half implosion, Yale seemed poised to pull off the upset. But in the end, whether the outcome was due to the Bulldogs' failings or to Penn's superiority, all that mattered was that the Quakers won again. Close call or not, they were winning their league games by an average of 27.8 points. Still, one wondered if Yale hadn't exposed some fissures in Penn's invincibility. The Quakers' victories had occurred in the familiar surroundings of the Palestra. Four of Penn's next five games were on the road. The Quakers now had to prove they could sustain their dominance away from home.

Chapter 15

Brothers
in Arms

I
f it is true that basketball is in the blood, then perhaps it is no surprise that over the years there have been several sets of brothers pac-
ing the sidelines: the Ibas (Hall of Fame coach Hank and younger
brother Clarence), the McGuires (Al and Dick), the Browns (Larry and
Herb), the Van Gundys (Jeff and Stan), the Valvanos (Jim and Bob), the
Herrions (Bill and Tom), the Thompsons (John III and Ronny), and the
Wachters (Ed and Leonard), who coached Harvard and Dartmouth,
respectively, from the mid- to late-1920s. With a few exceptions—most
notably Hank Iba, who had a 16–4 record against Clarence—these brothers were wise enough not to compete against one another on a regular
basis. The Ibas are believed to be the last pair of brothers to coach within
the same conference until the Joneses (James and Joe).

When Joe Jones was hired at Columbia in 2003, lost in his euphoria
over becoming a Division I head basketball coach was the realization that
he would face his brother twice a year. Joe is the younger-by-fourteen-
months brother of Yale coach James Jones. James, who had been in the

league four years when Joe arrived at Columbia, encouraged his brother to pursue the job. Yet until they had to face each other on opposite benches, neither man fully considered what it meant to have a brother coaching a league rival.

"It's always hard," Joe said. "It gets harder all the time. It's something I didn't give a lot of thought to when I took the job. I didn't give a lot of thought to I'm going to be playing against my brother. . . . It's weird. It's a really weird feeling. Then once the games start, you don't focus on that so much." "We would definitely not schedule each other because somebody's got to lose," James said. "Why would you want to do that to the other person? There's nothing worse than losing. Now you've got to lose to your brother. You don't want that. What's worse than that?"

James and Joe grew up on Long Island and were teammates at Half Hollow Hills West High School in Dix Hills, New York, before going their separate ways to college—James to SUNY-Albany and Joe to SUNY-Oswego. After college, James became a salesman, selling computers. He planned to get his MBA and then work on Wall Street. Joe went immediately into coaching, taking a job as a middle-school guidance counselor and coaching a ninth-grade team. "That was fun. Aw, man, that was some fun stuff," Joe said. "I was twenty-three. It was just awesome. [James] would come to practices to work with the kids. He came to my first game. He was just a good brother."

Pretty soon, it wasn't enough for James to help out Joe's team. He wanted to coach his own players. He took a pay cut and returned to his alma mater, becoming the junior varsity coach at Albany. His first team went 17–3. "I thought coaching was easy," James said. "What's amazing to me, it was one of my most successful seasons I ever coached, and I really didn't know a lot. The more I learn in coaching, the more I know I don't know." James spent five seasons at Albany before becoming an assistant at Yale in 1995. He joined the coaching staff at Ohio University two years later, then returned to New Haven as the Bulldogs' head coach in 1999.

Meanwhile, Joe became the head coach at Comsewogue High School in Port Jefferson Station, New York. He left the high school ranks after three years, joining Jay Wright's staff at Hofstra in 1994. In 1997, he went to Villanova and stayed there six seasons before becoming Columbia's head coach.

Basketball has brought the brothers—who share lean builds, shaved heads, and engaging smiles—closer. Their current situation, however, makes them careful what they say to one another. Some things one brother normally would share with the other can wind up being something he wouldn't want a rival coach to know. That doesn't stop them from talking several times a week. "I'm the older brother," James said. "He kind of vents a little bit to me. He does a little bit more talking than I do with him. I think he needs to get it out, to have somebody who understands. . . . I give him brotherly advice. At the same time, you're saying to yourself, well, jeez, you don't want to give him too much advice."

Joe has called James a lot lately. The 2005–2006 season had been much more difficult than he anticipated. Columbia was a young team—eleven of the fourteen players had a year or less of college experience—which meant a lot of growing pains. Then there were the injuries. Joe never expected his players to suffer as many ailments as they have—everything from knees to feet to backs to shingles. (Kashif Sweet, a sophomore guard out of Austin, Texas, lost seventeen pounds after a bout with the virus and slowly was working his way back into the lineup.) For a time, Columbia was down to eight healthy players, which made going five-on-five in practice impossible. The injuries, coupled with the Lions' inexperience, had been their downfall. They had lost eleven of their previous fourteen games.

"This year I've probably shared more with him than I normally do about my team," Joe said. "Because I'm searching for answers, trying to get this thing going. He's been helpful. We've talked about doing certain things with our programs and not so much the team as much as the program. We've shared a lot of ideas. When you lose, you're searching for answers. You're trying to get better. You can't act like you know everything."

Some might wonder how these two competitors can remain close, brotherly even, while competing and recruiting against one another. "What I don't like is I can't be happy for his success," James said. "It makes it hard to be happy. That bothers me that I can't be happy for his success. I've struggled dealing with that."

One incident nearly derailed their close relationship. When Joe applied for the Columbia job, James shared with him his top recruiting list, an inventory of players he had targeted for Yale. James knew this information would impress Columbia's search committee. He didn't expect Joe to use the list after he was hired. Before James could set up a visit with one of the recruits on the list, however, Joe arranged for that player to take a trip to Columbia. When James found out about the visit, he called Joe to ask him how it had happened. Joe gave him the brushoff. "I'm really angry," James said. "This is my brother talking to me. This is not some dude. This is my brother." After seething for a while, James called Joe back and the two men had it out. In the end, Joe apologized. The recruit, Ben Nwachukwu, whose ambition is to become a heart surgeon, eventually chose Columbia and had become one of Joe's better players.

James had lost only once in four meetings to his younger brother. That setback came Joe's first season at Columbia. Dragutin Kravic, the smooth shooter from Serbia, made eight three pointers and scored thirty-five points in a double-overtime win for the Lions. "Every time [Kravic] made [a three-point basket] Joe would stick his arms up," James said. "We hugged each other after the game, but knowing him as well as I do, and smirk is the wrong word, but he had a look on his face that I know that he knew that he got me. That hurt." "When he lost that game, the second game of our first year, that wasn't easy going over to shake his hand and seeing the disappointment on his face," Joe said. "It was the last game of the year. He's very competitive. That wasn't easy, watching him being that upset."

James didn't need the extra motivation of beating his brother to spur his team in this game. The Yale players were still smarting from the discouraging losses to Penn and Princeton the previous weekend. With three league losses, they knew their chances at winning an Ivy title were fading. The Bulldogs, who were in fifth place, also would have to find a way to win without their second-leading scorer, Sam Kaplan. The sneaker fanatic from Worcester, Massachusetts, injured his wrist in practice Tuesday and would not be playing. Freshman Ross Morin, the former high-school water-polo player from Cincinnati, would start in his place. Columbia was missing a player, too: Mack Montgomery was out with a knee injury.

Because of an Ivy League rule prohibiting Columbia from traveling to Yale the day before the game, the Lions rode the bus to New Haven on game day. It wasn't a long trip, but they nonetheless looked tired at the start of the game as Yale raced to a 14–0 lead. By the time it was 24–7, Joe had used two time-outs to try to wake his team out of its stupor. Nothing was going right for Columbia. Then Justin Armstrong, a sophomore guard from San Diego, scored on consecutive possessions, and his baskets seemed to ignite the Lions' offense. Columbia pulled to 31–29 before Yale closed out the half on an 8–2 run.

In the second half, the Bulldogs struggled to pull away from the Lions. Eventually, Yale prevailed, 74–67, improving James's record against his younger brother to 4–1. Disappointed by the loss, Joe nevertheless was pleased with the way his team competed. "We came out tonight, and we talked nothing about trying to win the game," Joe said. "We wanted to go out and have people respect our program. And if we can get that, and we play with some heart, then eventually we have good enough players; we're going to win. But first we have to play Columbia basketball. We have to learn what that's all about. We're learning that, and that's why I'm proud the way these guys came out tonight and tried to play. I know they were trying to win the game because it's my brother. And I told them I don't care about that. I'd rather them play hard and do the right things than to win tonight. Because once they figure that out then they're going to be fine, and we need to figure that out first."

The loss left Columbia mired in a four-game losing streak. At 1–6 in Ivy play and tied with Dartmouth for last place, the Lions were all but mathematically eliminated from the league title race. Seven games remained on the schedule, and other than pride, they had nothing left to play for. "The hardest thing now is to lose a game and get ready to play tomorrow night," Joe said.

When the league schedule was released, the Harvard-Penn game was the one nearly everyone circled on the calendar. Although Harvard had stumbled a couple of times and was tied with Cornell for third place, the Crimson still was seen as having the best chance to knock off the Quakers. First up, though, was Princeton, which had dominated Harvard over the years. The Tigers led the series, 117–36, and had won nine of the previous ten. But the previous five games at Lavietes between these teams had been decided by a total of eighteen points, and three of Princeton's victories had been by two points or less. Harvard, which was returning home after not having played there in a month, seemed due for a win.

For whatever reason—perhaps the Crimson was looking ahead to Penn or it was still in shock over its loss at Cornell—Harvard came out sluggish. The Crimson eventually shook off its listlessness and trailed just 27–25 at halftime, then appeared to take control of the game early in the second half. With just over a minute remaining, Harvard seemed on its way to victory. Then everything unraveled.

Princeton, which had cut Harvard's lead to four with less than a minute remaining, blanketed the Crimson with a swarming defense. Harvard's Drew Housman, trying to get the ball up the court, threw a long, high pass to Brian Cusworth. In a collision near midcourt, Princeton's Noah Savage tipped the ball away from Cusworth to Kyle Koncz. Harvard pleaded for a foul, to no avail. Scott Greenman, Harvard senior Zach Martin's good friend, sank a three-point basket to make it a one-point game with twenty-nine seconds to play. Princeton's stifling defense worked again as Jim Goffredo's pass was deflected into Justin Conway's hands. Again, Harvard wanted a foul, but the referees' whistles remained silent. Down by one, with no time-outs left, Princeton was about out of options. Greenman, looking for anyone who was open, spotted Savage along the baseline. Savage caught Greenman's pass with his back to the basket, spun around his defender, and lofted a fadeaway jumper over the outstretched arm of seven-footer Cusworth. The ball fell through the net with two-tenths of a second remaining, lifting the Tigers to a 60–59 victory.

For the second time in as many games, Harvard had squandered a lead in the final minute and lost. For the Crimson, those two minutes of poor play at the end of the Cornell and Princeton games meant the difference between a 6–1 record and a 4–3 record. Harvard coach Frank Sullivan told reporters after the game that the loss to Princeton was not only the most heartbreaking loss of the season but in a while.

After its stunning win over Harvard that kept it in second place, Princeton nearly suffered a letdown against Dartmouth. The Tigers squandered a ten-point second-half lead by making just one basket in the final ten minutes of the game. With thirteen seconds to play, Mike Lang sank a jump shot to pull the Big Green to 46–45. Accurate free-throw shooting by Princeton, however, prevented Dartmouth from picking up its second Ivy win of the season and moving out of the basement in the standings. The Tigers escaped with a 52–49 victory, while the Big Green suffered its eighteenth overall loss.

Princeton had won four in a row, had swept another Ivy weekend, and had done it on the road, no less, but there was no time to celebrate. A nor'easter was bearing down on the East Coast, which would make for a long bus trip from New Hampshire to New Jersey. The Tigers would not arrive home until 4:30 A.M. on Sunday, leaving them little time to prepare for Tuesday's showdown with league-leader Penn. Princeton trailed the Quakers by only one game in the standings, which meant once again the Penn-Princeton game would determine the top team in the league.

With the momentums of the two teams headed in opposite directions, the Harvard-Penn game lacked the luster it once had. Penn, which easily dispatched Dartmouth, 70–51, the previous night, was brimming with confidence. The Quakers had won seven of its last eight and remained undefeated in league play. Meantime, Harvard was reeling from back-to-back dispiriting losses.

A slow start doomed Harvard once again. The Crimson, which was four for twenty-two when trailing at halftime over the past two years, missed eighteen of its first twenty shots and turned the ball over seven times to open the game. Penn capitalized on Harvard's poor play and

Mark Zoller's outside shooting to sprint out to a 25–7 lead. "Zoller was a tad unconscious out there in the first half, making shots from everywhere," Penn coach Fran Dunphy said. "That certainly got us off to a great start."

Penn increased its lead to twenty-four points when the Quakers suddenly appeared to lose interest. The Crimson outscored Penn in the second half, but its first-half deficit was too great to overcome, and the Quakers won, 81–68. The top two contenders for Ivy League player of the year, Harvard's Matt Stehle and Penn's Ibrahim Jaaber, were spectacular in this game. Stehle scored a career-high twenty-eight points—twenty-two came in the second half—and grabbed fifteen rebounds. Jaaber finished with twenty-three points and six steals.

Dunphy wasn't pleased with Penn's finish. The Quakers may have won by double digits, but Dunphy saw too many mistakes in the final minutes. He watched Steve Danley be duped into picking up his fifth foul by Stehle. He saw Jaaber overplay Housman in an attempt to steal the ball, only to have Housman go in for a layup and Jaaber foul him trying to make up for his mistake. Penn was undefeated in Ivy League play and atop the standings, but you wouldn't know it listening to Dunphy. "We might be one of the dumber teams in America sometimes," Dunphy said. "We're not sure how to close things out. All we've got to do is keep the ball moving, give a thought to time and score. We didn't do a good job with that. . . . I think we're getting better in stretches and, hopefully, getting smarter throughout. We still do dumb things that drive a coach crazy."

Unintelligent play by his team was only one of Dunphy's concerns after this game. Starting point guard Eric Osmundson had injured his shoulder in a collision with Michael Beal toward the end of the game. Not a good sign, especially with the Princeton game looming. With a nor'easter that would close down the city for days about to hit Boston, Penn was eager to begin its long trip home. There was some discussion about stopping in Hartford and waiting for the storm to pass. Instead, the Quakers spent the night on a bus crawling down Interstate 95 to Philadelphia. They arrived home at 5 A.M., with less than sixty-three hours to prepare for their game against their biggest rival, Princeton.

For Harvard, unlike its previous two losses, this defeat did not occur in the final seconds, but that didn't mean it didn't sting just as much. Sullivan was doing his best to put a positive spin on the setback, but he knew the reality of the situation. Three consecutive losses had all but eliminated the Crimson from the Ivy League title race. "We lost to the first-place team in the league [Penn] by the smallest margin of anybody in the league," Sullivan said. "We lost to the second-place team

[Princeton] at the buzzer. And we lost to the third-place team [Cornell] at the buzzer. Our guys just need to get through that mentally and not get too defeated by it."

But the players' spirits were broken. All they had worked for had slipped away. Barring a total collapse by the four teams ahead of it in the standings, the Crimson was out of the race. Two months ago, Harvard was receiving votes in the top 25 poll. And now, the Crimson had nothing left to play for—no league championship, no trip to the NCAA tournament. This realization left the players hollow. As they slowly emerged from the locker room, their faces were a mixture of hurt, disbelief, and desolation. "I don't know what to say," Zach Martin said in a low voice. "It was really tough last night [losing to Princeton]. I was heartbroken. Like Coach said, the first couple minutes when we went down nine [to Penn], it was a shot to our heart. We couldn't bounce back."

At a time like this, most Ivy League teams quit, especially the seniors. They become more interested in preparing for job interviews than for opponents. And who can blame them? It is hard to keep putting in maximum effort for so little in return. Martin had seen it happen before, and he was adamant it would not happen with this Harvard team. No one was going to accuse these three seniors of being quitters. "While we were waiting in the locker room before Coach came in, Matt got up and said, 'Don't quit.' That's what we've been saying," Martin said. "We said it at the Cornell game: 'Don't anybody give up.' Because when we were freshmen, that's what a lot of people think—the seniors quit. Quit on us once they got four losses. A lot of people thought Harvard just quit. That's definitely not going to happen this year. We learned from that, us seniors. We definitely learned from that."

Coaches always say a game isn't won or lost in the final seconds. It's what happens throughout the entirety of the game that determines the outcome. A player who missed free throws at the end of the game isn't any more culpable for the loss than the player who missed a jump shot in the opening minutes. Yet it is hard not to look at Harvard's losses, especially the ones to Cornell and Princeton, and wonder what might have been. What if Lenny Collins had missed his three-point shot and Cornell had been forced to foul to get the ball back? Maybe Harvard would have made its free throws and won the game. Or what if Noah Savage's baseline jumper had been slightly off rather than on target? The Crimson would have escaped with a one-point win rather than suffered a one-point defeat. And maybe buoyed by its victory over Princeton, Harvard would have been more competitive early against Penn. The difference between Harvard's 4–4 record and a 6–2 or 7–1 record appeared incremental to the players and coaches.

"We're just as good as anybody out here," Martin said. "Like Coach said, today we weren't gelling like we have been. We were kind of falling apart. I think it was partly because we were a little bit disappointed from our past two games. Then they [Penn] come out here fired up, getting after us. We started to drift a little bit, but I think that we'll be all right. . . . If we played thirty-nine-minute fifty-five-second games, we'd be 6–2. We'd be in great shape. It is a little bit of bad luck."

Chapter 16

A Rivalry
Like No
Other

The first Penn-Princeton game of the 2005–2006 season marked the midpoint of the Ivy League schedule for the two teams. Penn was a perfect 6–0, and Princeton's only imperfection was its loss to Cornell a month ago. As usual, this game would determine first place in the league standings. A Princeton win would mean the two teams would be tied. A Penn win would give the Quakers a two-game lead in the race.

"The sense around here [Penn] is that the basketball gods have put things back in order [with] Penn on top," Quakers forward Steve Danley said. "We all came here knowing that we were going to play Princeton in big games to try to take the league lead. That's why we came here. That was kind of the deal when they recruited us. We were going to have to beat Princeton to win the league. That's the way it should be."

As *Philadelphia Daily News* columnist Dick Jerardi once wrote: "The Quakers rule the Ivy League. And when they don't, Princeton does."

Penn and Princeton have won or shared the league title forty-four times during the fifty-year history of the league, which is why the contest between the schools has long been a high-stakes game that has fueled the rivalry between them. The only time one of them won a title without beating the other during a season was in 2002 when the league had an unprecedented three teams tie for first place. Princeton lost twice to the Quakers that year, but shared the title with Penn and Yale. The Quakers beat Yale in a playoff to earn the league's NCAA tournament berth.

Rivalries grow out of the passions aroused in the participants and their fans, and college sports abound with some truly great ones: Alabama-Auburn football, Army-Navy football, Michigan-Ohio State football, and Duke-North Carolina basketball, to name a few. But these rivalries can't compare to Penn-Princeton basketball. While the emotions these two Ivy League teams provoke may be no fiercer than those inspired by the other rivalries, their contests feature a winner-take-all element the others lack. As has been the case for most of the last half century, these games decide who goes to the NCAA tournament and who stays home. For the most part, the other rivalries are merely about bragging rights. Duke can lose to North Carolina three times in a season and still go to the NCAA tournament. While the Blue Devils must endure the taunts of the Tar Heels, they at least will be playing in March. If Penn loses twice to Princeton, the Quakers could win every other game on their schedule, but they'll miss out on the NCAA tournament.

The stakes are just a part of what makes this rivalry intense. If you were to throw all the ingredients of Penn versus Princeton into a pot—urban versus suburban, team versus individual, one school's academic reputation versus the other—and boil the mixture down to its essential elements, what would remain would be one inanimate object and one very animate being. On one side would be the Palestra, one of the most storied venues in which to watch a college basketball game. On the other would be Pete Carril, the curmudgeonly former coach of Princeton.

Carril didn't light the fire that made this rivalry burn, but he sure fueled it. His histrionics on the sidelines made him the perfect foil for Penn fans. He would gesture animatedly or slump on the bench, depending on how Princeton was faring. "He became a character," said Steve Bilsky, a former Penn point guard who went on to become the school's athletics director. "From the standpoint of how our fans reacted to that, you couldn't have asked for somebody to be a better target. The 'Sit down, Pete' [chant] started here."

Sideline demeanor aside, Carril—who looks less like a basketball coach than a professor in the philosophy department—was ferociously competitive during his twenty-nine seasons at Princeton. More than anything, he wanted to win Ivy League titles. And the team that usually prevented him from achieving that goal was Penn. The Penn-Princeton rivalry "was probably most intense when Pete Carril was at Princeton, because he made it intense," said Alexander Wolff, a senior writer for *Sports Illustrated* and Princeton graduate. "He didn't have much use for Penn and made it clear he didn't."

Some of Carril's ire stemmed from his view that the Penn admissions department was more lenient than Princeton's. "He had some real issues at the time" with Penn's recruiting, said Art Hyland, Princeton's captain in 1963 and a former assistant to Carril. "They could recruit some players that we couldn't." Carril addressed Penn's recruiting and admission practices in his 1997 book, *The Smart Take from the Strong.* In it, he wrote: "My comment on that is that each school has its own way of doing what it needs to do, its own mission, its own sense of economy. Whatever Penn does is its own business and only should be noticed and mentioned when there's a violation of the rules. The rest of it is just crap."

Carril retired from Princeton in 1996 soon after recording the biggest upset of his career, the Tigers' 43–41 victory over defending champion UCLA in the first round of the NCAA tournament. He was inducted into the Naismith Memorial Basketball Hall of Fame two years later, having won 514 games and thirteen Ivy League titles and made eleven NCAA tournament appearances at Princeton—all without athletic scholarships. But for all his achievements, Carril finished with a losing record (27–34) against Penn.

When it comes to basketball arenas, few compare with the Palestra. It is a rare jewel in a crown that contains such precious gems as Pauley Pavilion, Rupp Arena, Allen Fieldhouse, Cameron Indoor Stadium, Hinkle Fieldhouse, and the Pit. Built in 1927 and named after the Olympic complex where athletes trained in ancient Greece, the red-brick building set back from South Thirty-Third Street evokes a bygone era and serves as a living museum of Philadelphia basketball. Penn may call the Palestra home, but it has long shared this venerable treasure with the City of Brotherly Love. The school turned the concourse into a gallery of Philadelphia hoops lore, paying homage to the players and coaches as well as the traditions that made this city crazy about its basketball.

From the enormous steel arches that soar above the court to the intimate bleacher seating, the Palestra is a grand old dame who grows more beautiful with age. Her magnificence inspires adulation, causing even the most jaded cynics to swoon. "It's a place where you feel the game the moment you step inside," author John Feinstein wrote in *A Season Inside.* Hall of Fame coach Chuck Daly reportedly said: "The Palestra is like having warm maple syrup poured all over you." With the Palestra as a backdrop, even the ugliest games are worth watching.

Almost since its doors opened, the Palestra has been home not only to Penn basketball but to Big 5 doubleheaders and NCAA tournaments. It was the site of the first NCAA championship in 1939 and has hosted more NCAA games than any other facility. Many memorable games have been played at the Palestra, including Princeton's stunning 50–49 victory over Penn on Feb. 9, 1999. If one game could encapsulate the rivalry between the schools, it would be this one. It had everything: unrestrained elation, profound despair, improbable runs, breathtaking shots, and torturous misses. Princeton was favored to win that day, even though the game was being played at the Palestra and the teams were tied atop the standings. The Tigers were riding a thirty-five-game Ivy League win streak, a run that had lasted three years.

Yet, anyone wandering into the Palestra that night without any knowledge of the teams would have thought Penn was clearly superior. Princeton had opened the game with a long jump shot by Brian Earl to give the Tigers a 3–0 lead. That basket would account for half of the field goals the Tigers made in the first twenty minutes. With Princeton misplacing its shooting touch, Penn scored twenty-nine unanswered points and went into halftime leading, 33–9.

The second half couldn't have been more different than the first. Princeton fell behind 40–13 before slowly whittling away the Quakers' lead. As Princeton athletic director Gary Walters described it to *Princeton Alumni Weekly* in a March 10, 1999, article: "It was like an imperceptible riptide. You couldn't see it on the surface, but it was dragging them out and dragging us in." Fans who gave up at halftime and left would come to regret their decision. Princeton mounted the fourth-largest comeback in Division I history to defeat Penn, 50–49. Earl watches replays of the game to this day. "What sticks out the most in the first half was we couldn't make a shot, and they hit everything," he said. "The crowd was going wild. It was the worst way you could go. You never want to be down twenty-seven at the Palestra. Nothing could go worse. I was just so angry, and I just wanted to go out there and basically save face. Then the second half was just the complete opposite. You start making a run, and all of a sudden you have all this energy. I felt like I could play another game after [it was over]. I wasn't tired at all."

Penn exacted the ultimate revenge. The Quakers did not lose another Ivy game. They closed out the season with a 73–48 victory over Princeton, won the league, and went to the NCAA tournament. Coming off the emotional victory, Princeton lost to Yale three days later, ending its string of consecutive Ivy victories at thirty-six. The Tigers would lose three league games that year and finish second behind Penn in the standings.

Unlike that 1999 game, this Penn-Princeton contest didn't turn out to be one of the classics. Weariness might have played a factor. The teams met at the Palestra just two days after returning from their Harvard-Dartmouth road trip, a journey made more grueling by the blinding snowstorm that assaulted the northeastern seaboard. Princeton coach Joe Scott decided his players needed a rest and gave them Sunday off, leaving the team only one day to prepare for the Quakers. Penn coach Fran Dunphy had his players practice Sunday and Monday. "The practices before Princeton are completely different than the practices before any other game during the year," Danley said. "We go through all their sets, their defensive philosophies. There's a lot of things we do specifically against Princeton. . . . The feeling is that you have to beat the Princeton system more than beat the Princeton players."

Penn had ripped through the first half of its Ivy League schedule with the relentless, destructive force of a tornado, pummeling its opponents by an average margin of 23.8 points per game. Of the 120 second-half minutes played, the Quakers had trailed for only forty-five seconds. In every league game, they had held a lead of at least twenty points. For most teams, this dominance over opponents would have created a sense of invincibility. Not Penn. Whatever the Quakers had done against the rest of the league meant nothing when it came to Princeton. To stumble against the Tigers could prove Penn's undoing. "We're looking at it as if we can't lose this game because we don't want to come down to the last game against them," Eric Osmundson said. "We want [the league race] to be over with before that."

Most felt Princeton was lucky to be in this position, given how the Tigers had foundered in their nonconference schedule. A modest four-game winning streak that included a dramatic win at Harvard had revived their season. They were playing more cohesively. They were beginning to shoot the ball better, especially from behind the arc. And their matchup zone defense finally was starting to cause opponents problems. All that said, however, Princeton remained a long shot to knock off Penn. And yet, anything can happen when rivals meet. The better team doesn't always win.

The Penn students, out in full force for the big game, stoked the boisterous atmosphere with their chants and signs. The Red-and-Blue Crew is best known for its "rollouts"—banners, several feet long, which are unfurled and then rolled out from the top of the student section to the bottom. Some of the signs are quite clever; others are crude. All are designed to rattle Princeton. Most took shots at the Tigers' recent scoring difficulties: "Penn scored 100 points last month. Princeton scored 100 last Nixon Administration." "Only Dick Cheney Shoots Worse than Princeton," a reference to the vice president's hunting incident the previous day. (Cheney accidentally shot a fellow hunter during a quail hunt.) "Why Arrest Five Princeton Players? They Weren't Over 21," a reference to Princeton's score against Monmouth. "You Can't Dance With a 6–4 Center," a reference to Justin Conway.

As usually happens in games between rivals, both teams came out tense and started slow. Many Penn fans—including Pennsylvania Governor Edward Rendell, a Penn alumnus who sat courtside—became anxious after the Quakers' only basket in the first eight minutes was a tip-in by Danley. Just two Princeton shots fell in, a three-pointer by Noah Savage and a jumper by Luke Owings. With the score stuck interminably on 5–2, it quickly became clear that baskets would be at a premium on this night—a circumstance that appeared to favor the Tigers. A low score would give Princeton a chance to keep the game close, and in a tight contest, anything can happen.

The game began to turn in Penn's favor midway through the first half. Joe Scott received his first technical foul of the season by coming onto the court and arguing a ten-second violation against the Tigers. The resulting free throws began a 10–3 run by the Quakers that enabled them to go into halftime up 23–13, a double-digit lead they never relinquished. The second half saw the teams engaged in an endless parade to the free-throw line, combining to make thirty-six of forty-one foul shots. In the end, Princeton's inability to generate enough offense cost the Tigers the win. Their defense held Penn to its lowest scoring output in an Ivy League game this season. Yet, Penn won, 60–41, because the Quakers put the ball in the basket and Princeton did not.

"We missed some critical layups in the beginning of the game, in the first half, that might have changed the complexion [of the game]," Scott said. "They were good looks for us, and they didn't go in. We've struggled with that all year." Only three players—Owings, Savage, and Scott Greenman—made a basket for Princeton. The Tigers shot less than 32 percent from the floor and finished with six more turnovers than made field goals.

The rivalry was beginning to turn one-sided. Since Princeton's twenty-seven-point comeback in 1999, Penn had won eleven of the previous fourteen meetings between the schools. Penn's victory brought more talk of an undefeated season. No team had yet challenged the Quakers, and none appeared on the verge of doing so. It was looking more and more like Penn would sail through its Ivy schedule without a blemish, just as it did three years ago. Coach Fran Dunphy tried his best to muzzle any discussions on this topic. "Obviously we can't do better than we're doing right now," he said. "We need to continue this push, this surge. It's going to be a tough weekend on the road. Columbia and Cornell will be more than ready for us. We need to keep focus. We need to understand that we've got seven really tough games left. And hopefully, we'll be ready and focused."

Chapter 17

Topsy-
Turvy
Weekend

At 7–0, Penn was halfway to its eighth perfect league season, and it didn't appear that any Ivy team was going to prevent the Quakers from reaching that milestone—certainly not Columbia, their next opponent. The Lions were on a five-game skid, had won only one Ivy game this season, and had lost to Penn by thirty-two points a month earlier. The Quakers had every reason to feel confident. No player on Penn's roster had lost to the Lions during his career.

The first time Penn went undefeated through an Ivy League season was in 1970. Back then, the Quakers weren't just the best team in the league; they were among the best teams in the country. Dick Harter, who played for Penn in the early 1950s, was the coach at the time. After leading the Quakers to a second consecutive undefeated Ivy season in 1971 and a No. 3 ranking in the Associated Press poll, Harter left to become Oregon's head coach. He later would join the NBA coaching ranks.

Future Naismith Memorial Basketball Hall of Fame member and NBA champion coach Chuck Daly followed Harter. Daly lost only ten Ivy games during his six years at the school, but he never went undefeated. He came close three times, going 13–1 in 1972, 1974, and 1975.

The only coach besides Harter to lead Penn to a perfect league record was Fran Dunphy. Under Dunphy, the Quakers have achieved Ivy perfection five times: in 1993, 1994, 1995, 2000, and 2003. Their streak of forty-eight consecutive Ivy wins—which ran from their final game of the 1992 season until February 9, 1996, when Dartmouth beat them, 54–53—is eclipsed only by UCLA's fifty-game Pac-8 winning streak from 1970 to 1974. Penn, UCLA, and Nebraska (1912–1914) are the only Division I teams to record three consecutive undefeated conference seasons.

Penn's game at Columbia fell on the school's inaugural athletic Hall of Fame weekend. For the first time, the Lions were honoring some of the greatest student-athletes in their history, several of them posthumously. Lou Gehrig, Sid Luckman, Chet Forte, Jim McMillian, and the entire 1967–1968 men's basketball team were among those inducted at an event in Low Memorial Library. Many of the inductees would be at Francis A. Levien Gymnasium watching Columbia take on Penn. With such an august gathering on hand to see them play, the Lions were not about to embarrass themselves or their school.

It was a game of runs. First, Columbia surged in front. Then Penn answered, going ahead by thirteen late in the first half. The Lions closed out the half strong, trailing by five at halftime. The Quakers built their lead back to double digits, only to have Columbia storm back to make it a two-point game. Because of the back-and-forth nature of this contest, neither team ever felt out of it.

Coming into the game, Columbia coach Joe Jones knew his team would struggle to guard Penn man-to-man. He had nightmares of Ibrahim Jaaber driving to the basket for uncontested layups. Jones figured the best way to slow down the Quakers would be to play a zone defense against them. It was a risky move. Penn's shooters could feast on a zone, but it was a gamble he was willing to take.

Early on, Jones's strategy seemed ill advised. Penn made seven three-point baskets in the first half. But those shots stopped falling after halftime. Rather than switch offensive strategies, the Quakers continued to shoot from behind the three-point arc. They would take more than half of their field goal attempts from three-point range, and their stubbornness would cost them.

Justin Armstrong, who had been in and out of the starting lineup all season, came off the bench to lead Columbia's final charge. Penn seemed to bring out the best in the sophomore guard. He had been the only player to score in double figures in the Lions' 87–55 loss to the Quakers in January, finishing with sixteen points. This game, he brought Columbia back from a ten-point second-half deficit by scoring ten points in less than ten minutes. Armstrong finished with a career-high twenty-three points.

Penn's final basket—a layup by Steve Danley—came with more than four-and-a-half minutes remaining in the game. The Quakers did not score again, and yet they still nearly won. With the score tied at 57, Mark Zoller was driving to the basket when he was called for a charge against John Baumann. The foul—Zoller's fifth—put him on the bench for the game's decisive play. Mack Montgomery tried to win the game for the Lions, but his jump shot hit the rim. Without Zoller underneath the basket to block him out, Ben Nwachukwu was free to position himself to make the tip-in. With one second remaining, the ball left his fingertips. As it fell through the net, the students rushed the court. Columbia had pulled off the biggest upset of the Ivy season. The 59–57 loss ended Penn's perfect season and gave the Lions their second Ivy win of the year.

The most disconcerting aspect of Penn's defeat was not that the Quakers squandered their chance to go undefeated in the league. Rather, their inability to beat the last-place team in the league indicated the Quakers were not nearly as powerful as their early Ivy results led one to believe. Those impressive wins had come at home. Now that they were going on the road, Penn suddenly appeared vulnerable. Was this the beginning of an implosion or merely a stumble?

February 17 would go down as Black Friday in the Ivy League. Last-place Columbia knocked off first-place Penn. Dartmouth, which was sharing the cellar with Columbia, upset third-place Yale. Brown beat fast-sinking Harvard, and Cornell lost at home to Princeton. At one arena when the scores were announced, some wondered if the public address announcer had mistakenly read the women's and not the men's scores. In one night, the whole league went topsy-turvy. As teams made a second swing through the league, their familiarity with one another led to the unpredictable results.

Princeton's victory over Cornell wasn't as big an upset. The second-place Tigers were separated from the third-place Big Red by a mere half-game in the standings. And it wasn't even the biggest game in Ithaca that night. The Cornell hockey team's contest against Dartmouth was a sellout. But this game would go down as one of the more memorable of the Ivy season.

Early on, it appeared as if Cornell would breeze to an easy victory and record its second consecutive sweep of Princeton—a feat the Big Red had not accomplished since the 1940s, pre–Ivy League. When Justin Conway picked up his third and fourth fouls within two seconds early in the second half, Princeton's chances of winning looked grim. Then, inexplicably, the teams' fortunes reversed. Cornell, which early on had scored so easily, strained to make a basket. The Tigers, who had struggled with their shot, sank nearly everything. Princeton trailed by just two points when Edwin Buffmire fouled Ryan Rourke to stop the clock at thirteen seconds. If Rourke made both free throws, Cornell would be up four, a seemingly insurmountable margin. Rourke made the first and missed the second.

The Tigers needed a three-pointer to tie the score and send the game into overtime. The play they ran was designed for Scott Greenman to get the ball and shoot it from behind a high screen. It worked perfectly. But when the ball left his hands, Greenman doubted it was going in. "It didn't feel great," he said. "I thought it was going to be a little short. I was kind of running under it as I shot it to check it out, the trajectory of it. But I'll take it feeling bad and going in rather than the other way around." With 1.1 seconds on the clock, the ball fell through the net. The Tigers had not led in this game, yet they were going to overtime.

Usually when a team loses a big lead in the final minutes of regulation it fares poorly in overtime. The momentum has swung the other way, and the team that forced the overtime typically goes on to win. But Cornell proved to be a resilient bunch. The Big Red had been through too much over the past month, and it was not going down easily. After the first two minutes, it appeared that the overtime would be a draw. Neither team could score. Finally, Andrew Naeve dunked to put Cornell ahead. With twenty-two seconds to play and the Big Red leading by one, Princeton once again sent Rourke to the free-throw line. This time, he made both foul shots.

There was no way the Big Red was going to let Greenman tie this game again with another three-pointer. No way. Except he did. Finding himself caught in front of Princeton's bench with time running out, Greenman dribbled through two defenders, snaked his body around Graham Dow, and launched an off-balance heave from one foot that somehow lurched through the rim with one second remaining. His three-point shot tied the score at 64 and sent the game to its second overtime. Princeton still hadn't led in this game. "I looked up, like 'Damn, I've got to do something,'" Greenman said. "I was dribbling out there. I don't really see anything. So I just tried to find an open area near the three-point line where I can get off a decent look, and I kind of snuck in there. I guess it helps that I'm only five-nine."

Greenman, who was shooting a woeful 17 percent from behind the arc after the first Ivy weekend, had made two of the biggest three-point shots in Princeton's season and perhaps his life. "The first one that sent it into overtime, that was a play—we ran it perfectly to get him that shot," Joe Scott said. "The second one, that's Hail Mary stuff. But like I told him, it's a good thing he's a lefty. Only a lefty could make that shot."

Princeton took its first lead forty-eight seconds into the second overtime on a layup by Luke Owings. The final minutes of this tense game were played out at the free-throw line. The Tigers missed only one foul shot to outlast the Big Red, 76–68. Princeton, which learned of Penn's loss at Columbia after the game, wasn't shy about admitting the role luck played in its victory. "We had good fortune, but I think our guys did something to maybe have some good fortune shine on us," Scott said. "This group of guys, I think they deserve some good fortune after what we've been through. And then we get double good fortune because nobody thought what was going to happen in New York [Penn's loss to Columbia] was going to happen, so that just makes tomorrow night's game [important]. Obviously, every night the season's on the line in this league, and the season's on the line tomorrow night."

Of course, Cornell was no less deserving of good luck after the tragedy the Big Red had suffered. But on this night, Princeton proved the more resilient team. "Early in the year, nobody would have said that about us," Scott said. "We would lose every game. We would do things that would give us no opportunity to even have a chance. We're a young team, and we're breaking through on that front. We're learning what it takes to win. We've had some success. Our guys believe in us, in themselves."

Princeton's victory did not come without a price. For the second weekend in a row, the Tigers played an emotionally punishing game on Friday night, and this one went two overtimes. Just seven players played, and all but two logged thirty-two or more minutes. Greenman played all fifty. Rather than make the long bus trip to New York and stay in a hotel, Scott decided to return to Princeton so the players could sleep in their own beds. They would travel on game day, taking the bus to New York on Saturday afternoon for their game that night against Columbia. It is one of the most difficult challenges in sports: following a big emotional win with another win. Columbia and Princeton were both coming off stirring victories. Now they had to be physically and mentally ready to play Saturday's game—no easy feat given the short turnaround time. The Lions wanted to prove their upset over Penn was no fluke. The Tigers knew they couldn't afford a letdown if they were to keep their Ivy League title hopes alive.

Columbia clearly had the advantage of playing at home and not having traveled overnight. The Lions scored at will in the first half, making 67 percent of their shots. Princeton, weary from its journey, sank only nine of its first twenty-three shot attempts and trailed by ten points at halftime. The Tigers' fatigue was evident not only in the layups they missed, but also in the number of fouls they accumulated. Tired players are often a step slow on defense. Princeton finished with twenty-two fouls, nine more than Columbia, and sent the Lions to the foul line twenty-eight times. The Tigers attempted only nine free throws.

Justin Armstrong followed up his spectacular performance against Penn with another strong showing against Princeton. He sank a pull-up jumper with eleven seconds on the clock to put Columbia ahead by one. The Tigers, having been in plenty of close games lately, were not rattled. Greenman, who ended up playing all forty minutes of this game after playing fifty minutes against Cornell, drove down the court. As he approached the basket, he drew three defenders. Spotting Noah Savage open on the wing, he threw him the ball. Savage mishandled the pass but recovered in time to shoot. That bobble was enough to alter his rhythm and cause the shot to fall short. After seven ties and sixteen lead changes, Columbia prevailed, 65–64, avenging their agonizing loss at Jadwin back in January. In his third season in the league, Joe Jones had finally beaten every Ivy opponent at least once.

It was only the third time since 1989 that Penn and Princeton had been beaten on consecutive nights by the same Ivy opponent: Yale had done it in 2005 and Columbia in 2001. Hardly surprising that the one team to accomplish this feat twice during this seventeen-year period was part of the worst road trip in the league. That doesn't diminish the Lions' accomplishment. Columbia came into the weekend tied with Dartmouth for last place in the league. The Lions' only league win to that point was against Cornell. To beat the top two teams in the league on consecutive nights showed the fortitude of the players. Yet in a season bereft of highlights, the players refused to count these victories as anything more than what they were. "You don't want to have a season justified by one weekend, saying 'Hey, you guys beat Penn and Princeton. That's great,'" John Baumann said. "That's a step, and we just need to keep improving. That was a great building block for our last two weekends, and it would really be awesome if we could carry that effort over and improve and ultimately end the season on a high note."

Despite Columbia's successful weekend, Penn's 67–56 win at Cornell mathematically eliminated the Lions from title contention with two weeks remaining in the league season. In a sense, they had nothing left to play for—no conference tournament, no postseason. At best, if they won their remaining four games, they would finish at .500 in the league and with an overall winning record. That would be quite an accomplishment, considering Columbia hadn't been 7–7 in the league in five years and hadn't finished above .500 overall in thirteen years. But those exploits hardly were worth bragging about to friends. It would have been easy for the players to call it quits and go through the motions in the last few games. "While the common person might say you don't technically have anything to play for because everybody's playing for the Ivy League championship, we have everything in the world to play for—the coaches, the people around us, Columbia," Baumann said. "We try to treat it like that. . . . We've worked so hard. We know we're going to be able to get something out of this."

Not surprisingly, both Baumann and Nwachukwu would like to see the Ivy League adopt a conference tournament to determine its league champion and NCAA tournament representative. "I definitely think it would be really good to have a conference tournament, but I don't know if the Ivy League would ever go for that," Nwachukwu said. "It's one of those things that it's bittersweet that we're playing well toward the end of the season because if we have a conference tournament, things would be in our favor right now. We're kind of starting to build a little momentum. It would be nice."

"I'd personally like to have a tournament just because you're technically never really out of it," Baumann said. "It makes your season a little longer. At the same time, I really understand where the league is coming from. It makes our league so unique. Every regular season conference game is effectively a tournament. I think that's what makes our league so competitive and unique. From a player's standpoint, especially on a team right now where we're out of it, obviously, of course, I'd love it just to have a shot."

One argument for a postseason tournament is that players would show more interest in late-season games. But as Columbia demonstrated, even teams out of the league race can still play meaningful games. "It would be really unfair to say that we'd play a game differently because we have a title on the line," Baumann said.

Though the topic occasionally is considered by the Ivy presidents, who have the final say in the matter, it appears unlikely they will ever embrace a league tournament. "Well, it makes the Ivy League championship then highly magnified as a goal, and that from our perspective, was always a very good thing," said Hunter R. Rawlings III, the president of Cornell from 1995 to 2003 and its interim president from 2005 to 2006. "It makes the championship of the Ivy League the elite goal each year, and it puts a high premium on each league game because you're not worrying about a postseason. . . . Of course, it's great to go and play in the NCAA tournament but realistically we know that Ivy teams are not going to go far in that tournament. They might win a game or two, but even that's a little unusual, I think. The only alternative to that is to start recruiting student-athletes who are radically different from the student body because that's the only way, frankly, you can achieve that kind of competitiveness in the sport of basketball.

"You have to also realize that these presidents are quite aware of what's going on in the rest of the country. They see the problems that emerge, unfortunately with some frequency, in the big-time programs, and they don't want any part of that."

After three straight losses—two of which were by a total of three points—Harvard coach Frank Sullivan decided his team needed a respite. He scaled back the practices in the week leading up to the Brown and Yale games. Since it had already gone through the league once, the Crimson didn't need to spend as much time on scouting reports. It already was familiar with the strengths and weaknesses of its coming opponents. This would give the players a chance to rest their minds and bodies and maybe revive the season.

Harvard would host Brown first. The Bears seemed to be the perfect opponent for the struggling Crimson. Harvard had won at Brown, 75–58, less than three weeks ago. The Bears had yet to win an Ivy road game, and they had a three-game losing streak against Harvard. None of that mattered. Harvard, plagued by another slow start, fell behind early. As had become its trademark, the Crimson made a furious second-half rally only to fall short. Brown never trailed in its 79–66 win.

Matt Stehle's frustration boiled over in this game. The normally stoic senior threw the basketball, hitting a Brown player in the stomach, and was assessed a technical foul. Stehle wasn't the only one having a bad night. Brown thoroughly outplayed Harvard, outscoring the Crimson, 43–26, around the basket despite Harvard's height advantage, and the Bears' reserves, led by freshman forward Chris Skrelja, outscored Harvard's, 38–8.

The loss left Harvard in disarray. Nothing was going right for the Crimson, and it couldn't seem to find the answer to its problems. Yale had its own woes. The Bulldogs hadn't won an Ivy League away game this season—they lost, 72–64, at Dartmouth on Friday night—a skid of eight straight Ivy road games. They also hadn't won at Lavietes in three years. Once again, it seemed a perfect opportunity for Harvard. The Crimson could avenge its loss in New Haven and end its four-game losing skid. Instead, Yale swept Harvard for the first time in three years, winning, 77–66, to give the Bulldogs their first Ivy League road win in two years. Yale shot nearly 50 percent from the floor while the Crimson made less than 35 percent of its shots. Matt Stehle, following one frustrating game with another, missed ten of eleven shot attempts, his worst shooting performance as a starter.

Harvard's players were at a loss to explain how things had gone south so quickly—three consecutive double-digit defeats, four straight losses at home, and a five-game losing streak. "I thought we were into it. We had been playing pretty well during practice," Zach Martin said. "In shootaround and everything, we seemed like we had a lot of energy and we were ready to go. It just came to game time and we just [came out flat] in both games."

Despite appearances to the contrary, Martin claimed that the team had not given up. "I really don't feel we were just like 'Wow, the season's over now. We can't win anything,'" Martin said. "We had other goals. It was still mathematically possible for us to win [the league title going into this weekend]. And everybody knew that. Even if we don't win the Ivy League championship, we were still thinking about other things, like the NIT or we still actually have a shot for setting the school record for most Division I wins in a season. We will tie if we win out. We had other goals. It's not just, 'Oh wow, we're packing it in because the chance of us winning the Ivy League championship is slim.'"

Martin felt that part of the team's problem against Brown and Yale was that it didn't prepare as much as it had in the past. Though the relaxed practices were intended to refresh the players, they had the opposite effect, and he met with Sullivan to discuss his concerns. "I feel like this week in practice will be a little more intense than it was last week because I told Coach what I feel about not [practicing] as much," Martin said. "I feel that that kind of hurt us. The past three years we've gone to Penn and Princeton and lost. All three times, all [six] games that we've played there. It's something that our seniors would really like to win both these games this weekend. We still have goals. There's no reason for anybody to pack it in."

After the agonizing losses to Yale and Brown, Harvard's season had gone from hopeful to hopeless. Sullivan decided to meet with the players in an effort to salvage what they could out of the remaining four games. He also revised the practices for that week. "He told us we don't deserve this," Beal said. "He feels bad for us in a way. We worked very hard and things didn't go our way, but he didn't leave it on that. Tuesday, Wednesday, Thursday [leading up to the Penn and Princeton games], those were awful practices. It was back to preseason. We ran sidelines, which is what we do when we get in trouble. He was like, 'You know we need to get back to that.' He's like, 'I don't care if your legs are tired, you're not going to come out here being soft. You need to get back to competing.'"

Sullivan said the hard practices were intended to shake the players up, shake them out of their doldrums. "Everybody goes through that the last two weeks," Sullivan said. "There is no light at the end of the tunnel. You talk about signing up for all twenty-seven [games], but it's hard sometimes when you get to this point in the season. This is the time of year in our league, the final three weeks, where guys start heading for the exits. We talked to the team about that. We can't punch the card out just now. We're here for the duration."

Chapter 18

Dreams
Deferred

I n the week leading up to Harvard's games at Penn and Princeton, the *Harvard Crimson*, the school's student newspaper, published an article on the team's failure to live up to expectations. Although the writer found fault with the players and coaching staff, he laid most of the blame on Harvard's administration for its lack of support and for insisting on a higher Academic Index requirement than the rest of the Ivies. He also went on to say that firing Coach Frank Sullivan would not bring Harvard any closer to an Ivy League basketball title. Already, rumors were circulating that Sullivan was on his way out because of the team's collapse.

Against this backdrop, Harvard made its final road trip of the season. With four games remaining on the schedule, Harvard could finish above .500 overall for the first time in four years if it won two out of four. By winning all four, the Crimson would tie the school's mark for most Division I wins (sixteen). Yet, in order to do that, Harvard would have to sweep Penn and Princeton—a feat it hadn't accomplished since 1985.

Moreover, the Crimson hadn't won at the Palestra since 1991, and its last win at Jadwin came in 1989.

Given Harvard's last few performances, it was widely thought that the Crimson didn't stand a chance against first-place Penn. Most observers assumed this game would be a blowout. It wasn't. Harvard came out uncharacteristically strong in the first half, looking every bit like the team picked to contend for the league championship. Here was the game everyone expected to see from these two teams. As the contest wore on, it turned more and more physical. Penn's Friedrich Ebede left with a strained groin late in the first half. His teammate Steve Danley went to the bench with a broken nose. Even though none of them ended up on the injured list, the Harvard players seemed more perturbed than the Penn players by the lack of fouls. They complained unsuccessfully to the officials. They weren't getting any sympathy from their coach either. During a time-out late in the first half, Sullivan took them to task for not being physical and for whining to the referees. "I thought the team was way too upset early in the game," Sullivan said. "Our guys wanted to get into a debate [with the officials]. Once we got past the fact that there's not going to be a debate, they're going to let you play . . . we were all appreciative—I know I was—[t]he refs let the game go. They let the kids play, and it wound up being a terrific basketball game."

Every time Penn tried to build a lead, Harvard stormed back. The Crimson may have fallen into a fifth-place tie with Brown in the standings, but the players were showing a resoluteness that had been missing the past month. They were scrappy and fearless. The Palestra crowd, stunned by the turn of events, was in a frenzy. Yet, the Harvard players weren't rattled. The Quakers maintained a slim lead over the final few minutes, but the Crimson didn't fold. Down by three with less than a minute remaining, Harvard needed a three-pointer to keep it in the game. Jim Goffredo was the obvious candidate to shoot it. Instead, Brian Cusworth, Harvard's seven-footer, lofted a shot from behind the arc that fell through the net. "We were trying to get Jimmy," Sullivan said. "We had trouble getting Jimmy open all night long. [Cusworth] just had the wherewithal and, actually, guts to take it. He took a page out of Mark Zoller's book at Harvard and sank some threes."

When the center starts knocking down threes, a team has to feel pretty good about its chances. Still, with the score tied at 62, Penn had one final opportunity to win the game in regulation. Harvard, haunted by recent last-second collapses to Cornell and Princeton, was not about to let this chance to redeem its season slip away. Yet it nearly did. Ibrahim Jaaber, the last player the Crimson wanted to have the ball, found a way to get a shot off with six seconds to play. For what seemed like the first time all season, Harvard caught a break. The ball did not go through the net. The buzzer sounded, and the game went to overtime. With Ebede and Danley on the bench nursing injuries, Penn looked in bad shape heading into its first extra session of the season, and when the Crimson took the early lead, it appeared the Quakers were going to lose for the second time in three games.

But Penn had no intention of falling on its home court. The Quakers, still fuming over their ruined perfect Ivy season, methodically seized control. Penn didn't make a basket the final two and a half minutes of overtime; it didn't need to. The Quakers made seven of ten free throws in the final minutes to seal their 74–71 victory. Coach Fran Dunphy was thrilled to escape with a win, especially with Penn down to five healthy bodies in its seven-man rotation. "It's a great win," said Dunphy, whose team finished a perfect 7–0 at home for the second consecutive Ivy season and the eighth time since 1993. "We were obviously in the soup a couple of times. . . . Finding a way to win is a nice thing. Obviously, we're in a situation where everybody wants to beat us. In all honesty, it is an enviable position."

For Harvard, it was yet another loss—no more or less devastating than those that came before it. And in the end, it didn't matter that the Crimson had played Penn evenly. A close loss counted the same as a blowout. "It was a big litmus test for our guys," Sullivan said. "They were so disappointed with last weekend, the weekend before. . . . It was a real positive for us to see we had the fight. I thought we were a tough out tonight. I thought both teams were a tough out. It was a tremendous Ivy League basketball game that represents the highest standards of play. For us, it's still a loss, though, and it's very painful."

Once again, Jaaber had rescued his team from an almost certain defeat. The junior guard and Ivy League player of the year favorite tied a career high with thirty-one points. He made a career-high six three-pointers and played forty-four minutes without turning the ball over. Without his performance, Penn certainly would have suffered its second Ivy setback of the season. Instead, Harvard was left to ponder how it let another game slip away.

"Obviously, it's better than last weekend because that was horrible," Michael Beal said. "For me, it's still a loss. . . . It was good to see us come out here and stick it to them, really [make them] earn it. . . . The thing I'm most proud of, if we're going take any pride from it, is not just the beginning but halftime, when we were down eight. That's another opportunity for us to quit—say, 'Hey, we gave it our best shot.' We didn't do that. We kept going. We kept fighting till the very end. Some things don't go our way, but at least we know that we gave it our all, and more importantly, we know that we didn't quit. If I'd gone out a quitter, I couldn't live with myself."

Fairly or unfairly, Harvard was being labeled as a bunch of quitters after losing six in a row. For a team many felt would contend for an Ivy League title, the Crimson's slide was inexplicable. Yet, even as Harvard's decline continued, the seniors maintained that they had goals they wanted to accomplish. "We came into a program that was strong," Beal said. "We went down our freshman year, and we're trying to get it back where it needs to be. So the work that we're putting in, it's not just for ourselves, that we can hold our head high when we graduate, but it is also for the freshmen so that they know what to do and what not to do. I think our sophomore year, after the things that happened our freshman year, there was a lag. We just have to make sure not to do that.

"One thing that was very different [this year] was that we were getting respect, and that's something that doesn't happen in this program, that I haven't seen in this program for a long time, getting respect from the outside public. It makes it a lot easier to play better when people respect you, when fans respect you. We really want to get that back and show people that, whatever happened—I can't explain it, nobody can explain it—that's not us. We're still a great team."

The seniors desperately needed to salvage what they could from this season. A win against Princeton at Jadwin would go a long way toward that goal. Mustering the energy to knock off the Tigers after such a draining loss to Penn wouldn't be easy though. "We just have to make sure that we don't let down for Princeton tomorrow night, and I don't think that we will," Beal said. "I think that a lot of people in our program are very angry at Princeton for that buzzer-beater [at Lavietes]. I think that sent us on a tumult. Cornell and Princeton—we have something for both of them."

Whatever Harvard had in mind for Princeton, the Crimson never got a chance to show the Tigers. A month ago, Princeton could barely run its offense with any efficiency. Against Harvard, the Tigers put on a clinic. They were nearly flawless. Everyone understood their roles and executed them to near perfection. If they weren't making a backdoor cut for a layup, they were knocking down a three-point basket. Princeton finished with twenty-one assists on twenty-five field goals. "We've been playing pretty well obviously for a month or more," Princeton coach Joe Scott said. "But at different times, we've played well for twenty minutes at a clip. Tonight obviously, we did it for the whole game. . . . Offensively, we played terrific, whether it was open threes, whether it was backdoor layups, whether it was individual drives, whether it was post moves. It was a complete game, I'd say."

Princeton's 75–48 victory further illustrated how quickly the two teams' fortunes had reversed. The setback—Harvard's worst league defeat in two years—dropped the Crimson's overall record below .500. After a strong start to the season, Harvard was in a free fall. Princeton, which had struggled early on, was playing its best basketball of the season. "We've been executing so much better," Scott said. "Obviously, guys feel comfortable playing with each other. They know what each other is going to do. We have a point guard who's playing really well. We have a center, if you want to call him that, playing extremely well. I'd say that in any program in the country, if you have a point guard playing well—and especially in our program, a point guard and a center playing well—I think you have a good chance to be playing well. If you're going to be honest about it, when we were going through our struggles, we didn't have a point guard and we were trying to find a center."

As well as Princeton played, everyone acknowledged that Harvard's overtime loss to Penn had a bearing on the outcome. "Last night, obviously, Harvard played extremely well. They had their chance down there [against Penn]," Scott said. "Somewhere in there is the battle of the Friday-Saturday, and it helped us somehow tonight. We played well, and they probably didn't play as well as they're capable of."

Harvard had to overcome more than just the strain that comes from playing an overtime game on the road. Playing what have traditionally been the two toughest teams in the league with their different styles of play on back-to-back nights on their home courts has never been easy. Since 1969, Penn and Princeton are 444–35 at home against the other six Ivy teams. Only two teams have swept the Tigers and the Quakers on their home courts in those thirty-seven years—Harvard in 1985 and Yale in 1987. "It's been the classic question that's been asked from year to year: what's the difference between the two styles of play, how much energy is required on Friday and does that zap you for Saturday," Sullivan said. "Take nothing away from Princeton. We were beaten, beaten fair, beaten square, beaten solidly. I think the forty-eight-hour period required more stamina certainly on the back end tonight than we were able to put into the weekend."

As Harvard limped home to finish its season, Princeton was left to consider its title possibilities. The Tigers, the hottest team in the Ivy League, were in second place, two games behind Penn with three games left for each team. Hard as this was to imagine a month ago, Princeton could be playing Penn for the league championship in the final game of the season. The Tigers would have to win their next two games—at Brown and at Yale—for that to happen. "We're in the race until the final weekend," Scott said. "We are the only other team that can say that.

Who knows what that is going to mean? We still have work to do, but we're the other team that's in the race on the final weekend. I think that says the most about what our guys have done, how far they've come, how well they've played, and the kind of kids they've been. That's what they should get the most credit for, putting themselves in this situation."

It was hard to believe that the same team that scored only twenty-one points in the loss to Monmouth and lost to Division III Carnegie Mellon was the same team now vying for an Ivy League championship. Those dark days seemed long ago. "I give credit to Greenman and Owings," Scott said. "Scottie [Greenman] as a senior—not playing, being injured, coming back, shooting horrendously—to be the way that he was during that time, to sort of bring the team with him, and Luke [Owings] somewhere around the Rice game to just say, 'We're just going to do whatever the coaches ask us to do, and we're going to do it as hard as we can' at a time when we weren't doing so well, I think that says a lot about those guys. I think it was their leadership that [led to the turnaround]. Obviously, the other guys were involved with it, but I've got to give credit to those two guys."

Had it not been for a couple buzzer-beaters and late swoons, Cornell would be contending for the Ivy championship as well. Take away Dragutin Kravic's last-second shot, Scott Greenman's two three-pointers, and the Big Red's late-game meltdowns against Yale and Penn, and Cornell would be tied with the first-place Quakers in the league standings. Instead, the Big Red occupied fourth place after losing three in a row. At the time, Khaliq Gant's terrifying injury shook Cornell, but it also galvanized the players and coaches. Now, however, the emotion from this traumatic event had flagged, and the Big Red was back to being the team it was before the tragedy—that is to say, wildly inconsistent and prone to unexplainable lapses.

Yale, which had sent Cornell on its downward spiral two weeks ago, was coming to Ithaca, and the Big Red was eager to pay the Bulldogs back for its 74–65 loss at New Haven. A win would move Cornell into a tie for third place with Yale. It also was Senior Weekend. Cornell's three seniors—Lenny Collins, David Lisle, and Ryan Rourke—would be playing their final two home games. They wanted nothing more than to end their careers at Newman Arena with a pair of victories.

The Yale-Cornell contest was an evenly matched game with neither team's lead reaching double digits. Cornell went ahead by nine in the second half, then Yale rallied to keep the game close. With just under two minutes to play, Dominick Martin pulled the Bulldogs within three by converting a three-point play. This was usually about the time Cornell went into one of its stupors. But in a surprising turn of events, the Big Red closed out the game strong to win, 68–64. The victory snapped Cornell's three-game skid and moved it into a tie for third place with Yale. Lisle, whose career at Cornell could best be described as quiet, made a splash against Yale. The pre-med major came off the bench to score a career-high sixteen points, twelve of which came during the decisive second half. He was part of a strong showing by Big Red reserves in this game. Freshman Brian Kreefer finished with ten points, and Jason Hartford added nine as the Cornell reserves outscored their Yale counterparts, 39–13.

Cornell coach Steve Donahue, recognizing how tired both teams were late in the season, elected to rotate fresh bodies liberally during the game to wear down Yale. It turned out to be a sound strategy. The Big Red had enough in reserve to make a late push to win the game. "What we've struggled with is closing out games," Lisle told the *Cornell Daily Sun* after the game. "We've had pretty much every game in the Ivy League this season—with the exception of Penn—where we were up with four or five minutes left and the game kind of falls away from us. So we knew we had to close out hard, and I think we stepped up and did that tonight."

After such a rousing victory, Cornell should have had no trouble dispatching Brown the next night. And yet, for some reason, the Big Red did not bring the same intensity to this game that the Bears did. Even the emotion of Senior Night—Collins, Lisle, and Rourke were honored before the game—was not enough to motivate Cornell. Brown was having one of those nights when it made nearly every shot. No matter what defense the Big Red tried—zone, man-to-man—nothing worked. Everything the Bears threw at the basket fell through the net. Cornell matched Brown's torrid shooting for a half, but after halftime, the Big Red's offense cooled. Sixteen lead changes later, the Bears held on for a 69–64 victory. Brown, which started 2–5 in the league, had won three of its last five games.

Cornell's loss—coupled with Penn's win against Dartmouth—mathematically eliminated the Big Red from the Ivy championship race. At best, Cornell could finish 8–6, matching its league record from last season. If the Big Red did beat Harvard and Dartmouth next weekend, its eight Ivy wins in back-to-back seasons would be a first in eighteen years. Yet, knowing how close Cornell came to vying for the league title, this achievement would be a small consolation to the players and coaches.

Chapter 19

And the
Winner
Is . . .

O nly two of the eight teams still had a shot at the Ivy League
championship, and given the history of the league, most out-
siders were not surprised those two were Penn and Princeton.
Ivy insiders, however, knew how unlikely the Tigers' position really was.
Princeton needed help if it was to win the title. The Tigers had to win
their next three games and needed the Quakers to lose one of their next
two. Two weeks ago, it looked as if Penn would have no trouble winning
its tenth title under Fran Dunphy. But the Quakers were not the same
team they were the first half of the Ivy season, when they won their first
seven league games by an average of twenty-three points. Penn had lost
at Columbia, needed second-half heroics by Ibrahim Jaaber to win at
Cornell, and then escaped with an overtime win against Harvard at home.
The Quakers' only convincing win during this stretch came at home

against Dartmouth, the worst team in the league. Rather than finishing strong, they were staggering to the end.

Injuries to key players were taking their toll on Penn. Friedrich Ebede would not play this weekend because of a groin strain. Steve Danley would wear a protective mask on his face because of his broken nose. Eric Osmundson hadn't scored in double figures since injuring his shoulder at Harvard back on February 11. With Dunphy's seven-man rotation, Penn had to hope that its few healthy bodies were enough against Yale and Brown. Unfortunately for the Quakers, they were going to one of the toughest venues to play in the Ivy League and a place where they hadn't experienced much success recently. Penn was 1–3 in its last four trips to New Haven.

Yale was eager to return to Lee Amphitheater after going 2–2 on its four-game road trip. The Bulldogs had lost at Dartmouth and Cornell but beat Harvard and Columbia. (James Jones improved to 5–1 against his younger brother Joe.) Yale was in third place in the Ivy standings but had no chance to win the league. Still, a strong finish combined with a Princeton swoon could vault the Bulldogs into second place, their best finish since tying for the Ivy championship in 2002, and give them an outside chance at an NIT bid. Yale had plenty riding on this game and certainly seemed to have the psychological edge against Penn at home.

Which is why it is difficult to explain the Bulldogs' poor play in the first half. For a team that clearly benefited from home-court advantage, Yale might as well have been playing in a hostile arena. Penn looked far more comfortable at Lee Amphitheater than the Bulldogs did. While Yale missed nineteen of its first twenty-eight shots, Penn built a twelve-point halftime lead. Four minutes into the second half, the Quakers were ahead by eighteen.

Then the momentum began to shift. The Bulldogs were surging as Penn was fading. The Quakers went through another late-game drought, failing to make a basket for the final eight minutes. All of a sudden the clock wasn't moving fast enough for Penn. Yale continued to chip away at the Quakers' lead until the Bulldogs were within two points, with two seconds left on the clock. They had just enough time for a steal and a quick shot. Penn's Brian Grandieri tried to throw a long pass to Eric Osmundson, but the ball sailed over his head and was intercepted by Dominick Martin who zipped it to sophomore guard Eric Flato at the top of the key. With time about to expire, Flato heaved the ball at the basket. If his three-point attempt fell through the net, Yale would win. Instead, the shot was off to the right, and Penn escaped with a 57–55 victory. "I caught it, turned, and shot all in one motion," said Flato, one of the better three-point shooters in the league. "If I had more time, I would have been able to get my feet set."

Although Dunphy denied that exhaustion played a factor in Penn's recent close games, there was every indication that the Quakers were a tired bunch—most notably, Ibrahim Jaaber, the Ivy League's leading scorer. He failed to score in double figures for the second consecutive game and only the third time this season. Held in check for most of the game by Casey Hughes, Jaaber scored just nine points. After the game, Penn learned that Princeton was trailing Brown. A Tigers loss would mean an Ivy League championship and a trip to the NCAA tournament for the Quakers.

Notwithstanding Princeton's impressive performance against Harvard, which left everyone wondering whether it could pull off one of the more spectacular in-season turnarounds in recent memory, the Tigers were still a wobbly team, winning games more by luck than by skill. More than half of Princeton's Ivy victories had been by the smallest of margins: the overtime win against Columbia at home, the last-second shot at Harvard, the three-point escape from Dartmouth, the two-overtime thriller at Cornell and another three-point close call against Dartmouth. Pulling out wins such as they had left the Tigers feeling nearly invincible, but their razor-thin margins of victory showed how vulnerable they actually were.

While the current buzz around the league centered on Princeton's revival, few were taking notice of Brown's quiet transformation. The Bears had won three of their last five games, including an impressive 69–64 victory at Cornell the past weekend, which moved them into fifth place. After losing two of their more experienced players early in the league season—junior forward Sam Manhanga to a foot injury and senior forward Luke Ruscoe to an ankle injury—Brown's young starting lineup of three sophomores, a freshman, and a junior was beginning to coalesce just as the season was ending. Keenan Jeppesen, a sophomore forward from Stoney Creek, Ontario, had emerged as the Bears' most consistent scorer, averaging 15.7 points per game, third best in the league. Freshman Scott Friske was the reigning Ivy League rookie of the week after scoring twenty-three points at Cornell, and Damon Huffman, last year's Ivy rookie of the year, seemed to have regained his shooting touch following his ten-of-eighteen performance from behind the arc the previous weekend. A bright future seemed ahead for the Bears.

Careless play by Princeton set the tone of this game from the beginning. The Tigers turned the ball over twice on their first two possessions, once on a shot-clock violation. After taking much better care of the ball over the last few weeks, they were sloppy and out of sorts. Brown capitalized on Princeton's clumsiness, turning twenty-one Tigers turn-overs into twenty-three points. "What you don't see is a Princeton team turn the ball over as many times as they did," Brown coach Glen Miller said. "In a game that's going to have less possessions than most games, every possession is critical, and you can't turn the ball over."

The Bears clogged the area around the basket, making it difficult for Princeton to score on layups and backdoor cuts. As a result, the Tigers settled for long jump shots, few of which were falling through the net. Of their sixteen shot attempts before halftime, eight were from three-point range and only one was good. Overall, Princeton took more than half of its shots from behind the arc but made only three—a woeful 16.7 percent. "Our focus always with them is—and it's not always executed—is that for the most part they're looking to get layups or three-pointers," Miller said. "They start to feel really good about themselves when they get a mixture of both. Our focus was to shut down the lane, take away the layup and their paint scores, and make them beat us over the top."

Brown, which had scored a season-low thirty-seven points the first time it had played Princeton, appeared better prepared to face Princeton's matchup zone defense this time around. The Bears were more aggressive than Princeton, driving to the basket and drawing fouls. They scored almost a third of their total points at the free-throw line. "In my opinion, that's how you have to beat that type of defense," Miller said. "You have to get post play. You have to get dribble penetration. You have to get points in the paint. Our main focus offensively was to attack them inside."

By beating Princeton, 61–46, Brown had split its series with every Ivy team it played except Penn, which the Bears would close out the season against on Saturday night. The Princeton and Harvard results were the most dramatic; they represented thirty-point swings between games. "The funny thing is most of the teams when they beat us the first time they beat us badly," Damon Huffman said. "And we turned around and took it to them the second time."

Brown also had split every weekend series in the league except one —the two road games against Penn and Princeton. Winning back-to-back games on consecutive nights wasn't something this young team had mastered yet. "A lot of times, the second night in the Ivy League, both teams are extremely fatigued," Huffman said. "So it really comes down to mental breakdowns and things like that. I mean a lot of times we would lose on the second night [because] we just weren't focusing. Tonight we were all mentally there, because Princeton's offense—you have to know their stuff. The thing with them [is] they make you work. If you have a mental breakdown or you're not in the right place at the right time, they're going to find you."

Without a superstar player who could take over games, Brown discovered it needed everyone to contribute this season. Sometimes the Bears put forth a team effort, sometimes they didn't, which is why they would finish with a poor overall record. A win against Penn on Saturday would put them at .500 in Ivy play—a modest achievement but an accomplishment nonetheless for this young team. "It's huge," Huffman said. "Not only is it beating the first-place team in the league, it gets us to .500. It carries momentum into the off-season. If you lose your last game, you just have a bad taste in your mouth. But if you win, you can ride it. You know you can beat the first-place team in the league."

It may seem odd that the players and Miller would be thrilled with a .500 finish, but it really was an indication of how after falling into the Ivy League basement, the Bears had the wherewithal to pull themselves out of it. "I'm very happy with these guys," Miller said. "I've stressed all along through our struggles that don't expect to be a good team next year just because we're a year older. You've got to make the most of every practice, every game. I started preaching that in December. These guys have really bought into that. We lost [2003–2004 Ivy League player of the year] Jason Forte from last year. Arguably our best player [Luke Ruscoe] hasn't really played in the conference. This would be a big accomplishment [to finish at .500]. It already is good progress."

Princeton's limited rotation of essentially six players—compounded by the illnesses of Edwin Buffmire and Noah Savage—was ravaged by foul trouble throughout the game. Four of the seven players who were on the court for the Tigers finished with four or more fouls. Kyle Koncz fouled out. "Losing a junior who is playing well, who is tough, it's not like our program now—it's in good shape, but it's not like it's just pick who's going in," Joe Scott said. "It's obvious that over the course of this month that it's been a nucleus of guys who have done it. Not having [Buffmire] and saying to Mike Strittmatter, 'Hey, now you have to be a thirty-minute guy.' He's not. He's a twelve- to fifteen-minute-a-game guy. Savage has been feeling horrendous. He didn't practice this week. He's got major, major health problems. He hasn't felt well, and he hasn't gotten better over the course of the season. At some point in time, you'd like to get healthy, and when you never get healthy, that stuff wears on you. It's definitely worn on him."

While Scott felt hamstrung by his rotation, it wasn't as if he didn't have players on the bench who could have played against Brown. Patrick Ekeruo, Harrison Schaen, and Kevin Steuerer had started games earlier in the season. (Steuerer would play two minutes near the end of the game.) He simply refused to put those players on the court. "What we do is we watch practice. The guys that are playing are the guys that play," Scott said. "None of that's changed. At this point in the year, you are what you are. That's okay for us. I'm happy with what we are. . . . Obviously at this juncture [more depth] might help us, but at this time of the year when you look at most teams they're down to seven guys and eight guys, because you have your rotation—you've been successful with it, and you stay with it, and you hope somebody doesn't get mono. It's called bad luck."

Scott's unwillingness to overlook his players' shortcomings aggravated his bad luck. It could be argued that Scott should have done more to develop the reserves so that when a player went down, another was ready to take his place. Instead, Scott was content to succeed or fail with the players who embraced his way of doing things. Although disappointed by the outcome at Brown, Scott wasn't surprised by it. "I don't know if I thought I had gotten [the poor play] out of our system," he said. "I was wondering when it was coming back."

Once Penn heard the Princeton result—about twenty minutes after its game against Yale ended—the Quakers cheered as only they could when their biggest rival's failing led to their ultimate reward. There was no trophy presentation; no nets were cut down. Only lots of smiles on a night when they felt lucky to escape New Haven with a win. It made the bus trip to Providence for their game against Brown the next night that much more palatable.

"It never gets old," Fran Dunphy said after the Quakers became the first in the NCAA tournament's sixty-five-team field. "It is always exciting to be able to watch the selection show on Sunday afternoon and wonder where you are going and who you are going to play. That is what college basketball is all about."

"I'm just glad we got this victory" over Yale, Eric Osmundson told the *Philadelphia Inquirer.* "The NCAAs are what you dream about as a kid, more so than the NBA. Now we want to take that next step and win one."

Brown carried the momentum—and, more important, its defense—from its impressive victory over Princeton into its game against Penn. For a game that appeared meaningless to anyone outside of the Pizzitola Center, it had all the drama of a contest where the championship was on the line. The Bears completely disrupted the Quakers' offense by mixing their defenses and keeping them off balance throughout the game. Penn managed to make only nine of its first twenty-nine field-goal attempts and trailed by eight points at halftime. The only way Penn kept this game close was by forcing Brown into twenty-three turnovers.

With his team down by three with twenty-one seconds to play, Brown's Marcus Becker spotted an open Huffman—the team's leading scorer and best three-point shooter—and tried to throw him the ball.

But Jaaber anticipated the pass and stole it. Instead of running out the clock or waiting to be fouled, Jaaber threw the ball ahead to Grandieri. While it would have been more sensible for Grandieri to dribble until time expired or he was fouled, he did what most basketball players would do and went to the basket for a layup. Becker, still smarting from his bad pass, atoned for his mistake by blocking the shot. Friske grabbed the ball, brought it up the court and threw it to Becker who had raced to the corner and was waiting to take the three-pointer. The shot fell through the net with four-tenths of a second remaining on the clock, tying the score at 60 and sending the game to overtime. For a team with no postseason to play for, Brown certainly showed great intensity and passion.

Penn, which led for less than five minutes in the forty-five-minute game, ultimately escaped with a 74–68 victory. The weekend had proved far more challenging than the Quakers anticipated, and they were relieved to slip away unscathed. Yet once again, the close games showed how fragile Penn was. This was not a team heading into the NCAA tournament with much momentum.

Brown, though disappointed not to have upset the top team in the league, wasn't hanging its head over the setback. "This game was very important to our future," Miller told reporters after the loss. "Even though we lost the game, I feel we accomplished a lot. This was a championship team, going to the NCAA tournament with one loss in our conference. Our guys deserved to win the game. They're very confident that we can compete next year. . . . We'll have probably the best postseason that we've had here in seven years. These guys are believers, and they want to be good."

Cornell was on the verge of becoming the feel-good story of the Ivy League when the Big Red's season drifted off course. The team had lost four of its last five and dropped into fourth place heading into the final weekend. Injuries certainly contributed to the Big Red's inconsistency. Its backcourt was hit particularly hard. The same week Khaliq Gant was hurt, freshman guard Jason Battle went down with a high ankle sprain. The wear and tear of back-to-back games had aggravated point guard Graham Dow's injury. Given Cornell's hodgepodge lineup, it was remarkable the team had done as well as it had.

The Big Red closed out its season with its most taxing Ivy road trip: games at Harvard and Dartmouth. Losing at either of them—or, worse yet, at both—would make an already long bus trip even more unbearable. Cornell had reason to be optimistic, though. The Big Red, which had done poorly on opponents' home courts in the nonconference season, was the only team in the league that had fared better on the road than at home. It was 3–2 on Ivy opponents' home courts, but 3–4 at Newman Arena.

Just when it seemed Cornell's injury woes couldn't possibly get any worse, they did. Jason Hartford, who had missed games earlier in the year with a broken bone in his wrist, now had a broken bone in his foot. He would attend the games in a cast rather than a uniform. Fortunately for the Big Red, it didn't need Hartford against Harvard. Cornell delivered the first blow—making its first five shots, all from three-point range—to stagger the Crimson and then battered them from long range (making eleven of twenty-three shots from behind the arc) until Harvard succumbed to a 71–44 defeat, the Big Red's most lopsided Ivy win of the season.

Cornell, which had swept only one weekend series all season, did its best to give away the game to Dartmouth the next night. The Big Red didn't make a field goal the final eight minutes yet somehow managed to hold on for a 64–60 victory. Cornell finished 8–6, matching its Ivy record from the previous season and good enough for third place. It was the first time since 1987 and 1988 that the Big Red had back-to-back winning Ivy seasons. Adam Gore, who set the school's single-season record by making 83 three-pointers, would earn the Ivy League's freshman of the year award.

The Harvard seniors didn't know what it was like to win the final game of the season. For three years, they had ended each season with a loss. For the past month, losing was all they had known. "Me, Matt, and Mike, we said we can't go out on a loss," Zach Martin said. "Every year we've gone out on a loss. It's such a downer. Especially this year, I feel like this is the best team I've ever been on. We had to go out on a winning note." A victory wouldn't assuage the painful conclusion to their careers, but it was one last goal they could achieve. If nothing else, they wanted to prove to themselves and everyone else that Harvard was not the team that lost to Cornell in its penultimate game of the season. "Last night was just embarrassing," Matt Stehle said. "We got our asses handed to us."

In a ceremony before the game, each senior was escorted onto the court by his parents. As they walked out in alphabetical order led by Michael Beal, the public address announcer read each player's list of accomplishments. Beal and Martin acknowledged the appreciative crowd with small waves. Stehle tried to remain stoic. But as the poignancy of the moment struck him, he found it difficult to hold back his tears. "When I woke up this morning, I didn't think there was going to be too much emotion," Stehle said. "I thought I'd be able to keep it in check.

But then during the pregame ceremony, going out with your parents, bringing in the huddle, saying the whole pregame thing for the last time, seeing all the guys, probably the last time we'll all be together, definitely it was real emotional for me."

Because it was his last game, Zach Martin was given a spot in the starting lineup, taking freshman Drew Housman's place. Whether the lineup change gave the Crimson a spark or just knowing this was the season finale, Harvard enjoyed its best start to a game in a long time. The Crimson jumped to a 12–3 lead and went ahead 20–8 midway through the half. It took a ten-point lead into halftime before Columbia pulled within two on Dragutin Kravic's layup in the second half. Harvard dug in and pushed the lead back up to ten before holding on for a 69–64 win. "It's good to finish with a win," Coach Sullivan said. "It became more important, because of the losing streak at the end of the season, that we finished with a victory. The music is back on tonight. The guys feel better about themselves. It would have been a devastating way to finish out for the seniors, a tough way to finish out the season."

The mood in the locker room was jubilant after the game. The players were hugging one another and the coaches. The seniors were telling everyone how much they would miss them. Stehle became choked up again. Martin tried to lighten the mood by teasing Stehle: "You're on the all-smart team. You're wicked smart!" a reference to Stehle being selected to the Academic All-America second team, one of fifteen players in Division I basketball recognized for their performances on the court and in the classroom.

Bruce Springsteen's "I'm Goin' Down" bellowed forth amid the shouts and laughter. The Jersey rocker resonated with the players even though the song was released before some of them were born. Back when Harvard was winning, "I'm Goin' Down" was its anthem after victories. Now it was the Crimson's farewell refrain to an unfulfilled season. "After a win, that's what gets played," Martin said. "I'm from New Jersey. Bruce is the man. [Brian] Darcy's a huge fan. Matt's a huge fan. Then it just grew on everybody. Even Mike. That's not his style of music."

"I'm going to listen to it when I'm at work and working like eighty-hour weeks," Beal said. "It will probably make me happy, nostalgic."

It had been a long time since Harvard had anything to be happy about. The 2005–2006 season had been enormously disappointing. The three seniors, in particular, took the Crimson's eight-game slide hard. They had put so much pressure on themselves to win Harvard's first Ivy League championship that instead of shrugging off the early mishaps, they agonized over them. Each failure compounded the next. They carried their defeats into their next games. These overachieving Ivy League kids whose answer to almost everything is to work harder didn't know how to let go.

Though they were accused of giving up on their season, they were undone instead by their passion and intensity. What should have fueled them caused them to burn up. It wasn't that they quit. They just cared too much. "I think that contributed to our downfall," Beal said. "We all were like, 'All right, we need to get this.' We put pressure on. We have to get it. And when [the shots weren't] going down or we got off to a slow start or they started hitting threes, it just got worse and worse. Even though we didn't turn on each other, we kind of turned on ourselves. . . . I mean it's a very different dynamic from anything I've ever been a part of. Obviously [the win against Columbia] doesn't take away the sting of this failed season. But I think what it does for us is it lets us know that we are still the team that we started off as. Even though we went through all this adversity, we still stuck together. For us to grit it out and get it tonight, I think that was really special. I know it was special for me, Matt, and Zach. I think it should be special for the rest of the guys to give them the confidence going into next year."

The cumulative effect of the losses over the past five weeks had drawn attention away from Harvard's achievements. The Crimson's 13–14 overall record was its best since 2001–2002. Beating Columbia not only prevented the Crimson from finishing last in the league, but it also meant Harvard ended with a win for the first time since 2001. While everyone had grander accomplishments in mind when the season started, some of the successes the Crimson should be proud of were being overlooked.

"That's the interesting thing about this season," Beal said. "Just because of how good we were, we have all these lofty goals and expectations that were really realistic, which have fallen so short, and I'm so upset about it. But we had the goals—getting into the NCAA tournament and winning the whole league—that in the process we kind of skipped over all the other things, you know, the little things that we've never done. I don't think we've had a winning season coming out of nonconference except my freshman year, being competitive going down to the Palestra, when was the last time we went down to the Palestra and didn't get blown out.

"As we digest this season, we're going to have to take some of those things out. As we get away from the pain of the dream deferred, then we'll start to look back and see the kind of positive things that came out. And on top of that, not quitting. I plan on going to have a conversation with Coach after this, sometime later next week, and just being like, 'Did we quit on you as seniors?' And making sure he didn't think that we did, because I don't think that we did. I think that we kept working. And I think that's something to hang our hats on, something to be proud of. Obviously the disappointment is going to be with us for years over our best opportunity. We came out with such goals, and we all worked so hard."

While Beal, Martin, and Stehle had their future to look forward to, Sullivan—the second-longest-tenured coach in the Ivy League—was hoping to keep his job. Harvard's director of athletics, Robert L. Scalise, had made it known how disappointed he was by the team's swoon. Sullivan expected to learn his fate in the next several weeks. In the meantime, he was left to try to explain why Harvard had stumbled badly late in the season. "I don't think anybody foresaw that we would be in the position that we're in, in the standings," Sullivan said. "It's highly disappointing. There's a million reasons why. A tip-in here, a play here, who knows? I think the example for everybody in the league this year was that anything can happen. This team [Columbia] beat Penn and Princeton, correct? I think this year in the Ivy League kind of showed everybody how fragile it is, how equal it is. You can be picked for anything in this league, and who knows what's going to happen. Princeton, us. How about Princeton starting like they did, us finishing like we did, Columbia getting back? I think it's a good illustration of how close we all are. I said to the players, 'This is why we don't have a tournament—because whoever is left standing at the end of this kind of activity deserves to be the Ivy League champion, according to the purists.'"

Only one game remained. Penn and Princeton would close out the 2005–2006 Ivy League season at Jadwin Gymnasium. Back in February, the first meeting between these longtime rivals had been devoid of drama, with the Quakers winning handily. Even with first place on the line, that game proved to be a dud. Other than Penn not wanting to head into the NCAA tournament after a loss and Princeton not wishing to end its tumultuous season with a setback, this game carried little meaning—except to those with a rooting interest in the teams, and for them, there are no insignificant games in this rivalry.

Because ESPNU was televising the game, it didn't tip off until 9 P.M. This later-than-usual start may have accounted for the low attendance, or perhaps Princeton's fair-weather fans decided that since their team had nothing to play for, they were staying home. Scott Greenman's family did its best to grow the crowd, turning out in force to watch him play his last game in a Tiger uniform. Princeton honored its lone senior before the game, but unlike some schools, it eschews an elaborate ceremony in favor of an understated tribute. After Greenman was recognized by the public address announcer, he hugged assistant coach Howard Levy and head coach Joe Scott and then shook hands with the other coaches and his teammates before walking out onto the court and waving to the crowd.

Penn had swept Princeton eight times under Fran Dunphy. But after barely escaping with wins against Yale and Brown, the Quakers hardly appeared ready to take on their rival. Princeton was exhausted, too. After stumbling against Brown, the Tigers beat Yale, 56–45. It had been a good win after such a bad loss to the Bears.

Though neither team played particularly well early, Princeton found its bearings first. The Tigers built a 10–1 advantage while the Quakers needed more than six and a half minutes to score their first point. Princeton's lead would balloon to eighteen points before the end of the first half on the strength of its 58 percent shooting. The Princeton student section began chanting "over-rated" at the Quakers with a minute remaining until halftime, and the Orange-and-Black fans gave the Tigers a standing ovation as they ran off the court.

Humbled by its poor first-half performance, Penn came out strong in the second half. With under seven minutes left to play, the Quakers pulled to 40–38 on David Whitehurst's layup. The Tigers pushed their lead back to seven with just over a minute remaining. Penn was nearly out of bodies: Mark Zoller fouled out with seven minutes to play; Steve Danley fouled out in the final minute, leaving the Quakers without their starting frontcourt. Yet, the Quakers managed to go on an 8–1 run in the final minute to tie the score at 50.

Everyone in the gym knew who was going to take the last shot for Princeton: Greenman. The senior had been the hero for the Tigers over the past couple weeks—finding Noah Savage at Harvard for the last-second basket and making three-pointers at Cornell to send the game into two overtimes. This was the last game of his college career. There was no more fitting way for him to go out than to score the game-winning basket against Penn. But it didn't happen that way. Greenman's baseline drive to the basket bounced around the rim and fell away, sending the game to overtime.

It should have been no surprise to anyone this game needed more time to be decided. Two of the previous five meetings between these teams had gone to overtime. Both teams, however, went into the extra period with depleted rosters. Danley and Zoller had fouled out for Penn, and Luke Owings—who hit nearly every big shot for Princeton and finished with thirteen points—went to the bench with his fifth foul late in regulation. Despite these deficiencies, neither team used more than seven players.

Penn scored first, taking its first lead of the game, and held that lead nearly the entire overtime. With less than ten seconds to play, Jaaber missed a layup but grabbed his own rebound and was fouled by Savage. Jaaber seemed intent on single-handedly winning this game for Penn. After going one for eight in the first half, he had scored twenty-three points in nearly twenty-five minutes. He missed his first foul shot but sank the second to put the Quakers ahead by one.

Once again, everyone in the gym knew exactly who was getting the ball once Princeton inbounded it. And yet, somehow, Greenman still ended up with it in his hands. Penn was momentarily confused about who was to guard him, and he took advantage of the Quakers' mix-up. He sprinted up the right sideline, toward Princeton's basket. As he approached, Justin Conway's defender left him to go stop Greenman's progress. Greenman spotted Conway, all alone underneath the basket, and threw him the ball. All Conway had to do was catch the pass and make the two-foot layup. In a gym, by himself, he makes that shot one hundred times out of one hundred. But this was different. Everyone was on his feet watching to see if Conway would make it. Not just this game but the entire Princeton season was riding on this one basket. With a preternatural calmness that had served him well all season, Conway sank the shot with 2.5 seconds left on the clock. The crowd was in a frenzy. Penn had one last chance to win, but Whitehurst's desperation heave missed its mark.

"Scottie did everything," said Conway who finished with a career-high twenty-one points and six assists. "I hope I could make that shot from under the basket. Granted, with two seconds left, it's a little harder than normal. But when I saw my guy go to Scottie, I just kind of stood there, knowing I was open, kind of looking at him to give me the ball then put it up." Conway had gone from little-known JV player to Princeton demigod in a matter of months. No one was more surprised than he at his newfound celebrity. "It's been a big change since the beginning of the season," Conway said. "I'm just so happy for the opportunity, and it means a lot to me to represent this program. That's the reason I'm here from the very beginning, so to be out on the court and help the team win that way, I mean, it's such a great feeling. I'm really proud that I had the opportunity to do that."

Princeton, which began the season 2–10, had finished 10–4 in the Ivy League, good enough for second place. Jadwin Gymnasium exploded in pandemonium. Princeton players were running around the court screaming while the Penn players trudged off the court. The students jumped up and down and hugged one another. It was the biggest, most dramatic win of the season for the Tigers, and a fitting ending to their year. "It's nice, to be honest with you, to be sitting next to these two guys and win that game and go 10–4," Coach Joe Scott said. "That's what makes me the happiest right now: that he [Greenman] threw the pass and was our captain, and that guy [Conway] caught the ball and made a layup. Because I don't know if you can say that's the way it's supposed to end, and for Penn and this rivalry, that's probably the way the game is supposed to go between the two of us."

Greenman played one of his worst games of the season in his last game for Princeton. He turned the ball over four times and missed seven of ten shots from the floor to finish with seven points. But when it mattered most, he was there for his team. "I'm extremely happy to have made that play at the end, and we won," Greenman said. "The rest of the game, I didn't exactly play too stellar. I had a lot of turnovers. I gave the ball away. Stuff I don't normally do. I think that made that last play even bigger. I would have been killing myself for the next—who knows how long?—years if that doesn't work out. It's a long ride, the whole four years. It's a grind, but it's what I love to do. It's been difficult to come to the realization that this is my last college game. I've just been through a lot here. It's tough. I was feeling different today through the game than I have in most other games."

Long after the game ended, late into the night, Greenman reflected on Princeton's turbulent season. He spoke almost wistfully, seeming not entirely ready to let go of his career. "It was difficult, obviously, in the beginning of the season. It was a lot of question marks because we were very inexperienced, and we didn't really have too many guys coming back who had played a lot of varsity minutes, the second year of a new coach, a lot of different things. Freshmen, trying to get everybody minutes. Then when I was injured, it was obviously tough. We struggled, had some groundbreaking losses. Stepping back from it, it might have given me a little different perspective on things, even made me cherish the fact that I only had fifteen games left. Then to come back and really have our team turn it around in the Ivy League season is just an unbelievable feeling. It's one of the best feelings in my life. This is what I love to do. My whole life, it's all I've been doing. It feels great to get a whole team to really come together and believe in a certain way and everything that comes along with that—the friendships and the memories and just hard work and great feelings after wins. It's the best thing ever."

Part III

TOURNAMENT
HOOPINESS

Chapter 20

The Wait of
Expectations

For college basketball players, Selection Sunday is akin to Christmas morning—a mixture of anticipation, excitement, and impatience. Just as a child must endure the long wait to open presents, the players and coaches must bide their time for the announcement of the NCAA tournament brackets. The day can't move fast enough.

Every team celebrates Selection Sunday differently. Some want it to be a private affair for members of the team only. Others make it an open celebration for fans and family as well. On this Selection Sunday, the Penn athletics department invited selected guests and media members to join the team at World Café Live, a restaurant/concert venue near campus. CBS stopped by, bringing a camera to provide a live reaction shot of the announcement. (Penn was one of nine schools to appear on the telecast.) At around 5 P.M., alumni, boosters, family members, and others began trickling into the downstairs auditorium reserved for the function. The players arrived wearing navy-blue long-sleeve T-shirts with "2006 Ivy League Basketball Champions" in red-and-white lettering and immediately dove into the buffet table of heavy hors d'oeuvres.

Everyone was trying to predict where Penn would be sent for its first-round game. Few expected the Quakers to remain in Philadelphia, one of the eight subregional sites. Southern California native Eric Osmundson had his fingers crossed that the team would go to San Diego. Others were picking Dayton or Greensboro. "We talk about this when we get together at the beginning of the year. We talk about wanting to have this party," Steve Danley said. "My family came up [from Maryland]. It's a festive environment. Some of my best friends are here. You want people to be here for this moment. You talk about this a lot as a kid. It's kind of fun to have it actually happen."

CBS announcer Greg Gumbel appeared on the enormous projection screen located on a stage in the front of the room. The players, gathered at a long table in the center, stared intently at the television. A hush fell over the room. The sixty-five-team field was about to be unveiled. More than three hundred schools begin each season dreaming of this moment, the chance to see their names on TV. The thirty-four schools like Penn that automatically qualified for the tournament by winning their conference's automatic bid wanted to know where they are going and who they are playing. The rest were hoping they had won enough games to impress the selection committee and earn an at-large bid. "Best day of the year when you're in it," Penn coach Fran Dunphy said. "And the most disappointing day when you're not. So we feel really good about it."

Gumbel announced the four No. 1 seeds: Duke, Connecticut, Villanova, and Memphis. Duke was the top seed in the Atlanta region, and Gumbel revealed that bracket first. The Blue Devils would play No. 16 seed Southern University in Greensboro. He continued listing the teams and whom they would play. After mentioning that Texas was the second seed in the region, he said: "And on Friday in Dallas, the No. 2–seeded Longhorns will play the champions of the Ivy League, the Penn Quakers."

As the Penn-Texas matchup flashed on the screen, the players' enthusiastic response was broadcast to the country. Everyone cheered for the cameras, but once the bright lights were switched off, the players admitted they were a bit disappointed. Penn was seeded No. 15, its lowest seed in nearly twenty years and the worst seed in Dunphy's tenure. The Quakers clearly didn't benefit from having Craig Littlepage, a former Penn player and head coach and onetime teammate of Penn athletic director Steve Bilsky, as the selection committee chairman. Having played a tough schedule, taking on two No. 1 seeds (Duke and Villanova), and finishing with the same record as last year (20–8) when the Quakers were a No. 13 seed, the players were baffled about why they dropped to a No. 15 seed. "It's kind of a slap in the face," Ibrahim Jaaber said.

"It's disappointing," added Osmundson, who was playing in his third NCAA tournament in five years. Osmundson was at Utah when the Utes went in 2002. "You see Texas go up there and you're like, 'Oh no.' . . . That's probably one of the toughest [No.] 2 matchups we could have gotten in the tournament."

In truth, Penn only had to look at its last seven games to understand why the Quakers didn't merit a higher seed. The selection committee rewards teams that finish strong, and Penn had limped to the finish. The Quakers had lost twice and needed overtime twice to pull out wins. Whatever the players felt about their seeding, Coach Dunphy wasn't the least bit perturbed about it. "It is what it is," he said. "Texas is a great team. It will be a tremendous challenge for us, but what a great opportunity."

As bad as it was that Penn had to play a No. 2 seed, the Quakers also had to play the Longhorns basically in their own backyard. The University of Texas is located in Austin, about a three-hour drive from Dallas—a much closer journey for its fans than Penn's. Not only that, the Longhorns were familiar with the arena. The Longhorns were at American Airlines Center, the site of the subregional, having just lost to Kansas there in the Big 12 Conference tournament title game an hour before the brackets were announced. Again, none of this troubled Dunphy. "First of all, it would be a challenge anywhere," he said. "If [the game] were in the Palestra, it would be a phenomenal challenge. Dallas is obviously not far from Austin, and there will be a pro-Texas crowd. We should be used to that by now. We've been on the road enough. The crowd portion of it is not what concerns you, although I'm sure they have great fans there. But more than that, the team concerns me. . . . They've got just great players. Every one of them is a great player."

Dunphy had plenty of reason to worry. Texas was big, strong, and athletic, with all-Americans and future NBA players in its lineup. It wasn't just the Longhorns' talented roster that left Dunphy anxious, though. He was uneasy about his team's play heading into the tournament. "I don't know that we're hitting on all cylinders," Dunphy said. "I think we were playing a little bit better earlier in the year. With Friedrich [Ebede] being out, that hasn't helped our rotation at all."

Penn's lone advantage against Texas might have been its anonymity. Because many of the Longhorns' games are broadcast on television, Penn's players—without watching any game film—could name Texas's starting five and give a description of each player. The Longhorn players probably could not do the same for Penn. Unless they happened to catch the Quakers' game against Duke, they likely had not seen them play. If nothing else, Penn would have the element of surprise on its side.

The Quakers' preparations for the NCAA tournament did not begin well. The first practice was a disaster. The coaches were barking at the players, and the players were sniping at each other. A foul mood prevailed. "The practice on Monday was kind of shaky for a number of different reasons, not just because guys were frustrated and tired of each other, but also because it's been a long road," Jaaber said. The petty slights that had built up over the course of the season were coming to a head. Everyone was irritable. Given how the team had splintered, it wasn't surprising Penn struggled the past few weeks to win games. Allowed to fester, this situation could prove disastrous. The Quakers needed to be united if they had any hope of upsetting Texas. Right now, they were in disarray.

And there were distractions. Steve Danley's mind was on his White House fellowship application. An hour and a half before Tuesday's practice, he popped into Penn sports information director Mike Mahoney's office and said: "I have an interview with the White House in fifteen minutes. Is there a phone I can use?" Temple coach John Chaney had resigned, and rumors swirled that Dunphy would be his successor, which was one reason four camera crews and several reporters showed up before Penn's practice on Tuesday.

After Dunphy deflected a question about the Temple job, he was asked about his team's chances against Texas. One reporter wondered if the Quakers would use their smarts to counteract the Longhorns' athleticism. "We have high IQs in the classroom; I don't know how many high IQs we have on the basketball court," Dunphy said. Dunphy may have dismissed the underdog tag the media wanted to apply to his team—"We're Penn playing Texas. I don't want to hear about this underdog stuff"—but he did list on the team's practice plan under "Thought for the day" a quotation by unknown: "A big shot is a little shot that kept shooting." As he was finishing up with the media, Dunphy noticed the players heading back into the locker room and asked one of the assistant coaches what was going on. When he was told it was a players-only meeting, Dunphy said: "I like those."

Friedrich Ebede, whose outspokenness sometimes made his teammates uncomfortable, had summoned the meeting. Free, as he was often called, was perhaps the last one on the team likely to initiate the gathering. Yet, as a senior whose college career was coming to an end, he understood best what was at stake. "If you look at the way we practiced [the last few weeks], we weren't really ready," Ebede said. "I was able to watch from the sidelines. You can tell. You can see. You can feel it. We needed to get everyone back together. Otherwise, Texas wouldn't give us a big margin of error."

Ebede's blunt manner stemmed from his unusual childhood. Born in Cameroon, Ebede is the son of Titus Edzoa, formerly a high-powered government official who, in 1997, was sentenced to fifteen years on embezzlement charges, although some say his imprisonment was politically motivated. As a teenager, Ebede tried to flee the country and was stopped. On his second attempt, he made it to Paris. After stops in Montreal and Washington, D.C., Ebede eventually landed in Wilmington, Delaware, where he finished high school and came to the attention of Penn. Ebede carries strong convictions and is never shy about speaking his mind. He once told a reporter: "I always try to honor some principle that is guarded by rationality and some sort of Cartesian philosophy. I don't want to tell people what they want to hear. I tell them the truth."

Ebede's agenda for the meeting was simple: clear the air. He told his teammates: "Listen, fellas. We're not going to play like any team we've been playing for the last couple months. The team we're going to be playing is one of the best teams in the country. If you want to go out and not just for show, you better be focused and ready because we don't have that potential where we can afford a big margin of error."

And though they tended to tune out Ebede's words in the past, this time the players took his words to heart. "I feel like we're pushing each other a lot more than we had been during the end of the Ivy stretch, when we had already clinched the Ivy title, had our NCAA bid," Jaaber said. "The meeting helped us refocus."

The next day, Penn flew to Dallas. For all the hoopla that surrounds the NCAA tournament, it is sometimes easy to forget there is a basketball game to be played. Teams that lose sight of this fact are the ones that go home early. Dunphy had been to the tournament enough times to know how to keep his players focused on the task at hand. Given that they had almost three full days in Dallas before the game, he wanted them staying busy. From the minute they arrived, he had them preparing for Texas. After a quick film session at the hotel, Penn boarded a bus to Jesuit College Preparatory School. Because the NCAA allots only a half-hour practice for each team at the arena, teams usually find alternate gyms to hold practices. Penn was lucky. One of their recruits for next season, Justin Reilly, attended Jesuit. His coach was more than happy to loan the Quakers the gym for their practice.

Because Penn's game was the last one of the Friday session—tip-off was set for 8:50 P.M.—the Quakers' practice time at the arena and press conference were scheduled late in the day on Thursday. This gave them the morning free. Dunphy, who tries to make every trip educational, took the players on a tour of the Sixth Floor Museum at Dealey Plaza, site of John F. Kennedy's assassination. The museum obviously resonated much more with Dunphy, who was a sophomore in high school when the president was shot, than with his players, but they clearly found the exhibit interesting—no one more so than Ebede, who got into an animated debate with assistant coach Shawn Trice about the theory of a second shooter.

After practicing at First Baptist Dallas's fitness facility, the team headed to American Airlines Center for its press conference and practice. On the podium, the players—Jaaber, Osmundson, Danley, and Mark Zoller—were relaxed and poised, not the least bit awestruck as the Texas media was expecting. "They were asking us what are we going to do because they don't think we can do much," Jaaber said. "They want to know what our plan is, just to see if we are thinking in the right direction, because they don't think we're going to win."

Texas coach Rick Barnes has known Dunphy since the two were assistant coaches working at rival Colonial Athletic Association schools in the 1980s. Barnes was at George Mason, and Dunphy was at American (now a member of the Patriot League), and the two often ran into each other while recruiting at various high school gyms in the Washington, D.C., area. Barnes went out of his way to praise the Penn coach. "From afar, I've always admired the job that Fran Dunphy's done since he's gone into that league," Barnes said. "He's probably one of the more underrated coaches in the country. He probably hasn't gotten his due in terms of how good he is. We all know how tough it is to work and play in that league."

After the press conference, the team headed out to the court to practice. The cavernous arena was close to empty, aside from a few family members and Penn supporters. While Texas had drawn a sizable crowd for its practice, apparently not many of them felt the need to watch the Longhorns' opponent. The Quakers spent most of their time on shooting drills. In an arena, the sightlines are much different than most college venues, which can cause problems for shooters. Dunphy wanted to make sure his players were comfortable with the baskets. The players appeared loose and carefree, not the least bit intimidated by what lay ahead.

Penn wasn't acting like the typical No. 15 seed. So often, the low-seeded teams are so thrilled to be in the tournament that how they fare becomes secondary. Not the Quakers. While Dunphy made sure to remind the players what a special opportunity it was for them, it was not unusual. Penn was making its twenty-second appearance in the NCAA tournament. Although the team's last Final Four appearance was twenty-seven years ago, the Quakers' starting five had played in last year's NCAA tournament game, and four of them had started it. Granted, it had been twelve years since Penn had won an NCAA tournament game— a 90–80 victory over Nebraska—and hardly anybody was giving them a chance against Texas—they were fifteen-point underdogs, according to the oddsmakers—but the Quakers believed they could compete with any team.

And they had learned from their experience a year ago. When they had been on this stage the previous year, the Quakers melted under the NCAA tournament's bright lights. Boston College thumped them, 85– 65, in a first-round game. "Last year we got blown out," Osmundson said. "We were pretty much embarrassed after the first half. I'm sure a lot of people turned off our [game] and started watching another game. I think there's a little added incentive to prove to people that we can play with these guys. . . . We know what to expect [this year]. Last year, we were kind of going in blind, like blindfolded. We didn't know what to expect. It's BC, a big ACC school. We were more timid."

Game day finally arrived. With Penn playing in the finale, the day stretched out like a Texas prairie. Dunphy tried to keep his players occu- pied. The Quakers were the only team to use its shootaround time at the arena on Friday morning. He also scheduled one last practice and film session for the afternoon. In between these activities, the players watched other games in their rooms. They saw Bucknell upset Arkansas and Northwestern State shock Iowa. Suddenly, Penn beating Texas didn't seem impossible.

By the end of practice that afternoon, Penn seemed to have absorbed every bit of knowledge the coaches had gleaned from dissecting hours and hours of game film. They knew Texas's offensive, defensive, and out- of-bounds plays. They knew the Longhorn players' tendencies and how to guard them. They couldn't have been more prepared for the game. At the end of the practice, Dunphy told the team: "We're now on the biggest stage that is out there. That is where we want to be. Take care of your teammates. Take care of one another. Play as hard as you possibly can. Be confident. Be sure of what we can do. Be ready to go. This is a tremendous opportunity."

Penn was the first team out of the locker room for warm-ups, and the Texas crowd was ready for the Quakers. Most of the 19,263 fans at the arena were wearing burnt orange, and it was clear where their sympathies lay. They showered Penn with pro forma boos that quickly turned to cheers as soon as they spotted the Longhorns running onto the court. None of this bothered Jaaber. He was listening to his MP3 player, off in his own world. The Quakers headed back to the locker room for final instructions from Dunphy. He told them: "Play hard, play smart, and have fun out there."

Neither team started well. Penn missed its first five shots, and Texas made only one of its first five. Finally, Jaaber made a three-point basket just over five minutes into the game to break the Quakers' scoring drought. It was a tighter-than-expected game for the Longhorns. Taking a page from the Princeton playbook, Penn slowed the tempo and lulled Texas into a half-court game. It was a smart strategy. By shortening the game, essentially creating fewer possessions for each team, Penn could keep it close. Dunphy later claimed that wasn't his intent. He feared turnovers would lead to easy transition baskets for the Longhorns. Penn turned the ball over only eight times, which led to just nine points for Texas. The Longhorns scored only two fast-break points before halftime. "It was more take care of each possession because I think that's how the game was dictated early," Dunphy said. "It was hard fought early and well played defensively early, so each possession became critical."

Dunphy may have been pleased with his team's effort, but Barnes was in agony. Penn was imposing its style of play, and it was not to the Longhorns' liking. "You get the feeling it's like going to the dentist," Barnes said. "It's going to be a long experience. You wanted Novocain, but they didn't have any."

Penn wasn't able to get near its basket because of Texas's hulking frontcourt, but at least its shots from the perimeter were falling. The Quakers went six of fourteen from three-point range in the first half but made only one of ten inside the arc. "They do a good job of forcing you to their big guys," Jaaber said. "You get in there and they're like trees. You're looking for somebody to pass the ball to, and you don't see [a teammate] because they're so big."

It was a physical game. Bodies were banging against one another and hitting the floor hard. Jaaber left the game midway through the first half, holding his temple. A couple minutes later, Zoller hobbled to the bench with an ankle injury. Ebede aggravated his groin injury. It wasn't even halftime, and the Quakers' bench resembled a triage unit. Osmundson survived relatively unscathed, but even he said later: "I felt the wrath of their strength."

The Quakers were holding their own, though. The small but enthusiastic Penn cheering section was almost hoarse from shouting, "Let's go Quakers," while the Texas fans sat in stunned silence. They couldn't believe the Longhorns were having trouble with an Ivy League team. Their disbelief grew when Penn took a 23–22 lead into halftime. "Don't be satisfied! Don't be satisfied!" Jaaber implored his teammates again and again when they filtered into the locker room.

NCAA tournament halftimes can seem to last an eternity, and Penn needed every minute of this one. The Quakers were beat up and worn down. They needed to rest and recuperate, but what they really wanted was to get back out on the court and play. "We were antsy," Osmundson said. "It was forever. You want to keep going. You have the momentum."

Texas switched strategies coming out of halftime. Guard Daniel Gibson opened the second half with a three-pointer, and the Longhorns attempted three of their first five shots from behind the arc. The move forced Penn to defend the Longhorns' shooters on the perimeter, which opened up the area underneath the basket. That's when their big men took over. LaMarcus Aldridge, Texas's six-foot-ten center who would go on to become the second pick in the NBA draft, keyed a run by the Longhorns that gave them a seven-point lead with ten minutes to play. The nervous Texas crowd, which had been waiting for something to cheer about, finally came alive. The Quakers remained unfazed. Osmundson sank a three-pointer; then Brian Grandieri made a layup to cut Texas's lead to 41–40 with six and a half minutes to play. "Keep hanging around baby," Zoller bellowed as he went to the bench. "Keep hanging around."

Penn called a time-out with under six minutes to play. The players were exhausted and needed a break. Dunphy had played essentially six players in the game. Doubled over, their hands tugging on their shorts, the Quakers were gasping for air. Their bodies, dripping with sweat, protested while their minds urged them to summon every ounce of energy. "With five minutes in your career left, the last thing you're going to do is start showing tired," Osmundson said.

The time-out turned out to be a disaster for Penn. Texas came back on the court with a burst of energy, while the Quakers looked drained. Penn didn't make a field goal for four and a half minutes while the Longhorns built a 51–42 lead. Then, just as it appeared the game was over, Jaaber banked a three-point shot from the top of the key to pull Penn within six with less than ninety seconds left on the clock. Texas didn't make another field goal, closing out its 60–52 victory at the free-throw line. Only a late rush by Texas prevented the Longhorns from becoming the fifth No. 2 seed in the history of the tournament to lose its first-round game.

Penn had lost its record eighth consecutive NCAA tournament game, but its tenaciousness belied its seeding. The Quakers—the only team in the tournament not to award athletic scholarships—had given Texas all it could handle. They never trailed by double digits and were within a point of the lead late in the game. No matter what the Long-horns threw at them, they never flinched. "They're a very good basket-ball team," Dunphy said of Texas. "It made me even more proud of our guys that we were where we were with six minutes to go."

The Quakers slowly made their way back to the locker room. Dunphy knew no words could console the players after the near miss. His first thought was of the seniors—Friedrich Ebede, Greg Kuchinski, and Eric Osmundson—who had played their final game for Penn. "What you talk about number one is the three seniors," Dunphy said. "It's their last time they put on a Penn uniform. You talk about how appreciative you are of their efforts. You talk about those guys who are coming back, who have an opportunity to get back to this stage again, and you talk about how hard it is to get there. Nobody's giving it to you. You've got to earn it. You've got to work at it. . . . You hope that we can get back to going to the NCAA tournament; then once we get here, hopefully we can win a game or two. That's always the hope. But it's hard to get here. It really is. It's a long arduous task. And it doesn't start in October. It starts probably in two or three weeks."

With so many returning players, Penn would be favored again to win the Ivy League. Yet everyone in the locker room that night realized nothing was assured. Getting back to the NCAA tournament would be their top priority, but so many things could go wrong in the meantime. This might have been their only opportunity to win an NCAA tourna-ment game, and it had slipped through their fingers.

"I've got a couple more years left, so it's not tough for me to take," sophomore David Whitehurst said. "But it's hard for me because the seniors didn't get a chance to win in the tournament. It's always easy to take your early years and say, 'Okay, I have next year.' But getting down to those last years—and I know how I am starting to feel it now—I only have a couple years, and who knows? Maybe this was my last chance. Maybe we don't win the Ivies next year. It's tough. It's tough to handle."

Epilogue

F ar too quickly, the 2005–2006 season ended. It is only in looking back that I now realize how that season presaged seismic changes within the league, most notably an upheaval in the coaching ranks. This once-steady conference has undergone some turbulent times of late. Of course, the coaching instability was only a part of the enduring story line. A team other than Penn or Princeton won the league for the first time in twenty years, and Cornell's Khaliq Gant made a remarkable recovery from his traumatic injury.

Fran Dunphy's decision to leave Penn for its Big 5 rival Temple began the turnover of Ivy coaches. Four weeks after John Chaney resigned and twenty-four days after Penn was knocked out of the NCAA tournament by Texas, Dunphy was introduced as Temple's coach. After all he had accomplished at Penn—ten Ivy League titles, nine NCAA tournament appearances, and 310 wins in seventeen seasons—the fifty-seven-year-old Dunphy was ready for something new. Not that moving across Philadelphia from University City to North Broad was an easy decision for him. Far from it. But the advantages Temple offered over Penn were too great, not the least of which were scholarships. No longer would Dunphy have to persuade parents to pay for their son's desire to play

Division I basketball. And he'd get more than twenty-four hours to prepare for a conference game.

It made sense that if Dunphy was going to leave Penn, he wasn't going to go far. Dunphy is as Philly as Tastykakes and cheesesteaks. He was born there, went to school there, and except for stints at Army and American, spent most of his coaching career there. Throughout the city, he is a hail-fellow-well-met. To walk down the street with the man is to stop and greet or be greeted by every other person. In this major metropolitan city, few people are strangers to Dunphy.

Which means he knew better than most how tricky it would be to take over for an icon. Chaney spent twenty-four seasons at Temple, winning 741 games and guiding the Owls to seventeen NCAA appearances. The coaches who came before Chaney weren't slouches, either. Dunphy was only the fourth basketball coach at Temple since World War II. Two of the previous coaches—Chaney and Harry Litwack—were in the Naismith Memorial Basketball Hall of Fame; the other, Don Casey, went on to the NBA. No wonder that at his news conference, Dunphy kept describing his new job as "a very daunting task."

Some wondered why Dunphy, who became the first to coach two Big 5 teams, left Penn for Temple. In some ways, it seemed a lateral career move. Temple had slipped the last five years under Chaney, and the Atlantic 10 Conference wasn't nearly as strong as in the past. A less obvious reason for his move may have been the chance to prove himself. There is no doubt that Dunphy is a good coach. His success at Penn bears that out. But because his accomplishments were in the Ivy League and because of Penn's long tradition of success, some may have questioned his coaching talents given Penn's inherent advantages in the league. Those same skeptics may have believed that any coach could have won at Penn. Temple was his chance to silence those critics.

Dunphy's departure opened a vacancy at Penn, one of the more coveted jobs in the Ivy League. In an unusual move, Penn athletic director Steve Bilsky stayed within the conference and plucked Glen Miller away from Brown. In some ways, the move made sense. No coach understands the nuances of the Ivy League better than one who is already in it. On the other hand, the awkwardness that accompanies playing your former team twice a year can't be overlooked, not to mention the hurt feelings of the players you left behind. Miller, who never won a game at the Palestra as a head coach, would now take over the defending Ivy League champions.

Miller's move to Penn created an opening at Brown. Director of athletics Michael Goldberger, following the lead of his Penn counterpart, tapped an Ivy League insider to replace Miller. Former Princeton standout Craig Robinson, who these days is best known as the brother-in-law of President Barack Obama rather than as a two-time Ivy League player of the year, was hired to coach the Bears. Robinson spent six years as an assistant coach to former Princeton coach Bill Carmody at Northwestern before Brown gave him his first collegiate head-coaching job. Robinson, who led Brown to a school-record nineteen victories in the 2007–2008 season, stayed just two years in Providence, Rhode Island, before leaving for Oregon State. Jesse Agel, Robinson's assistant at Brown, was promoted to head coach in June 2008.

Following the 2006–2007 season, two more Ivy League teams were searching for new head coaches. In a widely anticipated move, Harvard did not renew Frank Sullivan's contract after the Crimson went 12–16 overall and finished sixth in the league. Sullivan was replaced by former Duke standout and Michigan coach Tommy Amaker, making him the only African American head coach at Harvard and just the third to coach the basketball team. "We needed to hire a name coach who could prime the pump and bring excitement and energy back to the program," Harvard director of athletics Robert L. Scalise told the Associated Press. "When we hired Coach Amaker, we made a partnership with him to provide him with all of the resources he would need to be successful and bring championships to the school, and we will stand behind that commitment." All of a sudden, Harvard seemed to be taking its basketball program seriously. What Scalise didn't say at the time, but most Ivy observers wanted to know, was whether Harvard intended to relax its stringent academic requirements—the least flexible in the Ivy League—in order to bring in more talented recruits.

After the Crimson received commitments from what one analyst called the best recruiting class in Harvard's—if not the Ivy League's—history, a story appeared in the *New York Times* in March 2008 questioning the latitude the school had given Amaker. Scalise acknowledged to the paper that Harvard was recruiting players with lower academic profiles than it had in the past. "It's also a willingness to basically say, 'Okay, maybe we need to accept a few more kids, and maybe we need to go after a few more kids in the initial years when Tommy is trying to change the culture of the program,' " Scalise told the *Times*. "It's a willingness to say that we really do want to compete for the Ivy championship." The article also pointed out possible NCAA violations by an assistant coach. For a league that has always prided itself on its lack of recruiting or academic scandals, this was a crushing blow. And because it was Harvard, that venerable institution of higher learning, the story soon created a media storm. Pundits seized upon it to show how even the Ivy League isn't immune to the pressures of big-time college basketball.

The Ivy League investigated and later exonerated Harvard on both the NCAA violations and the charge that the school was admitting student-athletes with below-average Academic Indexes. Although the Crimson was vindicated, it doesn't change the fact that the school is putting a greater emphasis on winning. Some will say that's a good thing, that the administration's lack of support had held Harvard back all these years. But at what cost is the Crimson undertaking this mission to win Ivy League championships? By relaxing Harvard's standards to "change the culture of the program," as Scalise put it, the Crimson may be heading down a slippery slope and find it's hard to climb back up.

If Sullivan's exit was foreseen, Joe Scott's abrupt resignation came out of nowhere. It wasn't surprising that a growing number of Princeton fans wanted him gone after the Tigers' last-place finish in the Ivy League. Princeton went 11–17 overall and 2–12 in the league in Scott's final season, its worst Ivy record in program history. Irate fans created a Facebook group called "Fire Joe Scott," demanding Scott's removal. But Scott, who was 38–45 in three seasons at Princeton, wasn't forced out. He left on his own accord, returning to Colorado to coach at the University of Denver.

The stability Pete Carril brought to Princeton for twenty-nine seasons was becoming a distant memory. No Ivy program had gone through as many coaching changes as the Tigers had of late. In searching for its fourth coach in eleven seasons, Princeton once again kept its coaching hire within the family. The school turned to another former Tiger point guard, Sydney Johnson, which brought the number of African American head coaches in the Ivy League to six. Although Johnson's résumé was long on Princeton accolades—the only three-time team captain in program history, a part of the Tigers' stunning NCAA tournament win against UCLA in 1996, and the Ivy League player of the year in 1997—it was short on coaching experience: three years as an assistant to John Thompson III at Georgetown. With his limited coaching background, it will be interesting to see if Johnson can return Princeton to prominence in the league.

Cornell finally broke the Penn-Princeton stranglehold on the Ivy championship in 2008. Twenty years after it won its first and only league title, the Big Red went undefeated through the conference, becoming the first non–Penn or Princeton team to accomplish that feat. Led by sophomore point guard Louis Dale, the Ivy League player of the year, Cornell won a school-record twenty-two games and earned a No. 14 seed in the NCAA tournament. "The great thing about [Cornell winning the title] is that it wasn't a case of Penn and Princeton just slipping up and someone else lucking their way into an Ivy League title," said Jake Wilson, who runs the Web site ivy.basketball-u.com. Cornell "is every bit the equal of past Ivy League champions."

Cornell was the best team during the 2007–2008 season. The Big Red had experience, talent, depth, and for the first time in a while, few injuries. After years of building, Coach Steve Donahue finally put together a complete team. Taking nothing away from Cornell's fine season, it certainly didn't hurt the Big Red's title chances that neither Penn nor Princeton were at their usual level of excellence. It is too soon to speculate whether Cornell's resurgence means the demise of the Penn and Princeton dynasties. Though the programs have slipped, they both are showing signs of a renaissance. Miller and Johnson are recruiting talented players who, in a couple years or so, could have the Quakers and the Tigers once again vying for Ivy League championships.

Khaliq Gant, whose terrifying injury shook Cornell during the 2005–2006 season, took part in the Big Red's remarkable run to the title. Although he couldn't put on a uniform and join the players on the court, Gant remained a member of the team. His amazing recovery continued to be a source of inspiration for his teammates and coaches.

For his first twenty years, Gant was blissfully healthy. He never missed a game because of injury, never had surgery, never took any medication. He refused even aspirin for a headache. Having been born at home, the only time Gant had been in a hospital was to see his mom, a nurse, at work. He wanted nothing to do with being sick or injured, and for two decades, his body mostly complied. Except for a dislocated finger and a few stitches on his left eyebrow, Gant sailed through basketball unscathed. But on that fateful night in January 2006, everything changed. He went from Cornell basketball player to spinal-cord patient, from a world of classes and basketball to one filled with doctors, nurses, hospitals, and medications. Fiercely independent, Gant was now at the mercy of others. He needed help with the most basic tasks: eating, brushing his teeth, and scratching an itch. This loss of control over his life was more devastating to him than the loss of control over his limbs.

Gant's arrival at Atlanta's Shepherd Center in February coincided with the bleakest period of his recovery. While he had been in New York, Gant relied on his parents to help him. Dana Gant stayed at his bedside, constantly at his beck and call. Her soothing presence comforted him during anxious moments. That first night at Shepherd, Gant was by himself. The medical staff attended to his needs, but it wasn't the same as having his mom and dad look after him. As he lay awake in the darkness, paralyzed and unable to shut out the cacophony of the hospital, Gant grew more and more agitated. He began to make lists. A compulsive list-maker since childhood, Gant tallied everything that was happening to him so that he could tell his parents the next day.

"I remember the first night I was in Shepherd. Both my parents left. That was the worst night of my life," Gant said. "I don't want to think about it really. I couldn't do anything. I wasn't sleeping. . . . I was just lying awake. My nose would be running, and I couldn't wipe it. My arm would be uncomfortable or my gown would be wrapped under my arm. It was just a terrible night. I remember being really pissed off. I'm not the type of person who would just yell at somebody. I remember the next day my father came [to see him], just breaking down, freaking out, telling him what happened."

Gant hadn't had a good night's sleep since his injury. At best, he was sleeping an hour at a time. In addition to his lack of sleep, the surfeit of drugs coursing through his body—a body unaccustomed to medication—was wreaking havoc on his system. He became increasingly hyper, leading doctors to prescribe an antipsychotic to help quiet him down. With his erratic behavior, constant babbling, and inappropriate language, he was not the Khaliq he or anyone in his family recognized. "He was insane," Dana Gant said. "I was like, 'Who is this person?' I saw things in Khaliq I had never seen before. Those drugs were toxic to him."

The adverse reaction to his medication caused a delay in the start of his rehabilitation. When he finally calmed down, about a week into his stay at Shepherd, Gant started rehab slowly, too slowly for him. Passive resistance and stretching exercises, though challenging, were hardly the workouts he was accustomed to as a Division I athlete. He quickly mastered the sip-and-puff wheelchair and soon was zooming around the hallways in the hospital. Gant didn't hide his frustration with the pace of his rehab from his therapists. "I can be impatient. I'm usually a pretty fast learner," he said. "I was like, 'Why are you stopping me from doing this?'" It was pointed out that perhaps the medical staff was holding him back, taking it slow so that he didn't injure himself. "I guess that was their rationale," Gant said. "I disagree with that fully."

His father, Dean Gant, a self-employed music producer, essentially moved into the rehabilitation center, spending his days and nights there. Because he and his son share a love of music, Dean channeled that passion into Khaliq's rehab. He taught Khaliq keyboard exercises to help him rebuild the strength in his fingers. When they communicated, it was often through beatbox, rhyming, or song, allowing Khaliq to keep his mind active even when his body wasn't.

As his rehabilitation dragged on, one day blending into another, Gant became obsessed with his progress. There was no limit to his determination, no day wasted. He plotted out his rehab, setting goals for himself that exceeded his therapist's expectations. He knew how hard he could push himself. He had been pushing himself all his life to succeed at one thing or another. Rehab was no different. Each day he would try to do a little more, bringing himself that much closer to walking again. "Once I set my mind to something I will take the necessary steps to make it happen," Gant said. "Once I set my mind to rehab, I mean, I had nothing else to do."

Within a week of arriving at Shepherd, Gant began to wiggle his toes. A week later, he had movement in his legs. One day, while he was working on a stationary bike, the therapists helping him push his legs down on the pedals, the director of the spinal-cord-injury unit, Sarah Morrison, came to see how he was doing. Morrison took one look at Gant and right away noticed how advanced he was. She decided to challenge him. With her help, Gant stood on his own, just forty-five days after his injury. He looked a little wobbly, like a marionette with slack strings, but he was standing nonetheless. Dean Gant took a picture that Khaliq keeps to this day. He took his first steps a week and a half later.

By the time three of his teammates—Graham Dow, Kevin App, and Jason Mitchell—and two of his friends from Cornell, Louis Caras and Dave Porrell, made a road trip from Ithaca to Atlanta over spring break in late March, Gant had made tremendous progress. They watched him go through a rehab session and then went with him to eat at a restaurant near the hospital. It was during the meal that Gant surprised them. He got up from the table, and with his dad's help, walked to the bathroom. His friends may have thought he was showing off, but Gant insisted he just wanted to go to the bathroom without the cumbersome wheelchair. The Shepherd Center medical staff "didn't know I had done that. I wasn't supposed to do that, I don't think," Gant said. "It's not safe, obviously, to do something like that. It's kind of like the athlete mentality, you take a risk."

In early April, Gant moved into an apartment with his father near Shepherd to continue his rehab as an outpatient. Then, the first weekend in May, a little more than three months after his injury, Gant returned to Cornell for Slope Day, an annual outdoor festival at the school held on the last day of the spring semester. Though he needed crutches to get around, Gant had no intention of missing Slope Day. No injury was going to keep him away from this all-day party. Yet, coming back to Cornell, he found things had changed. "It was weird," Gant said. "I'm so used to being at Cornell and doing everything I normally did. I came back and everyone is like, 'Khaliq, how are you doing?' Random people coming up and talking to me. It was nice being so welcomed back. I remember I didn't think I mattered that much. Apparently, some people cared about me."

Gant is the first to say he was an unknown basketball player at Cornell. But after his injury, that all changed. It wasn't just the Cornell community that came to view him as a celebrity. The nationwide basketball community embraced him. The outpouring of support stunned him and his family. Harvard sent a poster signed by the players. Brown sent a signed basketball. Princeton's Scott Greenman posted a get-well wish on the Web site Cornell set up to send messages to Gant during his recovery. Atlanta Hawks forward Josh Smith and Orlando Magic forward Dwight Howard, both of whom played AAU basketball with Gant, stopped by Shepherd to visit him. North Carolina coach Roy Williams and Duke coach Mike Krzyzewski wrote letters. Arizona coach Lute Olson sent a hat and T-shirt. More T-shirts came from Virginia Tech and Saint Bonaventure, and another signed basketball arrived from Elon. Georgia Tech coach Paul Hewitt invited him to the NCAA tournament regional final in Atlanta. Small schools, big schools, and every school in between sent get-well wishes. "Some of these schools I didn't think even knew who I was," Gant said. "My room was just packed with stuff from people all over the country. That was definitely nice to be so popular."

He was particularly touched by the sentiments expressed by Bucknell coach Pat Flannery. Gant had been recruited strongly by Bucknell but chose Cornell. Flannery sent him a letter immediately after the injury and then, a year later, sent another letter to see how he was doing. "I wanted to thank him for that," Gant said. "I really respect him for that."

Friends from his high school sent cookies, others sent fruit baskets. The Gant family received so much food that they started sharing it with the nurses. But it wasn't just these tokens of support that moved him. It was also those people who told him he was an inspiration to them. Gant had a hard time seeing himself as inspirational. "I felt like I was doing something, not routine, but it's just like I'm trying to do something that needs to happen," Gant said. "When you're going through something, it's hard to put it in perspective."

Gant missed only a semester because of his injury but decided to take an extra year to finish his degree. He enjoyed college too much. He continued to be a part of the Cornell basketball team and was listed with the other players in the team's media guide. Gant came to the gym nearly every day to watch his teammates practice and play pickup. Occasionally, he shot baskets with them. He attended all home games and several away games. Asked why he would put himself through the misery of watching others play when he himself can't, Gant said: "All those guys are my best friends, I'm not going to not support them because I can't do something."

Gant refused to look at his injury as anything more than a mere set-back. Other than the scars on his neck, he displays almost no outward signs of his injury and has few limitations. Listening to him, you would think he had suffered nothing worse than a torn anterior cruciate ligament, not a 50 percent subluxation of his C4 and C5 vertebrae. Though he would not term it this way, Gant's ability to walk again is just short of miraculous. Even more remarkable, Gant never doubted he would walk again.

It is hard not to marvel at Gant's optimistic outlook throughout his ordeal. His father recalled a conversation with his son shortly after the injury occurred. "This was early in the process," Dean Gant said. "He is laying there, can't move anything, and then he tells me, 'Dad, you know what? I see this as a blessing.' I'm like, 'Huh?' He said, 'Well, I've never really been challenged in my life. Things have always come easy for me. You guys have always looked out for me. I've had it pretty good. This is the first time that I really feel like I'm faced with a challenge, with something that I really have to dig down deep and do. I think that's a blessing that I'm getting this opportunity to really be challenged and pushed to see what I can do. I know I'm going to overcome this, so I feel it's a blessing.'"

"I definitely think [the injury was] a blessing," Gant said. "Any time someone goes through a life-changing event, it makes them a stronger person. Having this happen to me has really changed my perspective. . . . What I went through has made me a little more mature. Seeing the out-pouring of emotion from people definitely helped me understand how great people can be. I think there's a lot of lessons I learned from it. Like the cliché, once you put your mind to something, you can definitely overcome it. For myself, I saw how strong-willed and powerful I can be. It gave me a great sense of confidence in myself and perspective . . . just to remember to not take anything for granted." Gant wiped his eyes and paused for a moment to collect himself. "Even when I watch the guys play, I'm thankful that they can do what they can do, and I'm thankful for what I can do now, just be able to walk."

When talking about his injury, Gant comes across as dispassionate, almost clinical—as if he is talking about someone else and not himself. It isn't until the subject turns to basketball that his steely exterior falls away and his emotions surface. Before the injury, Gant's coaches at times questioned his commitment to basketball. They sometimes felt his other interests pulled him away from the sport. But now that basketball has been taken away from him, it is clear just how much Gant loves basketball—and misses it. "I've been [playing basketball] all my life," said Gant, his voice thick with ache. "When I walked on the court and saw the guys play, it kind of hit me. I'm not going to play—yet."

Gant's playing career likely has ended. And he is dealing, prematurely, with what every Ivy player must eventually face: life after basketball. Some people may wonder how someone with an Ivy League degree can mourn the loss of a sport that demanded so much and gave so little in return. But just because a bright future lies ahead, that doesn't mean what you leave behind hurts any less. Just ask Seamus Lonergan, who played for Dartmouth from 1993 to 1997 and was captain his senior year. In many regards, Lonergan had a successful college basketball career. During his four years, the Big Green twice finished tied for second in the league. His sophomore season, Dartmouth went 10–4, but Penn won the league by going 14–0. Two years later, Dartmouth again went 10–4 but finished behind undefeated Princeton. Lonergan, who scored 1,651 points during his career, remains the second-leading scorer in school history.

Even though it's been more than a decade since he played in the league, Lonergan remembers the long bus trips in the snow and playing cards on the bus with his teammates as if it were yesterday. He recalls games at the Palestra and at Yale's "dungeon," as he calls it. "I have trouble watching college basketball these days because it makes me miss playing," said Lonergan, whose only outlet for his love of basketball has become pickup games. Nowadays, instead of dribbling around a basketball court, Lonergan can be found at Santa Clara Valley Medical Center in San Jose, California, where he is an emergency room physician. "One of the reasons why I picked [emergency medicine] was that it was kind of the closest thing I could get to playing basketball," he said. "Every patient is different, just like every game is different. . . . The teamwork, the communication, the quick decision-making—I was drawn to it for that."

Lonergan looks back fondly on his time playing basketball at Dartmouth. He talked about how playing basketball was a way to release the stress brought on by academics. When asked if there was any negative to playing basketball in the Ivy League, the only thing he could think of was the lack of a postseason tournament. More than ten years after his playing days have ended, he's still bitter about that. While there will always be some who say that sports at Ivy League schools should be contested only at the club or intramural level, it is former Ivy athletes like Lonergan who make the most persuasive argument for athletic competition at an academic institution. As he and others have shown, athletes can compete at the highest level and then go on to be successful outside athletics. "To take Division I sports out of the Ivy League would be an absolute disaster," Lonergan said. "You would lose some amazingly good people, some amazingly strong academic people and just people of strong character. I feel so strongly about that. What draws people to the league is to compete at the highest levels. We're not always a powerhouse conference in basketball, but we can definitely compete. We're proud of that, and the Ivy League should be proud of that."

Adherents of William Bowen's books disagree with Lonergan. They argue that the Ivy League is no place for big-time athletics. Instead, they believe the schools should focus solely on educating the best and the brightest. For a while, it seemed as if their arguments might sway the presidents. But these days, the presidents' tight rein on athletics, or at least on men's basketball, might be loosening. It is too early to tell, but Harvard's bold proclamations of its desire to win Ivy League championships may lead other schools to push the boundaries of what was acceptable in the past.

A win-at-all-costs mentality is unlikely to take hold of the league, but to what degree will the schools succumb to pressure from their alumni and fans to be the best? In the tug-of-war that exists between athletics and academics, the Ivy League, more so than just about every other conference, has managed to keep the weight evenly balanced on each side of the rope. In the past, the academic side may have had a bit more pull than the athletic side. Now it seems, the athletic side is gaining an advantage. That would be shortsighted. What makes this league unusual, what sets it apart, is that academics means just as much as athletics. If one side prevails over the other, all would be lost.

Let the rest of Division I college basketball deal with the problems that come from the culture of excess that surrounds the sport these days. The Ivy League doesn't need to go down that path to retain its legitimacy. It can remain true to its ideals and still be competitive. That may be wishful thinking. But it would be unfortunate if the league lost its identity trying to gain a bigger foothold on the college basketball landscape.

Acknowledgments

This book would not have been possible without the generosity and accessibility of the players and coaches in the Ivy League. Their enthusiasm for this book was more than I could have hoped for. I have so many wonderful memories from that season, and I will treasure them always.

As overworked (and underappreciated) as they are, the sports information directors always made time for me and my endless requests. I thank them: Brown's Chris Humm, Columbia's Darlene Camacho, Cornell's Jeremy Hartigan, Harvard's Kurt Svoboda, Penn's Mike Maloney, Princeton's Dave Rosenfeld and Jerry Price, Yale's Tim Bennett, and Dartmouth's Kathy Slattery Phillips, who died unexpectedly in November 2007. May she rest in peace.

I am grateful to the Ivy League office, executive director Jeff Orleans and his staff. Jake Wilson of ivy.basketball-u.com and Jon Solomon of Princeton Basketball News (princetonbasketball.com/blog/) helped me stay on top of everything going on in the league. Their insights on the Ivy League are far greater than mine.

When I approached John Feinstein for his advice on writing this book, I feared he would laugh in my face. Instead, he generously helped me begin, and I am indebted to him for his wisdom and guidance along the way.

I also owe much thanks to Christine Brennan for introducing me to the best agent in the business, Andrew Blauner, whose faith in this book never wavered, even when mine did at times. Bill Gildea and Karl Hente provided shrewd editorial counsel. Julie Tate lent her fact-checking expertise. The keen eyes of Beth Kressel and Molan Goldstein at Rutgers put the finishing touches on the manuscript.

It has been my privilege to work at the *Washington Post* and to learn from some of the best journalists in the newspaper business, in particular Emilio Garcia-Ruiz, George Solomon, Matt Vita, and Tracee Hamilton.

A special thanks to Matt Rennie, who was encouraging throughout, and to Steve Berkowitz, who sent me to my first Penn-Princeton game.

Not many cardiologists would let an author/patient schedule her open-heart surgery when it was convenient—say, when Harvard and Princeton took their exam breaks in January—and then make sure she was healthy enough to cover Fran Dunphy's three hundredth career win two weeks later. Allen Solomon and Douglas Murphy did. For that, and for keeping me healthy, I am grateful.

If not for the extraordinary support and encouragement of my parents, Audrey and Duane; my sister, Karen, and her family, who housed me on my many trips to Boston; my brother, David, who knew how to cheer me up when I was in despair; and my dear friends, Christine Searight, Gavin Francis, Liz Clarke, Tom Heath, and Polly Povejsil Heath, there would be no book.

Ivy League Rosters, 2005-2006 Season

BROWN BEARS

Head Coach: Glen Miller
Assistant Coaches: Kevin Jaskiewicz, Andy Partee, Mike Martin

PLAYER	YEAR	HOMETOWN
Marcus Becker	Junior	Martinsville, Va.
James Daniels	Sophomore	Oceanside, Calif.
Nathan Eads	Junior	Ellicott City, Md.
P. J. Flaherty	Junior	Merrimack, N.H.
Scott Friske	Freshman	Charlevoix, Mich.
Damon Huffman	Sophomore	Petoskey, Mich.
Keenan Jeppesen	Sophomore	Stony Creek, Ontario
Aaron Jimenez	Freshman	Franklin Park, Ill.
John Kresse	Freshman	Charleston, S.C.
Mark MacDonald	Sophomore	Lexington, Mass.
Sam Manhanga	Junior	Beira, Mozambique
Mark McAndrew	Sophomore	Barrington, R.I.
Luke Ruscoe	Senior	Nelson, New Zealand
Chris Skrelja	Freshman	Hastings-on-Hudson, Conn.

COLUMBIA LIONS

Head Coach: Joe Jones
Assistant Coaches: Jim Engles, Andrew Theokas, Joe Conefry

PLAYER	YEAR	HOMETOWN
Justin Armstrong	Sophomore	San Diego, Calif.
John Baumann	Sophomore	Westport, Conn.
Joe Bova	Freshman	Scotia, N.Y.
Dalen Cuff	Senior	Palm Harbor, Fla.
John-Michael Grzan	Senior	Rye Brook, N.Y.
Dragutin Kravic	Senior	Zrenjanin, Serbia
Brett Loscalzo	Sophomore	Ridgefield, Conn.
K. J. Matsui	Freshman	Tokyo, Japan
Jason Miller	Freshman	Hamilton, Ohio
Mack Montgomery	Sophomore	Clayton, N.C.
Leo Nolan	Freshman	Summit, N.J.
Ben Nwachukwu	Sophomore	Enugu, Nigeria
Kashif Sweet	Sophomore	Austin, Tex.
Daniel Trepanier	Freshman	Belle River, Ontario

CORNELL BIG RED

Head Coach: Steve Donahue
Assistant Coaches: Izzi Metz, Zach Spiker, Nat Graham

PLAYER	YEAR	HOMETOWN
Kevin App	Junior	Silver Spring, Md.
Jason Battle	Freshman	Wilmington, N.C.
Lenny Collins	Senior	San Juan Capistrano, Calif.
Graham Dow	Junior	Burlington, Ontario
Khaliq Gant	Sophomore	Norcross, Ga.
Adam Gore	Freshman	Monrovia, Ind.
Jason Hartford	Junior	Tillamook, Ore.
Ugo Ihekweazu	Junior	Houston, Tex.
Brian Kreefer	Freshman	East Liverpool, Ohio
David Lisle	Senior	Wingham, Ontario
Jason Mitchell	Junior	Saluda, S.C.
Conor Mullen	Freshman	Seattle, Wash.
Andrew Naeve	Junior	Miles, Iowa
Ryan Rourke	Senior	Bothell, Wash.

DARTMOUTH BIG GREEN

Head Coach: Terry Dunn
Assistant Coaches: Shay Berry, Tommy Deffebaugh, Ryan Hurd

PLAYER	YEAR	HOMETOWN
Calvin Arnold	Senior	Sebastopol, Calif.
Dominic Baker	Freshman	Homewood, Ill.
Johnathan Ball	Sophomore	Memphis, Tenn.
Alex Barnett	Freshman	St. Louis, Mo.
Dan Biber	Freshman	Lorain, Ohio
Paul Bode	Junior	Raleigh, N.C.
Chuck Flynn	Sophomore	Indianapolis, Ind.
Michael Giovacchini	Sophomore	Salt Lake City, Utah
Michael Lang	Senior	Chicago, Ill.
Jarrett Mathis	Freshman	Brooklyn, N.Y.
Brian McMillan	Sophomore	Valparaiso, Ind.
Jason Meyer	Senior	Covington, Ohio
DeVon Mosley	Freshman	Mesquite, Tex.
Leon Pattman	Junior	Memphis, Tenn.
Adam Powers	Freshman	Western Springs, Ill.
Marlon Sanders	Freshman	Cleveland Heights, Ohio
Reggie Schickel	Freshman	Charlotte, N.C.

HARVARD CRIMSON

Head Coach: Frank Sullivan
Assistant Coaches: Bill Holden, Lamar Reddicks

PLAYER	YEAR	HOMETOWN
Michael Beal	Senior	Brooklyn, N.Y.
Kenyon Churchwell	Freshman	Washington, D.C.
Brian Cusworth	Junior	St. Louis, Mo.
Brian Darcy	Junior	Shrewsbury, Mass.
Jim Goffredo	Junior	La Crescenta, Calif.
Erik Groszyk	Freshman	Salem, Mass.
Evan Harris	Freshman	Los Angeles, Calif.
Drew Housman	Freshman	Calabasas, Calif.
James Lambert	Sophomore	Huntington Beach, Calif.
Zach Martin	Senior	Medford, N.J.
Alex Pease	Freshman	Milwaukee, Wis.
Andrew Pusar	Freshman	West Orange, N.J.
Matt Stehle	Senior	Newton, Mass.
Brad Unger	Sophomore	Boyertown, Pa.
Ko Yada	Junior	Newport, Ore.

PENN QUAKERS

Head Coach: Fran Dunphy
Assistant Coaches: Dave Duke, Matt Langel, Shawn Trice

PLAYER	YEAR	HOMETOWN
Aron Cohen	Freshman	Huntingdon Valley, Pa.
Steve Danley	Junior	Germantown, Md.
Friedrich Ebede	Senior	Dovala, Cameroon
Kevin Egee	Freshman	Ridley, Pa.
Adam Franklin	Senior	New Castle, Del.
Joe Gill	Sophomore	Doylestown, Pa.
Brian Grandieri	Sophomore	Media, Pa.
Ibrahim Jaaber	Junior	Elizabeth, N.J.
Greg Kuchinski	Senior	Wall, N.J.
Cameron Lewis	Freshman	Washington, D.C.
Lorenz Manthey	Junior	Hamburg, Germany
Tommy McMahon	Freshman	Hillsboro, Calif.
Eric Osmundson	Senior	Carlsbad, Calif.
Brennan Votel	Freshman	Park Hills, Ky.
David Whitehurst	Sophomore	Tinton Falls, N.J.
Mark Zoller	Junior	Blue Bell, Pa.

PRINCETON TIGERS

Head Coach: Joe Scott
Assistant Coaches: Mike Brennan, Howard Levy, Tony Newsom

PLAYER	YEAR	HOMETOWN
Jason Briggs	Freshman	Olympia, Wash.
Edwin Buffmire	Junior	Scottsdale, Ariz.
Justin Conway	Junior	Sante Fe, N.M.
Patrick Ekeruo	Junior	Hayward, Calif.
Scott Greenman	Senior	Linwood, N.J.
Geoff Kestler	Freshman	Mt. Lebanon, Pa.
Kyle Koncz	Sophomore	Strongsville, Ohio
Noah Levine	Freshman	New York, N.Y.
Alex Okafor	Freshman	San Jose, Calif.
Luke Owings	Junior	Hyattsville, Md.
Matt Sargeant	Sophomore	Huntington Beach, Calif.
Noah Savage	Sophomore	Princeton, N.J.
Harrison Schaen	Sophomore	Huntington Beach, Calif.

PLAYER	YEAR	HOMETOWN
Max Schafer	Junior	Wayne, N.J.
Kevin Steuerer	Sophomore	Ossining, N.Y.
Michael Strittmatter	Freshman	Phoenix, Ariz.
Zach Woolridge	Sophomore	Sherman Oaks, Calif.

YALE BULLDOGS

Head Coach: James Jones
Assistant Coaches: Curtis Wilson, Jim McCarthy, Matt Kingsley

PLAYER	YEAR	HOMETOWN
Jason Abromaitis	Junior	Unionville, Conn.
Chris Andrews	Freshman	South Orange, N.J.
Eric Flato	Sophomore	Piedmont, Calif.
Ari Greenberg	Freshman	Fayetteville, N.Y.
Josh Greenberg	Senior	Fayetteville, N.Y.
Caleb Holmes	Sophomore	Olathe, Kans.
Nick Holmes	Sophomore	Olathe, Kans.
Casey Hughes	Junior	New Haven, Conn.
Sam Kaplan	Junior	Worcester, Mass.
Matt Kyle	Sophomore	North Myrtle Beach, S.C.
Dominick Martin	Senior	Asheville, N.C.
Ross Morin	Freshman	Cincinnati, Ohio
Travis Pinick	Freshman	Orange, Calif.
Ed White	Freshman	Los Angeles, Calif.
Reid Wittman	Freshman	New York, N.Y.

Index

About the Author

Kathy Orton has covered college basketball for the *Washington Post* for more than a decade. She also was the *Post* beat writer on the NFL's Baltimore Ravens for two seasons, including their Super Bowl season in 2000. She lives in Washington, D.C.